# The

# Lost Art

# of

# Walking

...........................

*The History, Science,*

*Philosophy, and Literature*

*of Pedestrianism*

GEOFF NICHOLSON

RIVERHEAD BOOKS

New York

RIVERHEAD BOOKS
Published by the Penguin Group
Penguin Group (USA) Inc.
375 Hudson Street, New York, New York 10014, USA
Penguin Group (Canada), 90 Eglinton Avenue East, Suite 700, Toronto, Ontario M4P 2Y3, Canada
(a division of Pearson Penguin Canada Inc.)
Penguin Books Ltd., 80 Strand, London WC2R 0RL, England
Penguin Group Ireland, 25 St. Stephen's Green, Dublin 2, Ireland (a division of Penguin Books Ltd.)
Penguin Group (Australia), 250 Camberwell Road, Camberwell, Victoria 3124, Australia
(a division of Pearson Australia Group Pty. Ltd.)
Penguin Books India Pvt Ltd., 11 Community Centre, Panchsheel Park, New Delhi—110 017, India
Penguin Group (NZ), 67 Apollo Drive, Rosedale, North Shore 0632, New Zealand
(a division of Pearson New Zealand Ltd.)
Penguin Books (South Africa) (Pty.) Ltd., 24 Sturdee Avenue, Rosebank, Johannesburg 2196,
South Africa

Penguin Books Ltd., Registered Offices: 80 Strand, London WC2R 0RL, England

The publisher does not have any control over and does not assume any responsibility for author or third-party websites or their content.

First Riverhead hardcover edition: November 2008
First Riverhead trade paperback edition: November 2009
Riverhead trade paperback ISBN: 978-1-59448-403-2

The Library of Congress has catalogued the Riverhead hardcover edition as follows:

Nicholson, Geoff, date.
The lost art of walking : the history, science, philosophy, and literature of pedestrianism /
Geoff Nicholson.
p. cm.
Includes bibliographical references.
ISBN: 978-1-59448-998-3
1. Walking. 2. Voyages and travels. I. Title.
GV199.5.N534 2008     2008025182
796.51—dc22

PRINTED IN THE UNITED STATES OF AMERICA

10  9  8  7  6  5  4  3  2  1

"Amusing...[Nicholson's] book is worth reading as a celebration of tangential and obsessive eccentricity. His curiosity, standard equipment for walkers, is contagious and brings him to unexpected places as well as expected oddballs." —*The Weekly Standard*

"[*The Lost Art of Walking*] is great fun—a mirthful ode to one of the most sustainable things a person can do." —*Plenty*

"[A] leisurely, charmingly obsessive literary stroll...Nicholson's genial exploration of this 'most ordinary, ubiquitous activity' is lively and entertaining." —*Publishers Weekly*

"An engaging and entertaining treatise on walking...Nicholson's witty style and distinct way of describing an ordinary activity make this a thoroughly enjoyable read. While by no means exhaustive, Nicholson does himself tread a lot of ground; readers may find the ultimate effect is that they are inspired to put the book down for a nice long walk with a newfound way of observing the scenery." —*Library Journal*

"Nicholson has written one of those charming titles that meanders in and out of history, geography, philosophy, and all manner of literary references in the way of Sarah Vowell and Roger Deakin. He makes it all seem so effortless that it is only later, after completing his invaluable 'walking bibliography,' that readers will grasp how well read he is....Nicholson flows readily from one subject to the next, carrying readers along on a smart and entertaining exploration of both physical action and cultural inquiry." —*Booklist*

"[Nicholson] delight[s] us with this discursive historical account of the who, what, where, why, when, and how of walking....Nicholson has walked everywhere from the Mojave Desert to the floor of Harrods, and many readers will wish they could join him on his next perambulation." —*Kirkus Reviews*

## ALSO BY GEOFF NICHOLSON

# Contents

· · · · · · · ·

The Lost Art of Walking

1
· · · · · · · ·

# AN INTRODUCTION:

## The Lost Art of Falling Down, When Bad Things Happen to Good Walkers, Some Fellow Travelers and Fellow Stumblers

*Walking isn't a lost art: one must,*
*by some means, get to the garage.*
—EVAN ESAR

A journey of a thousand miles begins with a single step," or so Lao-tzu, the Chinese Taoist sage, is often quoted as saying. In fact, this is a free translation of what he actually said, which was more like, "The journey of a thousand miles begins beneath your feet." My own feeling is that with most journeys, and especially the metaphoric sort, it's extremely difficult to decide where and when that first step occurs. We're already in motion before we know where we're going, before we even realize that we're on a journey at all. Designating a particular step as first or, for that matter, last is a tricky and often arbitrary business.

However, in my own case there was one particular step that was very different from any of the other steps I've ever taken in my life. It was a misstep, a stumble, a fall, a disagreement with gravity, a bone-breaking coming together of all-too-fragile body and all-too-solid earth.

Christmas was two days away, I was in Los Angeles, and I was feeling optimistic. I had decided to write a book about walking, my publisher had decided this was a fine idea, a commission was in the offing, and I was doing what could be construed as practical research. It was a warm, sunny California winter afternoon, and I was taking a long, hard walk in the Hollywood Hills.

That was where I lived at the time, and still do. It was, and is, one of my favorite places to walk in Los Angeles. It's intriguing and glossily peculiar territory, the craggy high ground up above the flatland of the city, a place with ascents and descents that are steep enough to get your heart and lungs pumping, which is the whole point. From up there you get panoramic views over the sprawl, occasionally you can see all the way to the ocean, and you regularly catch sight of the Hollywood sign. There are palm trees, cactus, and bougainvillea, and sometimes you turn a corner and are suddenly confronted by a coyote or a deer crossing the street, as though they, and you, were still out in the wild.

Yet the Hollywood Hills, like much of L.A., are still essentially suburban: the hedges are trimmed, freshly cleaned cars stand gleaming outside double or triple garages. Residents are house-proud, and they keep themselves to themselves, and that's one of the attractions. I was one of the few people who ever seemed to walk there. I encountered a few dog walkers, the odd person pushing a pram, the occasional jogger, a Mexican maid who didn't have transport, but I seldom saw anyone who was simply walking for the hell of it, as I was. I never saw anyone fall down.

Of course, I take full responsibility for my own actions and my own accident, but there remains something inscrutable about it. I was perfectly clean and sober, for instance; and it would surely have hurt less had I been drunk. True, I wasn't walking with any great care, but I wasn't so self-absorbed as to be oblivious to where I was putting my feet. And although I was in good spirits, I don't think there was any smugness or hubris in the equation. I certainly didn't think that nothing bad could happen to me.

I was walking along briskly, happily, the street had a steep downward slope, but there was nothing treacherous about it, nothing I hadn't successfully negotiated thousands of times before. There was even a sidewalk, by no means a given in many parts of L.A. But now, incomprehensibly, the negotiations broke down. I lost it. I tripped, I stumbled, I began to fall.

The older you get, the bigger a deal it is to fall down. When you're age five you can hit the deck, skin your knees, bleed profusely, and be up playing again in five minutes. The older falling man is so much more vulnerable. He's less supple, less resilient, less accustomed to the experience. He feels far more pain, embarrassment, and humiliation.

Even as I was falling I thought, Oh crap, I'm not really going to go all the way to the ground, am I? I'll stop myself somehow. I'll keep my footing. I'll regain my balance. And then I knew I was wrong about that. I was going all the way. I'd passed the tipping point. Oh crap, indeed.

Then there was the impact, a much greater, more generalized blow than I'd been anticipating. I was on the ground, winded, hurting all over, feeling like a fool, trying to breathe deeply and regularly, and thinking, possibly saying aloud, "Oh man, this really, really hurts, this is a bad one."

Even so, I didn't imagine I was actually going to do anything other than get up, dust myself off, and carry on walking. I thought I might have ripped a hole in my jeans, but that was all the damage I was expecting. So I made all the moves you'd make in order to stand up, using my arms to push myself off the ground, and then I realized I couldn't possibly do that: my right forearm was hurting far, far too much. And then I looked at the arm and saw that it appeared soft and spongy and was bent like a crescent roll. It was obviously, spectacularly broken. This was a brand-new experience. I hadn't lived an especially careful life. I'd had my share of accidents and impacts, but I'd never broken anything before. It seemed both shocking and unlikely.

Naturally, I've since tried to work out exactly what happened, and in the absolute sense, I don't know, and never will. But as far as I can tell, as I started to pitch forward, I reached out my right arm to break the fall. I had my camera in my left hand, and I was trying to protect it: a big mistake. All my weight and inertia homed in on my right wrist, with what now seems all-too-predictable results.

I lay on the ground unable to get up, and considered my options. If I'd had a cell phone with me I might have called 911 or, more likely, my wife, begging her to come pick me up, but I had no phone, just a camera, and I wondered if I could use the built-in flash as a distress signal. In the end it wasn't necessary.

I wasn't lying there very long before a guy getting into his car saw me on the ground, decided I wasn't a derelict or junkie, and came to my assistance. He hoisted me up and drove me to a nearby fire station. This was the smart way of doing things, he assured me. The firemen would be able to give me some immediate first aid, then drive me to a hospital, where, having arrived in an emergency vehicle, I'd be able to jump the line in the emergency room. All this, in due course, proved to be true.

I was taken care of by a young fireman who had his surname stitched onto the pocket of his uniform: the name was Finger. He was grimly impressed by the look of my arm. "How'd ya do that?" he asked. "Just walking," I said. He shook his head. It didn't seem right to him. It seemed downright weird. Normally, they only saw breaks like mine on people who'd fallen off ladders. He put me on a stretcher, put my arm in an inflatable splint, gave me enough morphine to disorientate me without quite killing the pain, and ferried me to a hospital, where everyone continued to respect the extremity of the injury.

The X-rays showed there wasn't just one break but three: two in the radius, one in the ulna, with huge displacement all round. I'd have to have some serious surgery, was the opinion of the X-ray guys, and I'd end up with metal pins in my arm. They were right about all this. And they, too, were impressed. They thought my injury was something out of the ordinary, as though I must be one wild and crazy dude to have done that to myself by whatever method. They said it looked like a skateboard injury, and this made me feel just a little better. Another dose of morphine made me feel better still.


A week later I had surgery at the Good Samaritan Hospital on Wilshire Boulevard. My doctor had a signed photograph of

Slash from Guns N' Roses on her wall, and Slash was obviously happy with the service.

Once I'd been operated on, put in a cast and splinted up, sent home, and begun the recovery period, I started meeting more people who asked what I'd done to myself. I sensed that they wanted to hear stories of knife fights, car wrecks, overturned Jet Skis, and I didn't want to disappoint them, though I didn't want to lie. I found myself saying, "The break was spectacular, even if the cause was pedestrian."

And there was always the big L.A. question: "Are you OK to drive?" Drive? Hell, I had problems enough walking. As a man working on a book on the subject, I felt I had a duty to try to keep pounding the streets, even with a broken arm. It didn't sound so hard. But walking with a broken arm is much more difficult than you, or certainly I, might imagine. For one thing, despite serious quantities of painkilling opiates, the arm continued to hurt like hell. There's a rich tradition of walking while enjoying opiate-induced sensory derangement—Baudelaire, De Quincey, Coleridge—but I didn't feel happily deranged; I simply hurt. And even if the arm didn't hurt when I set off walking, by the time I'd gone a few hundred yards the blood was circulating faster and setting off freshly revealed twinges and spasms.

More than that, walking while nursing an injured arm in a cast and sling throws off your balance and distorts the geometry of the walking body, creating various tensions and asymmetries that in themselves create further pain. My broken arm ached and it made the rest of my body ache, too. And that didn't end even when the cast came off. I was left nursing this tender, half-formed thing, something soft and without muscle: it was like having a week-old puppy dangling at the end of my arm, although in this case the puppy actually *was* the arm.

Worse, having fallen down once, I feared that I could all too easily do it again. It seemed my walking capabilities were no longer to be trusted. I still went out walking, but with a new attention to detail. I didn't go very far, and I made sure that I now wore ground-hugging, butt-ugly shoes. I walked more slowly, obsessively looked where my feet were going, and regarded curbs, steps, and changes in gradient as obstacles set specifically to undo me. Who knew walking was such a confidence game? Who knew it was so complicated and risky?

Well, quite a few people it turned out. I suddenly discovered that falling down while walking wasn't such a rare event. My friends and acquaintances turned out to be a poorly balanced crowd, and many of them had stories about getting a foot caught in a pothole in the street, losing their footing on slippery or uneven sidewalks, tumbling off wet stepping stones, or having pratfalls while walking across gravel driveways or parking lots. Sometimes, like me, they fell for no apparent reason whatsoever.

By some accounts, walking itself was a series of falls, a precarious balancing act that had the walker standing on one leg for most of the time, constantly pitching himself forward, transferring energy and weight in a reckless and dangerous manner, avoiding disaster only by constantly getting a foot down in the very nick of time.

Others said that spending your whole life on two legs was a downright odd thing to do. Plenty of mammals stand on two legs once in a while, but humans are the only ones ridiculous enough to do it all the time. The body just wasn't designed for it. All those bad backs and knees and feet and hips—we'd have had none of those things if only we'd remained on all fours. If a quadruped missed a step with one foot, there were three others right there to make up the difference. What was the big deal about bipedalism, anyway?

At one time, the explanation for bipedalism seemed simple enough, and was demonstrated in that old, familiar illustration: a line of rising, ever-more-human-looking creatures, a common ancestral ape at the far left-hand side, some chimplike critter walking on his knuckles in the middle, and a naked, spear-carrying *Homo sapiens* at the far right.

The text that accompanied this drawing would have told you that our ancient primate ancestors lived in trees and moved on all fours until a more sophisticated primate appeared, called *Ramapithecus*, that could stand up at least part of the time and could pick up things with its hands, probably rocks to throw at its enemies. Then, about five million years ago, *Australopithecus* came on the scene, tiny-brained but a proper upright walker who probably used stones or bones for specific tasks, though these didn't quite constitute "tools." Next, two and a half million years ago, along came "1470 man" with a better brain than any ape, and with the genuine ability to make and use tools. Standing on two legs is a great help when you want to use tools. *Homo erectus* arrived about half a million years ago, *Homo sapiens*, 250,000 years after that. The move was always onward and upward: four legs good, two legs better.

This narrative fits with what is known as the "savannah

hypothesis," which suggests that our ancestors were perfectly happy living in trees and would have remained there, but some profound ecological change occurred, leading to a catastrophic deforestation. Swinging from one tree to another was no longer possible because the trees were too far apart, and so a new form of travel was required. This new form involved some trial and error. At first we scrabbled on all fours, then raised ourselves a little, using our forearms and knuckles as necessary, and finally we made the breakthrough: we stood up and walked on two legs because that was the most efficient way of getting from nearby tree A to distant tree B.

Other theories of bipedalism suggest that walking on two legs simply uses less energy than walking on four: it's claimed that walking humans use 75 percent less energy than chimpanzees, for instance, and evolution favors efficiency. Another theory, the "thermoregulatory model," asserts that standing upright is advantageous because it keeps the body cooler, placing it in the vicinity of fresh, moving air. A different theory attributes bipedalism to changes in social and reproductive habits in early hominids. At a certain point in human development, males acquired the nurturing urge. They wanted to care for their families and to provide for them. They went out foraging and brought back what they'd gathered, carrying it in their arms. Since two limbs were engaged in the carrying, they were forced to walk on the other two.

These narratives don't strike me as mutually exclusive, though naturally there is fierce debate among supporters of the different theories. However, as a result of research done by two English scientists, Robin Crompton and Susannah Thorpe, the whole bipedal apple cart has now been upset. In the early 2000s, Crompton and Thorpe spent a year in the rain forests of Sumatra, studying and filming orangutans, a species that spends its entire life in trees, and therefore, one might have thought, a species with absolutely no use for bipedalism.

Well, it turns out the Sumatran orangutans are *extremely* bipedal. They may not walk on the ground, but they constantly stand on two legs and walk along tree branches, using their arms for balance and for gathering food. The conclusion is that we didn't come down from the trees and gradually adapt to walking on two feet, but that bipedalism was already part of the repertoire. Knuckle walking, therefore, wasn't an intermediate stage but a later development, necessitated in chimpanzees and gorillas because they're anatomically unable to straighten their legs.

If Crompton and Thorpe are correct, this information completely changes the way anthropologists are going to have to think about human development. It means, above all, that our ancestors didn't start walking upright approximately five million years ago, as previously thought, but more like ten or fifteen million years earlier. It also means that the precise "reasons" for bipedalism remain as obscure as ever.

I wasn't much cheered by all this theory. If my ancestors had been walking for fifteen to twenty million years, that really ought to be enough time to get the hang of it, to build the skill set into the race memory.

Things only got worse when I spoke to Dr. Martin Bax, an English pediatrician with an international reputation. Martin reckoned there was nothing difficult about walking. For instance, he told me, you can see the legs of unborn babies moving in the womb, making walking motions, from about seventeen weeks. This is a good sign and proof that the baby is healthy, mobile, and not tangled up in anything, but there's nothing very advanced about it: at seventeen weeks, the baby's cortex isn't fully formed, indicating that walking is a function of the spine or midbrain.

In the 1920s and '30s in Oxford, Martin said, an academic by the name of Sherington did experiments with decorticated cats. He removed their brains and found they were still able to walk perfectly well. Martin was also aware of some unpublished research done in England in the 1970s on aborted fetuses, and scientists had managed to get them walking, too. In other words, walking could be, quite literally, a brainless activity. You didn't even have to be alive to do it.

Once babies are out of the womb, Martin continued, they achieve "primary walking" at about six weeks of age. This isn't real walking because the babies have no sense of balance and no strength in their legs, so they can't stand up, but if you support them, they're able to make all the motions that are needed for walking. There are some extraordinary films and photographs, shot in the late 1920s by the German pediatrician Albrecht Peiper, in which given a certain kind of support, not only do babies walk on the ground, they can also walk up walls and on the ceiling.

In fact, there's a long artistic tradition of walking on the ceiling, often done by stage magicians. Ricky Jay writes about them in his *Journal of Anomalies.* Usually there's nothing very magical about the process. The illusion is created using suction cups, hidden ropes, or metal shoes that fit into grooves on the ceiling of a stage set.

More impressively, the Moscow Circus, in the 1960s, featured an act in which an acrobat walked upside down along the underside of a beam that was suspended above a cage full of tigers. Simultaneously, a tiger walked, upright, across the top of the beam. As the tiger walked, it triggered a series of hidden loops that dropped down from the underside of the beam: the upside-down acrobat then inserted his feet into the loops and walked along, too. This is an amazing feat not only of walking but also of coordination. The acrobat's steps had to match precisely those of the tiger.

A man might be forgiven for losing his footing in such circumstances, but what excuse did I have? If I couldn't even walk in the street without falling down and breaking my arm in three places, then I had to ask myself what my qualifications were for considering myself a walker.

The overriding one was that I liked walking: I liked it a lot. And I didn't just like it in the abstract, I liked *doing* it, and all through my life I'd always done it a lot, usually in an unorganized but nevertheless enthusiastic way, on four continents, at home and abroad, in town and country, in conditions that could be favorable or adverse.

Walking had certainly always been a pleasure, but it was more than that. For me walking has to do with exploration, a way of accommodating myself, of feeling at home. When I find myself in a new place I explore it on foot. It's the way I get to know that place. Maybe it's a way of marking territory, of beating the bounds. Setting foot in a street makes it yours in a way that driving down it never does.

Often I've walked for the simplest reasons, sometimes because I've had no choice. When I was younger and poorer, a three-mile walk home was the way I frequently rounded off an evening out. Sometimes walking is simply the most efficient way of getting from A to B. If you live in a big city, and for large chunks of my life I've lived in London and New York, walking is often infinitely preferable to using public transportation. When you walk you're your own boss.

On a very small number of occasions I've walked as an act of political protest, though I suspect my fellow protesters might have said they were on a "march" rather than a walk. These events pertained to the usual sorts of things—nuclear proliferation, the British poll tax, the "gate hours" at my old college, which prevented you from having girls in your room overnight. Actually the second and third of these protests might be thought to have been successful: both the poll tax and my college's gate hours were duly abandoned. The nuclear issue is evidently going to require a bit more walking.

I've also walked for charity, but that was some time ago, and even back then it struck me as a dubious thing to do. If people want to give money to charity, if they want to help fund a cure for AIDS or cancer or whatever, they should go right ahead and do it. They shouldn't have to wait for somebody else to promise to walk thirty miles and then sponsor them to do it. It suggests that walking is some eccentric and out-of-the ordinary activity, so rare that people would only do it for money, even if the money was going to a good cause. There's also the sense that walking is a form of suffering: by walking we share the pain and sorrow of the AIDS sufferer or the cancer patient. I object to both these propositions. Walking is special but it's not strange. It's not a stunt. It's worth doing for its own sake.

There is, of course, an environmental argument in favor of walking. Undoubtedly there would be green benefits if we all walked to work rather than drove there in our cars. Undoubtedly, also, we'd do less harm if we spent our leisure hours walking in quiet places rather than, say, off-roading in SUVs. However, the changes that would be needed to convert us into a nation of walkers rather than car users are so colossal that it seems to me we're not talking about promoting pedestrianism here, but rather about attempting to change human nature itself, which strikes me as, at best, an overambitious project. Yes, there was a time when everybody walked: they did it because they had no choice. The moment they had a choice, they chose not to do it.

If the pedestrian-advocate movement has a solution to this problem, I've yet to hear it. But the main problem I have with the activist walking lobby is that its members seek to make a hard and fast division between walkers and drivers: walkers are saints, drivers are pure evil. This doesn't match my experience of humanity. Most of us are both walkers and drivers. Sure, I find drivers annoying when I walk, but I also find pedestrians annoying when I drive. It's not clear to me that absolute virtue resides on either side.

More than that, even the most environmentally conscious walkers sometimes get in their cars and drive considerable distances in order to go walking. I can see the obvious contradiction in this, but I don't find it genuinely pernicious. Sometimes the neighborhood just isn't enough. In any case, my walking isn't intended to save the planet.

Great claims are also made for the health benefits of walking, for its capacity to make us lean and fit, but I have serious doubts about this. Clearly walking is better than nothing, and in general it does the body no harm (unless you happen to pull, sprain, twist, or break something, or get run down by a car). But the number of calories burned while walking is really unimpressive. A 180-pound man walking at four miles an hour burns up about 100 calories per mile. True, a 300-pound man walking at five miles an hour burns 218 calories per mile, but I suspect there are rather few 300-pound men who are capable of walking at five miles per hour even for brief periods.

The fact is, to the dismay of anyone who's ever tried to lose weight, a pound of body fat contains 3,500 calories. In other words, to lose a pound of flesh, you need to walk thirty-five miles. There must be easier ways of doing it. In any case, I don't walk in order to get or stay fit. If there's any such thing as a desirable "walker's physique," I have yet to see it.

I've never walked professionally, though I've had jobs that required me to do a fair amount of walking: garbageman, gardener, security man, drone in a department store. Actually, in the last case the walking wasn't so much work as a way of avoiding work. I was employed by Harrods in London, a vast and labyrinthine, multifloored department store, ripe for exploration. I discovered, as many had before me, that a man who displayed a false sense of purpose and held a piece of paper in his hand could wander just about anywhere in the place and everybody would always assume he was going about his proper business.

And so at Harrods I walked constantly, relentlessly, through airless, air-conditioned departments, up and down escalators and staircases, moving just purposefully enough to avoid giving the impression that I was loafing. I circulated through the pet department, ate samples in the food hall, went to the musical instrument department, where I admired the grand pianos. I investigated book and record departments, checked out men's suits. Sometimes I lurked in the electronics department and watched TV; on the odd occasion I even found myself in the bridal department admiring empire bodices and taffeta trains.

And although I wasn't being paid to walk, I did earn money while I was doing it, in the sense that I earned the same amount of money whether I was doing anything useful or not. Since I hated the job so much, every moment that I wasn't doing what I was supposed to be doing became a victory; a modest victory to be sure, but I took my satisfactions where I could find them. When I eventually returned to my own desk after what might have been an hour-long walking expedition, it was rare for anyone in the office to notice I'd even been away, although one Australian colleague did regularly accuse me of "going walkabout."

The word *walking* looks and sounds like a simple, honest, straightforward one, and in some ways it is. The dictionary tells us it has its origin in late Middle English, and therefore doesn't need a Greek or Latin precursor. Latin terms such as *ambulare* or *pedibus ire* seem needlessly fancy; the classical Greek *peripateo*, *stoicheo*, or *erchomai* are just downright unfamiliar.

Yet perhaps that very simplicity in English is why we need so many qualifiers, so many synonyms, or not quite synonyms, for walking, each word with its own shade and delineation of meaning. I found it revealing to see which of these words applied to my own walking and which didn't. Tell me how you walk and I'll tell you who you are.

For example, I've performed all the slack, idle, casual, purposeless forms of walking. I've strolled and wandered, pottered and tottered, dawdled and shuffled, mooched and sauntered and meandered.

I've certainly ambled, and I could be said to have rambled (though the British Ramblers' Association is made up of hale, out-doorsy hearties who would probably spit on my walking efforts and dismiss them as trifling), and probably I've also shambled, but I don't think I've ever gamboled.

I've definitely hiked, or at least I've definitely been on paths that call themselves hiking trails, but hiking conjures up a degree of seriousness, organization, and specialized clothing that I never quite trust. One of the minor but profound satisfactions of being on a grand, well-known hiking trail is to swan along in shorts, sneakers, and a T-shirt, and to encounter others who are dressed as though for an assault on Annapurna. By the same token I've also trekked.

I've trudged, tramped, and slogged, and in New York I've cer-tainly schlepped. As I say, I've never marched in any military or quasi-military sense. Incidentally, the phrase "Bolivian marching powder" as a euphemism for cocaine, much popularized by the literary firm of McInerney and Ellis in the 1980s, turns out to have a much earlier origin. In the First World War, British sol-diers were given cocaine-based tablets, known as "forced march tablets," though I'd have thought all marching is forced; the sol-diers wouldn't be doing it if they hadn't been ordered to.

At the time of the Falklands War, the people of England heard a lot about British soldiers "yomping" to Port Stanley. It's unwise for a civilian to offer a hard-and-fast opinion on army slang, but I believe yomping involves crossing rough terrain carrying a full pack, and is similar to, but significantly different from, "tabbing." Marines yomp; paratroopers tab, which according to some sources stands for "tactical advance to battle." Tabbing is about speed; yomping is about distance. Unless you've been a British soldier it would be unwise to claim to have done either.

A couple of times when suffering from tendonitis or bursitis (walkers' complaints) I've limped and hobbled. I've waded, which is walking in, though not on, water. I've occasionally, metaphorically, walked on air, and I have probably, again not literally, sometimes walked a tightrope and walked on eggshells. Apparently when I was a child I sleepwalked a few times, but I have no memory of it. When I was a would-be playwright we did walk-throughs of my plays. Occasionally I've been given my walking papers. I have never, Byronically, walked in beauty like the night.

I have certainly drifted. However, that's a word that contains one highly specialized meaning, coming from the French founders and followers of psychogeography, who speak of the *dérive*, which translates as drift, both noun and verb. Psychogeography, as a word, and sometimes as a practice, looms large over the contemporary, literary walker, including me. It was the brainchild of a Frenchman, Guy Debord, who defined it in 1955 as "the study of the precise laws and specific effects of the geographical environment." He and his fellow psychogeographers liked to think of themselves as flâneurs: urban and urbane, disciples of Baudelaire, bohemian dandies who walked around the city observing cool stuff, often stoned. There will be much more of this later, but essentially we're back in the realm of sensory derangement and heightened sensibility, a condition that may cause a man to stagger, roll, barrel, career, or careen. I've walked in some of these ways; maybe I've even floated. The extent to which this actually makes me, or anyone else, a flâneur is debatable.

I don't think I've ever cruised. I'm not sure that cruising is a thing a heterosexual man can do. I'm equally sure I've never trolled or minced. Edmund White tells us that whereas in English the word *cruise* is an exclusively gay term, the equivalent French word *drageur* is also heterosexual. "Straight people cruise one another in Paris," he writes, in a book called, tellingly, *The Flâneur*, "unlike Americans, who feel menaced or insulted by looks on the street." Ah, those poor, sensitive Americans.

There is, undoubtedly, a sexual component to walking. Actually having real sex while walking, that's just about impossible, but some people are very sexy when they walk, and a great many more people think about sex as they walk. In the days when I had a real job and a real place of work, I'd live for the lunch hour, when I could get out and walk the streets and look at all the women who were also walking the streets on their lunch hour. We're talking about the male gaze here, a dangerously ubiquitous phenomenon apparently, and one immortalized in the Frank Loesser song "Standing on the Corner":

> Brother you can't go to jail for what you're thinking
> Or for that "woooo" look in your eye...

Some would probably have it otherwise; and yes, walking is a very different prospect for men than for women.

I'm always fascinated by the female models in fashion shows, the ones who parade up and down on the runways and catwalks. They're sexy, all right, and it's got a lot to do with the way they walk, but it's a very specialized form of walking. They strut and stomp, they stride out, hammer their feet down, scissor their legs across each other, and look as though they're really determined to get somewhere, but of course they never really do get anywhere. They just get to the end of the runway and then they spin around on their stiletto heels and head back precisely where they came from. This only just counts as walking. And *runway* is such a strange term, because it sounds like they're at the airport, taxiing, getting ready to fly. But these fashion models never lift off. They don't even run on the runway.

*Streetwalker* is another term that doesn't quite describe the sexuality or the style of walking to which it refers. Yes, streetwalkers operate in the street, and, yes, they're on their feet, but how much walking do they actually do? Streetwalkers have always been the lowest of prostitutes. The *Oxford English Dictionary* dates the word to 1592, but even if the word was newfangled at the time, the practice surely was not. The streetwalker is, and always has been, the most vulnerable of sex professionals. The sight of a woman walking at night, whether she's selling herself or not, is enough to stir uncontrollable urges in some men. It has required some women to take back the night.

And yet, here and now in the West, women walkers are surely safer than they've ever been. That may not be saying a whole lot, but here's the Spanish feminist Margarita Nelken claiming that walking was the one thing that separated her, a twentieth-century woman, from her mother and grandmother. "This footing," she writes, "this morning walk—elastic step, rhythmic body in loose, comfortable clothing—of the girls that walk for hygiene in these clear and warm days of early spring...they have opened the windows of the sad room in which their grandmothers sat." She wrote that in 1923 in a magazine called *La Moda Elegante*.

There are, I think, certain ways in which sex and walking closely resemble each other. For one thing, they're both at heart basic, simple, repetitive activities that just about everybody does at one time or another. And yet despite being so ordinary and commonplace, they're both capable of great sophistication and elaboration. They can be completely banal and meaningless, and yet they can also involve great passions and adventures. Both can lead you into strange and previously unknown territories: a walk on the wild side.

So, if I have never cruised, catwalked, or streetwalked, I also hope I've never flounced, as in "flounced out of the room." *Stormed*, I think, is the preferred manly word here. Sometimes, less forcefully, I may have sloped off or stolen away. I have sidled, tiptoed, pussyfooted, perhaps even slunk.

I have hit the streets, pounded the pavement, worn out shoe leather, taken shank's pony, hotfooted it, legged it, strode out, loped, paced. So far I have never waddled, but as the years pass and the pounds pack on, it may be a fate awaiting me.

Otherwise I may well have promenaded, pedestrianized, peregrinated, ambulated, perambulated, circumambulated, hoofed, and locomoted, but these aren't words I'd ever normally use. And I've never said, as apparently they do in Cockney rhyming slang, "gone for a ball of chalk," although I've probably done the deed it describes, which is essentially to "get lost."

I'm sure I've strutted, but I'm pretty damn sure that I've never swaggered. In a notorious speech he made at the Republican National Convention in 2004, George W. Bush said, to the delight of the supportive crowd and the consternation of others, "Some folks look at me and see a certain swagger. In Texas we call it walkin'."

In fact, the word *swagger* has its origins in the Norwegian dialect word *svagga*, meaning to sway, which may not be quite what the ex-president had in mind. However, given the capacity of the English language to soak up words from elsewhere, it's hardly surprising that many of our words for walking originate in other tongues.

French gives us *promenade* and *march*, and the word *mooch* has its origins in the Old French *muchier*, meaning to hide or skulk. We get *shuffle* from the Low German *schüffeln*, and *tramp* from Old Teutonic. *Trek* comes from the Dutch, via South Africa. *Flounce* comes from *flunsa*, a Scandinavian word that means hurry in Norwegian and plunge in Swedish.

What's more surprising is that if you consult the *Oxford English Dictionary* to find where the words *trudge, stroll,* and *saunter* come from, you'll find them simply designated "origins obscure." *Hike* is "original dialect obscure." *Strut* is "obscure," and *ramble* is simply "origin unknown."

Some words, more comprehensibly, have been borrowed from other parts of English for their metaphoric possibilities.

*Ambling*, for instance, despite its historic Latin origins, was once a thing done only by horses; *meandering* was done only by rivers. The word *slope*, as in slope off, didn't contain the sense of walking at all until the mid-nineteenth century, and is one of the few genuine all-American coinages. *Pussyfoot* is another, even later one, being the nickname of one W. E. Johnson, a lecturer and advocate of Prohibition.

I began to wonder whether other languages have as many words for walking as English does. I put the question out among my polyglot friends and acquaintances and was impressed by their enthusiasm for the subject. Any misinformation in the paragraphs that follow is naturally all their fault.

A friend in São Paolo reported with dismay that his Portuguese thesaurus listed only eight synonyms for walking, and none of them approximated his favorite word, *trudge*. Another friend, whose Farsi is admittedly rusty, came up, via her mother and grandfather, with nine synonyms, including *kharamiden*—to walk elegantly, like a deer; *jahiden*—to walk percussively, like a frog; and *verjeh vorjeh karden*—to squirm about. The Norwegians seemed much better supplied. My source came up with over fifty synonyms, including *vagge*, *flakke*, *sjangle*, and *spankulere*.

From an American now living in Italy I learned such colorful walking phrases as *darsela a gambe* (to make with the legs) and *alzare i tacchi* (pick up the heels), both of which mean to run away. He also came up with the word *cammellare*, literally to walk like a camel, a style adopted by disaffected youths who slouch along, head down, creating a camel-like hump on their backs.

The Germans, I learned, have the quaint expression *auf Schuster's Rappen*, which means "on the shoemaker's black horses," pretty much the equivalent of shank's pony, and a particular favorite of mine is *Um den Pudding laufen*, which means to walk round the block or go the long way round, or literally "running around the pudding."

Instead of using various different words for walking, the Japanese use a common base verb, then add an assortment of phenomimes, which are used as adverbs. So *aruku* is the basic word meaning to walk, then *chokochoko aruku* is to toddle, *noronoro aruku* is to inch along, *furafura aruku* is to shamble or teeter, and *zorozoro aruku* is to swarm or cluster.

Sometimes, as in Russian, a reverse principle seems to be at work. Instead of having many words for walk, the word for walk itself can have many meanings other than simply putting one foot in front of the other. The Russian word *hodit'* is usually translated simply as to walk or to go, but it also contains the senses of sail, ply, move, visit, attend to a sick person, circulate money, wear, look after, take care of, nurse, step, straddle, foster children, play cards, scuff, scuffle, shin, flop along, tag along, herd, tend to, track, traffic, go at a crawl, and find one's feet.

The Dutch use one or two words that look a lot like their English counterparts—*lopen, wandelen, promeneren*, for instance—but they also have the wonderful *ijsberen*, which means pacing to and fro (*ijsbeer* being the Dutch word for polar bear). They also use *flaneren*, which brings us back to the French word *flâner*, and to psychogeography.

The French have really hit the conceptual jackpot with the word *flâner*, a truly wonderful word in that it means simultaneously to walk and to not walk. It can indeed mean to stroll, but it can also mean the act of simply hanging around, staying right where you are and not walking at all. There is something gloriously perverse about this, and it is, of course, the root of *flâneur*.

Another part of my qualifications for considering myself a walker was my familiarity with the standard texts on walking. The connection between walking and writing is an obvious one. Walkers write; writers walk. There are quite a number of usual suspects:

Thoreau, because he wrote the "book," or essay or lecture, called "Walking." And his fellow Americans Emerson and Hawthorne and Whitman, the last of whom wrote, "Afoot and lighthearted / I take to the open road."

And Wordsworth, and also his sister Dorothy, who walked with him and wrote about it in her diary: "March 30, 1798. Walked I know not where. March 31, 1798. Walked. April 1, 1798. Walked by moonlight." And their friend Coleridge, who calculated that Wordsworth had walked 180,000 miles over the course of his life. And De Quincey, and William Blake, and John Clare, and John Keats with an epistolary account of his walking tour of the Lake District and the Scottish Highlands.

And Boswell and Johnson touring the Western Isles, which must have been a strain, given Boswell's description of Johnson's physical condition: "His figure was large and well formed, and his countenance of the cast of an ancient statue; yet his appearance was rendered strange and somewhat uncouth, by convulsive cramps. . . . So morbid was his temperament, that he never knew the natural joy of a free and vigorous use of his limbs: when he walked, it was like the struggling gait of one in fetters."

And Mark Twain in the Alps, and Robert Frost in "The Road Not Taken," which is a wonderful work if you read it as a poem suggesting that you end up in much the same place regardless of which road you take, and you might think that's the only sensible way it can be read, yet there seem to be a lot of people who want to read it as a poem about strident individualism.

And Charles Dickens, naturally, passim, but especially in "Night Walks" and the opening of *The Old Curiosity Shop*, and there are the stories about him saying to guests at his house, "Let's have a walk before dinner," and then dragging them around the countryside for a few hours and coming home later after covering twelve or thirteen miles.

And Henri Michaux's poem "Marchand," which puns, in French, on *marchant* meaning walking and *merchant* meaning salesman. And Frank O'Hara's poem "Walking to Work," with the opening lines "It's going to be the sunny side / from now / on," and also his poem "Ode on Causality," which contains the phrase "standing still and walking in New York," which is also the title of a collection of his essays.

And there's Joyce's *Ulysses*, and Paul Auster's *New York Trilogy*, and Walter Benjamin, and Flaubert, and Proust in *Swann's Way*, and Borges in "The Garden of Forking Paths," and Samuel Beckett in *Lessness*—"One step in the ruins in the sand on his back in the endlessness he will make it."

I respect the great, more or less, contemporary nonfiction walkers, travel writers such as John Hillaby, Peter Jenkins, Edward Abbey, and Bill Bryson. And one or two of them, Sebastian Snow and Bruce Chatwin, I absolutely love. But I have a problem reading most of them. They make me feel guilty. They make me feel

I should be doing what they're doing. I should be out there walking, covering the miles, pitting myself against the elements, not sitting about reading.

Modern literary theory sees a similarity between walking and writing that I find persuasive: words inscribe a text in the same way that a walk inscribes space. In *The Practice of Everyday Life*, Michel de Certeau writes, "The act of walking...is a process of appropriation of the topographical system on the part of the pedestrian; it is a special acting-out of the place...and it implies relations among differentiated positions." I think this is a fancy way of saying that writing is one way of making the world our own, and that walking is another.

Being outside the loop of academic theory, I had never come across de Certeau until I read an essay by Markus Poetzsch, which I sought out because I was so impressed by its title, "Walks Alone and 'I know not where': Dorothy Wordsworth's Deviant Pedestrianism." As well as parsing de Certeau, Poetzsch writes, "No less than the physical act, the literary acts of Romantic pedestrianism are, from their earliest beginnings, bound up with notions of deviance and deviation, with a willful turning away from what is generically, or shall we say topographically, normative: the well-trodden path. From the 'devious feet' of William Wordsworth's speaker in 'An Evening Walk,' to the socially and 'self-leveling expeditions'...of Thelwall's 'Ambulator,' to the unsociable traveler in Hazlitt's 'On Going a Journey' who walks expressly 'to get rid of others'...to Clare's autobiographical account of his escape from High Beech asylum near Epping, the textualization of walking in the period is marked by a self-conscious nonconformism. The mere act of foregrounding this most taken-for-granted and familiar of motions signals unconventionality, for it ascribes to pedestrian activities hitherto unrealized significance."

As I sat in Los Angeles rereading the literature, nursing my broken arm, and doing rather little walking, I was at least becoming a student of my own condition, and I found one interesting local literary precedent. In the 1950s Aldous Huxley, author, explorer of inner space, knocker at the doors of perception, had lived in the Hollywood Hills, not far from where I did. The Hills reminded him of Greece.

Huxley was a walker, writer, and thinker in the great English literary tradition. David King Dunaway's *Huxley in Hollywood* describes a typical day in the life of Aldous Huxley: getting up, writing six to ten pages, eating the lunch prepared for him by his maid, and then at one-thirty setting off on a long walk through the Hollywood Hills, getting back home in time for tea.

He often walked with other people—his wife arranged a series of entertaining but inconsequential mistresses for him—but on at least one occasion he walked alone and had a nasty fall. The area was far less built up than now and Huxley fell among scrub and dirt, a soft landing compared to mine and one that didn't result in any breakages. However, Huxley's fall was also less unexpected than mine. He was an old man and half-blind. He had far better excuses than I did, but I still liked to think of him as a fellow traveler and tumbler.

A better precedent, I discovered, was Thomas Jefferson, a mad keen walker by all accounts but also an unfortunate one. In Paris, in 1785, he, too, fell over while walking and broke his right wrist. There are various accounts of the circumstances: that he fell while jumping over a wall, in the company of an unnamed friend, though sometimes the unnamed friend is an unnamed married woman and sometimes the wall becomes a kettle. These are all, it seems to me, variations on the same story, though another variant has the broken wrist caused by a fall off a horse, which definitely spoils things.

What seems certain is that Jefferson didn't get very good treatment from the doctors of Paris. His arm was completely out of action for several weeks and gave him trouble for the rest of his life. Much later, in 1821, just a few years before his death, he fell again, on a broken step while descending a staircase, and this time broke the left arm.

And then there is Jean-Jacques Rousseau, he of *The Reveries of the Solitary Walker*. On the second walk, he's on the road "down from Menilmontant almost opposite the Galant Jardinière," having spent an afternoon in "peaceful meditations," when he sees a Great Dane barreling toward him, running ahead of a carriage, which apparently was the style in those days. Rousseau decides that in order to avoid being knocked down he'll make a "great leap...so well timed that the dog would pass under me while I was still in the air."

History doesn't tell us how big the Great Dane was, but it couldn't have been very small if Rousseau thought it was going to knock him down, so say it was three feet tall; I don't know how much of an athlete Rousseau was, but if he was really thinking about jumping three feet straight up in the air from a standing start, he must have had a high regard for his own prowess. His abilities weren't put to the test. While he was doing his calculations about when and how to jump, the dog hit him and knocked him over and out. "I did not feel the blow, nor the fall, nor anything of what followed until the moment I came to," he wrote.

He was so stunned that he suffered from momentary amnesia, didn't know where he was, and couldn't even tell the people who picked him up where he lived. But eventually he remembered. Someone advised him to get a cab home, but he didn't, he *walked*, "easily and sprightly, feeling neither pain nor hurt, though I kept spitting out a lot of blood." And eventually he got home. "My wife's cries on seeing me made me understand I was worse off than I thought."

Fortunately, he wasn't as badly off as *some* people thought. The *Courier d'Avignon* on December 20, 1776, mistakenly reported that he was dead: "M. Jean-Jacques Rousseau has died from the after-effects of his fall. He lived in poverty; he died in misery; and the strangeness of his fate accompanied him all the way to the tomb."

Dying while out walking: it doesn't get much stranger than that. It's certainly much stranger and more epic than breaking an arm. And in some ways I found myself wishing that my own injuries had been stranger, or at least more dramatic. Nobody is impressed by or even very sympathetic toward a broken arm. Nobody, and I include myself in that category, understands how it might send you into a tailspin of melancholy. As I recuperated physically, I found myself becoming increasingly, and it seemed to me unjustifiably, gloomy and depressed. The intensity of the feelings seemed out of all proportion to the injury. OK, so I'd broken my arm; OK, so I couldn't walk as much as I wanted to; in fact, I was scarcely walking at all. But why would that plunge me into the kind of despair I was feeling? It seemed unfathomable.

And then I read Oliver Sacks's book *A Leg to Stand On*. It describes how he broke his leg while walking, and the long, surprisingly traumatic process of his recovery. The story of his break offered all the surface drama and excitement that my own lacked. He did it while walking on a mountain in Norway, and he fell while being chased by a bull. The injury was serious. He was alone on the mountain and it took him six hours to drag himself to anything like safety. He might easily have died.

Sacks's break was complicated, the convalescence infinitely more painful and protracted than mine. His triggered a personal and professional crisis, and although my own injury wasn't quite doing that, not yet anyway, I feared that it might, and I saw all too clearly how an injury that the world regarded as trivial, as little more than a simple repair job, could completely change your view of the world and yourself.

Sacks's case was complicated because he was a doctor who suddenly became a patient, a change of role and status that I imagine all members of the medical profession would find threatening. But he also experienced an anguish far more general, yet from where I was now standing (or slumping) far more recognizable than that. He writes, "Almost every patient who had had injury or surgery to a limb, and whose limb had been casted, out of sight, out of action, had experienced at least some degree of alienation: I heard of hands and feet which felt 'queer,' 'wrong,' 'strange,' 'unreal,' 'uncanny,' 'detached,' and 'cut off.'" . . . Yes, that seemed to be describing my own condition, but I'd have said it was more than that. I didn't just feel detached from my injured arm; I felt detached from the whole world.

As I sat around the house in L.A. nursing my broken arm, and doing no walking, I became increasingly dispirited. I was feeling depressed, and although there were some reasons for that, those reasons didn't seem great or serious enough to justify the scale of my feelings. I felt feeble, vulnerable, becalmed, utterly miserable. I was spending my time reading books about walking, but I thought I might never walk out of the house again. I considered myself a good and enthusiastic walker, a fully qualified pedestrian. I loved walking: it was a source of happiness, wonder, and enlightenment. Yet a walk to the end of the street now seemed as impossible as a journey of a thousand miles. I told myself I wasn't doing any walking because I was so depressed and enervated. And then I thought of something. Perhaps I was depressed and enervated precisely because I wasn't doing any walking.

I should have realized this much sooner. There was something very familiar about it. It was something I had worked out some time ago, then managed to forget. The truth is, the real reason I walk is because I have to. I walk because it keeps me sane. I had proved this to myself a couple of years back when I first arrived in Los Angeles.

# 2
· · · · · · · ·

## LOS ANGELES:
## Walking Wounded with Ray and Phil
## and Others

*I took the steps down Angel's Flight to Hill Street: a hundred and forty steps,*
*with tight fists, frightened of no man, but scared of the Third Street Tunnel,*
*scared to walk through it—claustrophobia. Scared of high places too, and of*
*blood, and of earthquakes; otherwise, quite fearless, excepting death, except*
*the fear I'll scream in a crowd, except the fear of appendicitis, except the fear*
*of heart trouble.*

—JOHN FANTE, *Ask the Dust*

John Paul Jones, the bass player of Led Zeppelin, has a
story that he still trots out in interviews, of how he was
arrested in the 1970s for leaving his hotel room and daring to
walk the streets of Los Angeles. "I didn't realize you're not supposed to walk anywhere," he says.

D. J. Waldie, author of *Holy Land*, writes about the one-mile
daily walk from his home to his office (actually in Lakewood, in
Los Angeles County, rather than the city). He describes being
"stopped by a sheriff's patrol car on a completely empty stretch

of suburban sidewalk, at midday, dressed in a coat and tie, and ordered to identify myself and explain my destination. As a pedestrian, I was a suspect."

Waldie was perhaps channeling Ray Bradbury, author of the dystopic science fiction short story "The Pedestrian," in which the hero is picked up by totalitarian cops who know he must be up to no good simply because he's a walker.

There are at least two pop songs—"Nobody Walks in L.A." by Ashford & Simpson, and "Walking in L.A." by Missing Persons—that express much the same sentiment, although the actual message of these songs is not so much that nobody walks in L.A., but rather that nobody who's *anybody* walks in L.A.

Jean Baudrillard, in his book *America*, writes, "As soon as you start walking in Los Angeles you are a threat to public order, like a dog wandering in the road."

All these add up to a fine and persuasive legend, and as they say in John Ford's *The Man Who Shot Liberty Valance*, "This is the West, sir. When the legend becomes fact, print the legend."


I had moved to Los Angeles with my then girlfriend, now wife, a few years earlier. We'd gone there partly for work, and partly in order to live out certain fantasies, both Epicurean and apocalyptic, about California. I admit I didn't go there for the walking.

We found a place to live, bought a couple of cheap cars, my girlfriend started her job, and I sat in the house, writing as ever, and then doing the sorts of things you do in L.A., going to Musso & Frank Grill, to the Getty, to a couple of Frank Lloyd Wright sites, to the Museum of Jurassic Technology, to the beach. Life was conspicuously good. I had nothing at all to complain about. And I became completely and utterly depressed.

Now, I know what some of you are thinking: "Good. Any halfway civilized man who's lived in Europe or on the East Coast of America and then chooses to move to the vacuous wastelands of Los Angeles *deserves* to be depressed by the thinness and vacuity of the culture, by the superficiality and prefabricated good looks of the people, perhaps simply by the ease of being in a place where the sun usually shines and the living is too easy." Well, only up to a point.

I soldiered on through my depression, didn't do the obvious L.A. thing, which would have been to see a therapist or have some mood-lightening plastic surgery. Instead, I tried to pretend it wasn't happening. I carried on with my housebound, sedentary writer's life. My writing was going well enough. I tried to be cheerful but it didn't work.

And then one day I was sitting gloomily in the sunroom reading the newspaper and I came across one of those "recent medical evidence shows" types of articles. The evidence came from Duke University and it concerned the treatment of depression. The research said that a twenty-minute walk three times a week was better medicine, and did patients more good, than all the antidepressants in the world.

This shouldn't have surprised me. Robert Burton, author of *The Anatomy of Melancholy* and a hero of mine, realized something similar in about 1621. He regards walking as a cure for melancholy, and says, "The most pleasant of all outward pastimes is that of Aretaeus, deambulatio per amoena loca (strolling through pleasant scenery), to make a petty progress, a merry journey now and then with some good companions, to visit friends, see cities, castles, towns ... to walk amongst orchards, bowers, mounts, and arbors, artificial wildernesses, green thickets, arches, groves, lawns, rivulets, fountains, and such-like pleasant places, like that Antiochian Daphne, brooks, pools, fishponds, between wood and water, in a fair meadow, by a river-side. . . ."

He's free-associating by this point, and you could draw a parallel between the obsessive, indirect yet forward movement of his prose and similar qualities found in the act of walking. The effect is spoiled, however, because although Burton says walking is the most *pleasant* way of banishing melancholy, he doesn't think it's superior to a great many other ways of doing it. He also highly rates watching a battle.

Duke and Burton aside, even I knew that exercise stimulates the production of endorphins, "nature's painkillers," and the fact was, just about the only exercise I'd ever done, certainly the only exercise I'd ever enjoyed, was walking.

A light went on.

For most of my adult life I'd lived in London and New York, which, we are constantly being told, are two of the world's great walking cities. In these places I hadn't just walked for twenty minutes three times a week, I'd walked every single day, sometimes for hours. It was how I got around. It was how I related to the city. In my spare time I'd head off to some unknown part of town and explore it on foot, alone or with other people.

I frequently met others who did very much the same. There was even a solid literary tradition. In London you had Dickens, De Quincey, Iain Sinclair; in New York you had Walt Whitman, Alfred Kazin, Paul Auster. Other great cities had their own great literary walkers. In Los Angeles it was different. I'd heard the pop songs, read Baudrillard and some John Paul Jones interviews. As far as I was aware back then, there was no tradition, no history, no literature of walking here. I now know that I was wrong (more of that later), but at the time I thought walking in L.A. was a foolish and freakish thing.

Be that as it may, for the sake of my own sanity, I started walking. And the truth is that the moment I started walking, I saw plenty of other people doing the same. There were people dog walking, streetwalking, power walking. There were always tourists, in Hollywood or Santa Monica or taking self-guided tours of downtown. People walked with their kids, kids walked by themselves, old people walked together. There were walkers everywhere.

Some, of course, may have been walking to their cars, having been forced to park some distance away from where they really wanted to be. Some may have walked unwillingly because they were simply too poor to own a car, because they had lousy jobs or were freshly immigrated, or both. Some of the walkers were homeless, pushing shopping carts full of recyclables. A few were simply mad. I joined them. I became an L.A. walker.


I had first set foot in Los Angeles in 1975. I'd got there by hitchhiking. When I was twenty-one years old I crossed the continental United States on foot. Sometimes I think I only ever did it so that sometime later I'd be able to say, "When I was twenty-one years old I crossed the continental United States on foot." It also had something to do with having read a lot, arguably too much, of Jack Kerouac.

The received wisdom about Kerouac back then had him as the king of the hippie hitchhikers. This, as we now know, was inaccurate in almost every way. He wasn't a hippie, and he wasn't a king, and although he did a certain amount of hitchhiking, he was just as likely to catch a bus or hop a freight train or be driven by Neal Cassady in a borrowed or stolen car. I was ready to experience all these modes of transport, but my initial plan was to stand by the American roadside with my thumb stuck out to get lifts along the way from Toronto (I had good, dull reasons to start there) to Isla Vista, in California, where I had a semilegal job lined up.

Today it sounds to me as absurd, difficult, and dangerous a plan as it must have sounded to my father at the time. To be fair to him, he didn't raise any objections on the grounds of personal safety. After all, he'd run off to join the Royal Navy when he was sixteen, in the middle of World War Two, and found himself in the thick of it on a minesweeper in the Mediterranean. His worries were more on the grounds of practicality.

I remember him saying to me, "But what if you don't get any lifts?"

The idea had literally never occurred to me.

"Of course I'll get lifts," I said.

My father thought about this. "Well, I hope so," he said. "I mean, if you had to get from here to London"—"here" was our home in Sheffield, in the north of England, 165 miles from the capital—"then I suppose you could get there eventually just by walking. But getting to California, well, it'd take you forever."

And, of course, I did get lifts, plenty of them, some of them colorful, only one of them with obvious lethal potential. I'll spare you most of my hitchhiking stories, but the fact is, when you hitchhike you do a lot of walking, far more than you want to. You get dropped off in places you don't want to be, in places where no other car would ever stop to pick you up. So you walk on to the next crossroads where more traffic joins the road, or to a nice long, clear stretch where a car can pull in easily, or two miles farther to a field where you can sleep for the night.

My best hitchhiking and walking moment came somewhere in semirural Oklahoma. There was a bleak, empty highway on my left and weed-strewn railway tracks on my right, and I admit that my memory may have made the image a little more cinematic than it really was, but the story is as true as I can make it.

A long way up ahead I saw an old black man walking toward me. He was lean, loose, in work clothes. His walk was solid and serviceable, but so very weary-looking. We were approaching each other for a good long time and we made eye contact long before we got within hailing distance. When we finally came face-to-face the old guy said, "I wish I was where you just comin' from." I've spent a lot of time over the years trying to think of some witty thing I should have said in reply.

Eventually, and a little reluctantly, my hitchhiking took me to Los Angeles. Even before I'd left England everybody had told me that L.A. was impossible without a car, and I saw no reason to doubt them. I'd even read Kerouac's opinion, in *On the Road*, that "Los Angeles is a jungle," and though I certainly wished he'd come up with a more interesting metaphor, I again thought it was probably true.

There are plenty of lacunae in my memories of that first visit, but I do remember the lift that took me into L.A. The driver, who looked like a hippie from Central Casting—bearded, mellow, soft-spoken, and pretty well-heeled, judging by his car—proudly pointed out as we approached the city that we were driving on a twelve-lane highway, and he made a detour so that he could drive down Sunset Boulevard and show me the Strip. He was especially keen that I see the huge billboards, and as I remember it they were of the Marlboro Man, Peter Frampton, and Joe Cocker, but again, time may have buffed up these memories.

My new pal dropped me off on Hollywood Boulevard, at a fleapit that called itself a "motor hotel," and even so cost far more than I could afford. I'd hoped that somewhere along the way I might have been befriended by fun-loving hippie chicks who'd invite me to stay in their commune in Laurel Canyon, but that hadn't materialized.

Hollywood Boulevard was a scary place in the mid-seventies, though no doubt I scared more easily then than I do now. There were a lot of people on the street who looked somewhat like hippies, but you could tell they weren't the mellow, peace-loving type of hippie. They were only there for the drugs and the sex, and you just knew they wanted bad drugs and bad sex.

And there were a lot of hookers, of both sexes, but predominantly male. Thanks to John Rechy, we now know that the real industrial-strength action was taking place not on Hollywood Boulevard but half a block south on Selma. The main drag, however, was quite action-packed enough for me. The hustlers walked up and down, wearing their cowboy hats and fringed suede jackets, looking like extras, or perhaps leads, from the movie *Midnight Cowboy*, or more feasibly Warhol's *Lonesome Cow-*

*boys.* As a matter of fact, I owned a fringed suede jacket at the time, and I was glad I hadn't brought it with me to America.

I remember seeing a street musician standing in a doorway somewhere near Vine Street playing a saxophone, and I stopped to listen to him. He had a great act. He'd start out playing a recognizable version of "My Favorite Things," and then veer off into ever wilder improvised Coltrane-style free-jazz squawking, until he fell on his knees writhing with the intense emotion of it all. Then he'd stop, stand up, and do it all over again. It impressed the hell out of me.

I did by chance meet a fun-loving woman who had a couple of tickets for a David Bowie concert at the Hollywood Bowl and offered me one of them, but the journey there seemed unimaginably difficult to both of us. We didn't have a car so we thought it was impossible.

Now I look at the map and see that you can walk from Boulevard to Bowl quite easily in half an hour at most, and I suppose a bit of careful map reading would have told me that at the time. But I believed the myth and the hype, that you couldn't get anywhere or do anything in L.A. without a car, and you were wiser not to try.

Three decades later, newly arrived in Los Angeles, I was ready to defy the wisdom. In the name of self-medication I began to take regular, long, sometimes arduous walks in L.A. In fact there are a few places in and around the city where people go walking: Griffith Park, Runyon Canyon, Venice Beach, the shopping streets of Beverly Hills, Santa Monica's Third Street Promenade, parts of downtown. A long drive may well be involved in getting to any of them.

There was something a bit obvious about walking in these places, but I didn't want to be completely self-denying or self-punishing, so I walked in all of them. Then, since I was living in a movie town it seemed natural enough to visit some movie sites: places where Hollywood stars lived or at least *had* lived and, in some cases, died. Is there any other city in the world where you can buy maps and guides telling you the locations of the homes of its most famous living citizens? I bought several.

If the data were to be believed you could, for instance, walk along Franklin Avenue, a largely unsung street, where Dorothy Dandridge had lived before she went bankrupt, where Gary Cooper had lodged with his parents, where Joan Didion had lived in her yellow Corvette period. Live stars were a bit thin on the ground on Franklin, however. For them it was recommended that you go to, say, Aldercreek Place in Westlake Village, where you could saunter past the home of Frankie Avalon, or to Folkstone Lane in Bel Air, where Tony Curtis lived, or to Cornell Road, the Agoura Hills site of chez Kelsey Grammer.

Once you started walking in Beverly Hills, the famous, and the ghosts of the famous, were to be found on every street: Greta Garbo on Chevy Chase Drive, Barbra Streisand on North Bedford Drive, everybody and his uncle on Roxbury: dead legends such as Lionel Barrymore, Lucille Ball, and Dorothy Parker, and live ones such as Mia Farrow and Peter Falk.

Inevitably these walks of mine didn't result in my seeing any movie stars. In many cases I didn't even get to see the houses because of high walls and hedges, and signs promising an armed response. But if you're the sort of person who's moved by the notion that somebody famous is (or was) here, then there's still a frisson to be had from looking at movie star homes. And some days, I'm that sort of person.

My star maps told me not to go knocking on doors and bothering the stars, and I didn't, and in a lot of cases I wasn't even sure the information was accurate. I felt sure that movie stars moved more often than these maps were updated. Which brings me to the story of the time I walked with Christina Ricci.

It was on Valley Oak Drive, a long, quiet, traffic-free dead end, like many of the streets in the Hollywood Hills. I walked all the way to the end of the street, then immediately turned and started walking back. It was the natural thing to do but I feared it made me look shifty and up to no good, as if I was casing the neighborhood.

As I turned on my heels I saw walking toward me down the middle of the street what at first appeared to be a child, or at best a very young teenage girl. She was incredibly thin, had brassy, dyed blond hair, and was wearing minute hot pants. She was looking lost and she spoke before I had a chance to.

"Have you seen a dog?" she asked me.

"No," I said, and then, even though I have no interest in dogs and can barely tell one breed from another, I asked, "What kind is it?"

Either sensing or sharing my indifference to dog breeds, the little girl said, "Oh, it's just a tiny dog," and she mimed holding a puppy that wasn't much more than a single handful.

It was then that I realized the little girl was a fully grown woman, was in fact the movie actress Christina Ricci. I'd have realized sooner if she hadn't had the blond hair. Of course I didn't tell her I knew who she was, but my eyes probably signaled recognition; I'd thought she was great in the Addams Family movies. She evidently lived nearby, and as I found out later, had just moved into a Lloyd Wright house on the street.

"Oh, well," said Christina Ricci, and she then seemed to be at a loose end. Having reached the dead end of the street, she, too, had to turn back, which would mean walking along with me.

I like to think I look reasonably presentable when I'm out walking. I don't think I look like a stalker or pervert, but as Christina Ricci had seen, I was certainly a man who had walked to the end of the street and then turned on his heel and started walking smartly back. Was that a man you could completely trust?

An odd, socially awkward, and in my experience unique, interaction took place. Christina Ricci and I walked half the length of Valley Oak Drive in each other's company. We weren't quite walking together, but we weren't quite walking separately either, and we both felt obliged to make some polite, stilted conversation as we went. We talked about dogs. It was excruciating. And as we walked, a chorus of canine barking came at us from behind various neighborhood gates and fences. None of the barks sounded as though it came from a dog of the size she apparently owned.

What I didn't tell her was that as I'd been walking that afternoon, I'd seen a lot of handmade signs attached to trees and lampposts: WANTED posters for lost dogs and cats. Some generous rewards were being offered. The fear, a reasonable one, in fact a strong probability, was that these family pets had been snatched by the coyotes that roamed wild in the area. If Christina Ricci was going to find her little dog, she had a strictly limited amount of time in which to do it.


I felt I was starting to get the hang of L.A. My walks, perverse and contradictory and laborious as they sometimes were, became a profound source of pleasure and satisfaction. I was making the city my own, asserting my own version, marking territory, beating the bounds, drawing my own map.

I was doing myself good. I was feeling much, much less depressed. I can't say that I finished each walk and thought to myself, ah yes, this is precisely the kind of serotonin-stimulating activity that those boffins at Duke University were talking about, but then I didn't need to. When you're not depressed you don't spend much time thinking about depression. And that was the state I was in when I went walking in the Hollywood Hills two days before Christmas, fell, broke my arm, stopped walking, and got depressed all over again.

So after a couple of months of nursing my arm, of inactivity and escalating misery, as the opiates ceased to deliver much in the way of painkilling, I knew I had to start self-medicating again. I did what I had to do, picked myself up, dusted myself off, and started walking again.

I undertook a series of long, unfocused but serious walks on the boulevards that run more or less east and west across L.A.: Pico, Olympic, Sunset, Santa Monica, Beverly, Melrose, Wilshire. I referred to the walks, only somewhat ironically, as "transits." There was nothing conceptually rigorous about these expeditions. I went at my own pace, without specific expectations or goals, and I noticed what I noticed.

One of my enduring memories of Sunset concerns a couple I saw walking along ahead of me, near the Hollywood Freeway. The man was middle-aged, lean, bearded, a bit raddled perhaps but essentially holding it together. His female companion was not. She was younger than him, as wide as a house, disheveled, with huge flopping, untethered breasts, and I guess she was suffering from some mental problems. Suddenly, she looked down to the side of the road, at something in the bushes, and she reacted with delight. I looked to see what she'd found. There were twenty or thirty medicine bottles lying there, empty as far as I could tell, but still containing some powdery residue. The woman swooped down on them with absolute joy, and the man wasn't able to stop her, though he tried. About a week later I happened to see them again, in a supermarket some miles away, and I fell into conversation with the man. He told me he liked my shirt. He said it was the kind of shirt worn by men of influence.

On Wilshire Boulevard I saw a man with no legs, indeed nothing at all below the pelvis, with a sort of thick plastic diaper around the bottom of his torso; he was not actually walking, I suppose, but he was propelling himself at some speed. He had a block of wood in each hand, like wooden door handles, so that his hands didn't have to touch the sidewalk, and as he moved they made a noise somewhere between the sound of clogs and high heels.

As I was walking down Rampart Boulevard, a car pulled up next to me. I looked over and saw the driver was a woman talking on her cell phone, with an unruly little girl bouncing around in the passenger seat. I thought the woman was lost and stopping to ask me for directions, but no, she'd actually stopped the car so she could give the little girl a good slapping, which she then did, with her cell phone still at her ear.

Some of these walks could be tough. It gets damned hot in the middle of the day in L.A. in the summer. I nearly got run down once or twice. Dogs endlessly snarled and yelped at me, and street people hassled me with varying degrees of seriousness.

On Los Feliz Boulevard, a young black man who appeared to have all his worldly goods scattered at his feet gave me a bright hello, which I returned, and when I was past him he called after me, "Dude! Are you in the movies?"

"Nah," I said laughing.

"You look just like that dude in *Die Hard* 2," he said.

For no good reason I said, "I wish," and then we both had a good laugh.

When I got home I went through the cast list of *Die Hard* 2 and I'm damned if I could see anybody there who might look like me. Not Bruce Willis, I think I can safely say. It'd be flattering to think it was Franco Nero, but putting all other objections aside, we aren't even remotely in the same age bracket. And surely not Dennis Franz. Surely. Not even my worst enemies would say I looked like him. Whatever my physical failings, I do have plenty of hair.

And then there was the time I was walking in downtown L.A., a place where a lot of others walk, too. It was a busy weekday lunchtime. The streets were full of people. There was a lot to look at, a lot of distractions, and that was why I wasn't paying much attention to the youngish, hippieish white guy who was standing not very far away from me as I was waiting to cross the street. He was a panhandler, however, and thought I was pointedly ignoring him. I might have if I'd been aware of him, but I wasn't. After failing to get my attention for a while, he said loudly, in a sneering tone of voice, "Hey, who do you think you are? Jack Kerouac?" As insults go, I couldn't have asked for better. I didn't respond. The light changed and I walked across the street smiling fit to bust.

I walked for a while in the footsteps of those two great Angelenos Raymond Chandler and his fictional alter ego Philip Marlowe. I had a partial list of the places Chandler had lived, based on information from his selected letters, from two Chandler biographies, plus a certain amount of anecdotal evidence. Chandler seems to have lived *everywhere*: Los Feliz, Santa Monica, Arcadia, Monrovia, Brentwood, Pacific Palisades, you name it, and all manner of places in between. It made for interesting but ultimately unsatisfying walking. It was easy enough to find the streets, some much meaner than others, but often I couldn't find the actual addresses. Times and the city had changed too much.

I went, for instance, to Loma Street in what is now MacArthur Park, where Chandler lived in 1916 when he worked as an accountant at the Los Angeles Creamery. The address no longer existed. Later a mailman tried very hard to help me find one of Chandler's old places on 12th Street, but our best efforts put his apartment exactly where there was now an alleyway that ran behind a Korean Presbyterian church. A bungalow court on Leeward shared an address with somewhere Chandler had once lived, but it was now a series of tightly packed bunkers, neat and recently repainted but thoroughly austere, and enclosed behind spiked iron railings and barbed wire, evoking captivity as much as security. It couldn't have been like that in Chandler's time.

My only really good score, easily walked to from my home, was the Spanish-style, ice cream–colored apartment block on Greenwood Place, where Chandler and his wife, Cissy, had lived when he wrote his first short stories for *Black Mask* magazine. At that time Chandler had lost his job as an oil executive because of alcoholism and its attendant problems, and I'd constructed quite the tragic and romantic picture for Chandler, and for myself. There are some very bleak apartment blocks in that area, and I guessed that Ray and Cissy, with no visible means of support, had holed up in one of these. I was quite wrong. There was nothing bleak about 4616 Greenwood. It looked like a very decent place to live. More than that, it looked like a fully authentic Chandler location: sun-drenched, lush, keeping its secrets. As I paced up and down outside, it was possible to entertain the fantasy that I was tracking down some vital clues about the man and his work. Finding clues, however, was a rarity.

I have since discovered that at the time I was doing these Chandler walks, an author named Judith Freeman was covering a lot of the same territory, researching a book about Chandler's marriage. She doesn't seem to have had much more luck than I did at locating genuine Chandler territory, but she wrote the book anyway.

Both of us must, at least occasionally, have walked where Chandler had once walked, and walking with Chandler was probably safer than driving with him, certainly safer than being on the sidewalk when he was behind the wheel. In a letter to Roger Machell, Chandler recalls driving home in his oil executive days, "plastered to the hairline in a most agreeable manner.... We missed pedestrians by a thin millimeter... laughing heartily at the idea of a man trying to walk on two legs."

Certainly Chandler's Marlowe thinks nothing of having a few stiff drinks before and even during a long drive, and we do tend to think of hard-boiled detectives as drivers rather than walkers, but in the course of his inquiries Marlowe, like any good gumshoe, did plenty of walking, too. I thought it might be more rewarding to walk in Marlowe's mythical city than in the remains of Chandler's historical one.

I tried, for a start, to find the house where Marlowe lives in *The Long Goodbye*, "in the Laurel Canyon district," a surprisingly bohemian area for a private eye, even in the 1940s. The description of Marlowe's house is what I've come to think of as pure Chandler. It sounds very convincingly specific and yet it's actually deceptively general. "It was a small hillside house on a dead end street with a long flight of redwood steps to the front door and a grove of eucalyptus trees across the way."

There is no Yucca Drive in Laurel Canyon, but there is a Yucca Trail (which is not a dead end), and sure enough when I walked there, I saw at least two houses that fit the bill in terms of steps and eucalyptus trees. Did Chandler scout this street, walk the neighborhood looking for a suitable fictional home for his detective? I do like to think so.

In the novel, Terry Lennox, the ambiguously appealing, white-haired, facially reconstructed semi-villain, walks to Marlowe's place from Fountain Avenue, a long and perilous ascent, steep as a ski slope in places, made more taxing by blind bends and drivers who have no expectation whatsoever of encountering anyone on foot.

Marlowe himself walks to Laurel Canyon in *The Big Sleep*, to the house of one Arthur Gwynne Geiger. He walks there from the Sternwood mansion in West Hollywood, first covering "ten blocks of curving, rain swept streets" until he "comes out at a service station," then adds, "I made it back to Geiger's house in something over half an hour of nimble walking."

I have walked various routes between various possible locations for both the mansion and Geiger's house, but convincing though Chandler's (and Marlowe's) account is, the geography of the book is a long way off from the real geography of the city. There are no ten curving blocks, there is no suitably placed gas station. The best guess has Geiger living on Kirkwood Terrace, a street off Laurel Canyon Boulevard, with the Sternwood mansion a ringer for the Doheny mansion, a mock Tudor extravaganza in Beverly Hills, sometimes used as a movie set (*Murder, She Wrote, The Witches of Eastwick, The Prestige*) and also the site of a real murder.

*The Big Sleep* is also the novel in which Marlowe follows on foot a customer from Geiger's bookstore, a sort of porno lending library, situated on the north side of Hollywood Boulevard near Las Palmas Avenue, a place that can be located today with some precision. Some sources place the bookstore in what is now the "new room" of Musso & Frank's restaurant, one of Chandler's favorite watering holes, a taste shared by such writer/drinkers as Fitzgerald, Faulkner, Parker, Hammett, and Bukowski.

Marlowe tails the customer, who gets increasingly panicky as he walks west on Hollywood Boulevard to Highland, then another block, then turns right and then left into a "narrow tree lined street with three bungalow courts," the second of which is called La Baba. Eventually the customer cracks, ditches the smut he's borrowed, and then saunters away, leaving Marlowe to retrieve the filthy goods.

The first part of the walk is easily replicated, but by the end you'll find yourself walking into Hollywood and Highland, a corporate, multistory shopping mall that by some accounts is responsible for the revitalization of Hollywood, but which nevertheless has the look of something that will be a slum in ten years' time. Chandler would have been horrified, and would have reveled in his horror.

However, my favorite Marlowe walking moment appears in *Farewell, My Lovely*, where he climbs the 280 steps up to Cabrillo Street in Montemar Vista, where he's got an appointment with a popinjay called Lindsay Marriott. "It was a nice walk if you like grunting," Marlowe says.

Cabrillo Street and Montemar Vista are Chandler's inventions, but if you're looking for a long trudge up a great many steps, Castellammare, on the Pacific Coast Highway, offers a very adequate substitute. I did the climb, and it's a struggle to find exactly 280 steps—some now lead into dead ends, some are crumbling wood—but you can do something that's not too far off the mark. The grunting is much as reported, but it really is a "nice" walk, if you like walking. On the way you pass the house where the actress Thelma Todd was murdered, and the view from the top is just about worth the effort.

There is in Los Angeles these days a place called Raymond Chandler Square. It isn't a square in the usual sense, but rather an intersection where Cahuenga and Hollywood boulevards meet. It's pleasing in a way that Raymond Chandler Square is so ordinary, so unfancy. It's the kind of place where the businesses don't seem to be in it for the long run; but the last time I looked, the four corners offered a Greek pizzeria, a Popeyes chicken and biscuits restaurant, a place for cashing checks, and, more substantially, a big, serious anonymous bank building that is a contender for the fictional Cahuenga Building, which was where Marlowe had an office in *Farewell, My Lovely*.

Hollywood Boulevard is one of the places where people *do* actually walk in Los Angeles. When people like me complain about the lack of street life in L.A., other Angelenos tend to say, "Go to Hollywood Boulevard if you want some street life, man." They mean that Hollywood street life is all about drugs and sex, runaways, people fresh off the bus, boys up to no good, the improbably and ill-advisedly transvestite, the kind of people who need piercing and tattooing parlors and smoke shops, who find themselves sitting on the sidewalk, with a dog on a string, eating pizza and bumming cigarettes, the mad, the lost, the winsomely deranged. One of my recent favorites was a guy, youngish, clean, healthy-looking, pushing a baby carriage full of his belongings and singing, "The devil's been defeated and you can all go to hell." Everyone, including me, will also tell you that it used to be a whole lot worse.

These days there are also plenty of tourists walking on Hollywood Boulevard as well, and many of them look frankly bemused. They know they're in Hollywood, they know that they're on the legendary Hollywood Walk of Fame, and yet they don't quite know what they're supposed to be doing there. Taking the names of people you admire and putting them in stars on the sidewalk where people can walk all over them still strikes me as an odd and not very respectful thing to do.

And of course some people do far worse than walk. You can imagine my ambivalent glee when I discovered the existence of something called the Hollywood Entertainment District Public Urination Map, charting every act of public urination observed by the area's security guards. You might think that part of a security guard's job might be to prevent public urination rather than merely observe it, but it's probably a hard thing to stop, certainly once the perpetrator is in full flow. No doubt a great deal of unobserved urination must go on, too. This is one of the unavoidable facts of walking on Hollywood Boulevard: anywhere you go not only has somebody walked there before you, somebody has probably pissed there as well.

If putting stars' names in the sidewalk is odd, then taking photographs of them seems even odder, yet every time I go along Hollywood Boulevard I see people snapping away at the ground, at the stars, sometimes even filming them. And I'm always amazed which names they choose to photograph. I began to take note. In quick succession I noticed people photographing the stars of Sylvester Stallone, Michael Jackson, and Olivia Newton-John. I'll let the historians of pop culture sort out the reasons.

The Walk of Fame runs east/west along the boulevard from Gower to La Brea, and north/south on Vine Street from Yucca to Sunset, forming a long, thin cross. The names at the far west end are Spanky McFarland and the Dead End Kids. At the eastern end it's Benny Goodman and Stanley Kramer. On Vine Street we run from Jeff Chandler and Texas Guinan in the north down to Franklin Pangborn and Edward Small.

If you protest that these are no longer household names, then I suppose that might be the whole point. The names are written in concrete (actually brass set in terrazzo), but their fame is no more permanent than if it were written in water. The Walk of Fame might remind you that showbiz just isn't the place to look for permanence.

I've often tried to determine whether there's any logic to the placement of the stars. The current A-list is certainly represented in the forecourt outside Grauman's Chinese and the Kodak Theatre, which is what you'd expect. And some of the stars outside the Capitol Records building on Vine certainly belong to recording artists, but by no means all.

Surely there's more insult than irony in the fact that Edith Head's star is outside Lady Studio Exotic Shoes. Why does the crew of Apollo 11 have four separate stars and why are they all at the intersection of Hollywood and Vine? And I wonder how Gary Cooper and Sylvia Sidney might have felt about having their stars placed outside the Frolic Room, a bar famous for its cheap beer and pickled eggs. But I imagine they'd be happier than Fritz Lang and Orson Welles, who for a long time were outside the entrance of the DMV until it moved recently.

There is one man who never walks down Hollywood Boulevard, and that's a man with no feet and one leg who polishes some of the stars. He does it of his own volition and he doesn't beg for money, but people who think he's doing a good job slip him a couple of dollars. And there are other people who adopt the star of their particular hero or heroine and keep it clean.

Even so there are a great many more stars than there are people who want to look after them. You can see why some of the obscure ones get neglected, but there are some very big names whose stars are in need of a bit of spit and polish. Nobody is taking care of Ava Gardner or Liza Minnelli, as far as I can see.

If there's a journey's end for the Hollywood Boulevard walk, it's Grauman's Chinese Theatre, where people congregate and pay a couple of dollars to have their pictures taken with a look-alike: a Marilyn, an Elvis, a Charlie Chaplin, a man in a Spider-Man suit, a woman dressed as Wonder Woman. Since changing facilities are limited on Hollywood Boulevard, most of the characters arrive already in costume, and in order to avoid commuting, many of them live in the area within walking distance of work. One of the best sights I know in Hollywood is to see Wonder Woman emerging from her apartment block on Las Palmas and striding up to Hollywood Boulevard, getting into character as she goes.

The most extreme Los Angeles walker I know (and he is a kind of superhero) is called Mudman, a persona of the artist Kim Jones. In order to become Mudman, Jones coats his body in mud, pulls a thick nylon stocking over his head, puts on a foam headdress, and then straps to his back a large lattice structure made of wooden slats, tree branches, wax, wire, tape, sponge, and whatnot. Sometimes he also wears a glove on his left hand from which a number of long wooden spikes protrude all the way to the ground. The effect is visually and conceptually compelling, especially if you see him walking toward you on a city street.

Mudman is a living, walking sculpture, one that invokes a whole raft of visual associations. He looks grotesque yet vulnerable, sinister perhaps but not humorless. The idea of a man made out of mud is as old as the golem or Adam, and certainly Jones's creation has elements of ancient religion, part shaman, part witch doctor, part Wicker Man. The structure on his back looks like broken wings, like a self-inflicted cross he has to bear.

But Mudman also looks like something out of pop culture, a blighted superhero, some kin of Swamp Thing or the Incredible Hulk, and it's not clear what superpowers he has, if any, apart from being able to walk. The stocking, without holes for eyes or mouth, serves as a blank mask, more inscrutable than Batman's or Spider-Man's, though like them he definitely seems to be hiding something. At the same time this very blankness allows viewers to project their own fantasies and interpretations onto him.

Mudman made his first appearances in and around Los Angeles in the mid-1970s, evolving out of a series of performances and installations, often in Venice Beach, where Jones lived at the time. Over the years he has walked as part of art events in San Francisco, Chicago, London, Rome, Germany, and Switzerland. Sometimes his own feces have been added to the mud, and in Rome he didn't use mud at all, preferring yogurt and cottage cheese.

Mudman's most famous example of art walking, however, consists of two twelve-hour walks along the full length of Wilshire Boulevard, about eighteen miles from downtown to the ocean in Santa Monica. He did the first walk on January 28, 1976, which was his birthday, from sunrise to sunset; then a week later, on February 4, he did it again from sunset to sunrise. Along the way he had the kind of encounters you might expect: a gas station attendant who wouldn't let him use the bathroom, a cop who told him to keep moving, and an old lady who asked him, "Does your mother know you're doing this?"

The walking artist is no novelty. Britain has two of the greatest walking artists in Richard Long and Hamish Fulton, and although Jones knows their work, he says his own art is more influenced by the work of Eva Hesse, Vito Acconci, and Joseph Beuys. And yet, for all the mythic aura surrounding Mudman, some of his origins are firmly rooted in Jones's autobiography. Between the ages of seven and ten he suffered from Perthes disease, one of nature's more savage little jokes, a condition that affects only children, restricting blood supply to the ball-and-socket joint at the top of the femur and causing the thigh bones to soften and break. It certainly puts a damper on any attempts to walk, and it's not strictly curable, though it will pass of its own accord if the body is protected and allowed to heal itself. Bed rest, leg braces, and wheelchairs tend to be part of the process and Jones endured all of them.

Jones recovered in due course. One of his legs is still a little shorter than the other, he tells me, but that doesn't stop him walking. Nor for that matter did it stop him enlisting as a marine in 1966 and going to Vietnam a year later. It's not entirely clear whether Jones had a good or a bad war. We know that it involved doing a certain amount of walking, or at least marching, but his main job was delivering mail. Mudman looks like a combatant but also like a war victim, like one of the walking wounded.

I asked Jones if he had any plans to do a Mudman walk in the near future, hoping I might walk along with him, or at least observe other people's reactions. "I still do Mudman," he said. "I haven't done it in a while, but I plan to do it as long as I can. My favorite time to do Mudman is when *no one* expects or knows that I'm going to do it."

Of course if you're in Los Angeles you could say that nobody ever expects anybody to do any walking at all, but the fact is, I now realize, that's simply not true. The longer I live in L.A., the more I become aware that the city does indeed have a rich tradition of walking: political, literary, artistic, recreational.

There is an annual Cesar Chavez Walk, for example, at which you're invited to "walk alongside Chavez family members, students, elected officials, celebrities, and community members." By walking you join "the call for social justice." Who could be so churlish as to walk against social justice? When Angelenos wanted to protest against the war in Iraq, they closed Hollywood Boulevard, and thousands took to it on foot. When they want to demonstrate in favor of Latino immigration, as they increasingly do, then Wilshire becomes a pedestrian precinct.

There is a long short story by Jim Harrison called "Westward Ho," in which a dubious Native American character known as Brown Dog attempts to cross the city on foot, from Cucamonga to Westwood, some forty-seven miles. Back home in Michigan, Brown Dog is known as a "walking fool." There's plenty of walking in the fiction of John Fante, and Charles Bukowski's novels contain a lot more walking than you might expect, much of it done when the hero's car has broken down.

There's a man called Neil Hopper who runs the website walkinginla.com. It features austere, minimalist records of his walks around the city. A typical walk might be called "June 23, 2007 Bell Gardens, Pico Rivera, Montebello" or "September 24, 2005 Normandie Ave, Venice Blvd," and that will be all the "text" he provides. It's as inscrutable as any art piece by Richard Long. There'll be a Google map showing his route, plus maybe half a dozen nondescript photographs showing, say, a liquor store, a stretch of freeway, a midcentury motel, a cool old car. Beyond that there will be no indication of why he walks or what he gets out of it. The fact that he doesn't even attempt to articulate his obvious pleasure strikes me as oddly noble.

Despite everything, some of us Angelenos keep on walking. It seems fair enough to question the essential wisdom and sanity of certain L.A. walkers, but for some of us it's not only a passion and a pleasure, it's also a necessary activity that keeps us (more or less) sane. We would be a great deal crazier, and certainly more depressed, if we didn't do it.

And so to return to the naysayers, to the likes of Jean Baudrillard and his assertion, "As soon as you start walking in Los Angeles you are a threat to public order, like a dog wandering in the road," the fact is, it takes rather more than a bit of pedestrianism to disrupt the public order of L.A. As far as that goes, L.A. can pretty much handle a dog wandering in the road, too. Print the legend if you must, but don't expect all us Angelenos to live it.

## ECCENTRICS, OBSESSIVES,

## ARTISTS:

## Walks with Richard Long,

## Captain Barclay, et al.

*Sidewalk's for regular walkin', not for fancy walkin'!*
—JASPER (in *The Simpsons*, "Who Shot
Mr. Burns?")

Looked at a certain way, walking is the most ordinary, natural, ubiquitous activity. What could be more commonplace or lacking in eccentricity than the act of walking? And yet we live in a world where plenty of people find the idea of walking for pleasure, much less for philosophical, aesthetic, or deeply personal reasons, to be not just odd but downright incomprehensible.

In 2005 when Steve Vaught, a four-hundred-pound ex-marine, began his walk across America, from San Diego to New York, the media tended to treat him as a weight-loss enthusiastic. He did the walk, and he did lose weight, just over a hundred pounds in thirteen months, and he did get to appear on *Oprah*. But his weight loss wasn't enough for some, and you could see their point: at three hundred pounds he wasn't the very best advertisement for walking as a weight-loss strategy. Vaught insisted that weight loss was only part of the story. He was also walking "to regain his life," he said, and by his own account he has. "I no longer manage business or pursue money beyond what I need," he says. "I've given away all my material things and live life out of two or three carry bags, and I recommend it highly."

Weight loss, at least, was identified as a "good reason" for walking, if not exactly natural. Walking naked, however natural in one sense, is still regarded as deeply odd. The most famous naked walker of recent years is the Englishman Steve Gough. He describes himself as "body positive" and claims that his extensive experience of walking naked in the world has given him a "connectedness" with others. He has now twice walked naked from Land's End to John o' Groat's, a traditional walking route, the longest distance between two points on the British mainland. He has spent a lot of time in court, and a certain amount of time in jail.

The British media only got interested in it when he did the Land's End to John o' Groat's walk for the second time and took his naked girlfriend, Melanie Roberts, with him. He also had a film crew with him. Cynics might think that without the naked girlfriend there might not have been a film crew.

The resulting documentary, made by Richard Macer, shows the British public's surprisingly extreme reactions to the naked pair, both positive and negative. Gough encounters a number of people who regard him as a harmless, likable, even admirable eccentric, part of a great British tradition, which is surely the only sensible way to regard him. This includes a group of women he encounters in a pub in Derbyshire who strip down to their underwear in a show of solidarity. By contrast, a working-class mother is shown seething with rage and disgust, afraid that the sight of a naked man and woman will have some hideously damaging effect on her innocent children. Her reaction is alarmingly, frighteningly extreme.

I wonder what the modern media might have made of the Old Leatherman, a nineteenth-century tramp who for just over thirty years, from 1858 to 1889, was in constant motion, dressed head to foot in leather, walking a three-hundred-mile circuit around parts of Connecticut and New York State. The route took him precisely thirty-four days: you could set your watch by him. In those three decades of walking he wasn't heard to utter a single intelligible word.

In fact, the media of the time did give the Old Leatherman a certain amount of attention. He was regularly photographed, and his image appeared on commercially available postcards. He was also invited to display himself in a New York City freak show, an opportunity he wisely declined. His reputation as an eccentric walker surely could not have survived long periods as a sedentary museum exhibit.

As for who the Leatherman was and why he walked, the best story we have, and best doesn't mean truest, is that he began life as Jules Bourglay (spellings differ) in Lyons, France. He was a young woodcarver, who fell in love above his station with the daughter of a wealthy leather merchant, surname Laron.

Bourglay asked for the girl's hand in marriage and Laron père didn't say yes, but he didn't dismiss the idea out of hand. He gave Bourglay a job in his leather business. If the young man proved himself in the course of the first year, he'd keep him on and approve the marriage.

The move was a disaster. The leather business was in trouble, and Bourglay made some bad decisions, buying leather at high prices just as the market value was going down. The decisions were so bad that Laron went bankrupt and lost his business. The wedding, understandably, was off. Devastated, Bourglay spent a year in a French monastery, then made his way to America, where he tried to expiate his guilt by walking.

That sounds thoroughly eccentric to me, and of course it may be untrue, but even as a myth from a different age it's interesting that the story was thought of as a reasonable explanation for why a man might walk regular three-hundred-mile circuits while dressed in full leather. Perhaps once eccentricity is understood it is no longer considered eccentric at all. So what is it that defines a walk and a walker as eccentric?


I once worked for a security company that provided guards for many of London's major art institutions, including the British Museum, the Royal Academy, and the Tate Gallery. My job was simple enough, to protect works of art from the public, and a basic level of vigilance was all that was required of me. But I did have to stay literally on my feet, and metaphorically on my toes, and so whole days, and eventually weeks and months, were spent pacing up and down one gallery or another trying to remain alert, looking at art, keeping an eye on the potentially troublesome public. Sometimes I fantasized about where my endless pacing might have taken me had I actually been going somewhere. But, of course, I wasn't being paid to go anywhere: I was being paid to walk back and forth.

Some of my colleagues in the museums and galleries complained about the boredom and the pain in their feet, but I never found this a problem. Long periods of time spent in the presence of a work of art, almost any bona-fide work of art, created rare and wonderful experiences, and that made it all worthwhile.

There was a moment in the Royal Academy, before it opened for the day, when I found myself alone in a gallery surrounded by thirty or so priceless Van Goghs, part of an exhibition on Post-Impressionism. As I walked up and down, waiting for the public to be let in, it was easy to entertain other fantasies: that the Van Goghs belonged to me, that I was some sort of James Bond villain who'd secreted these treasures, that I was walking in my own marble hall, a secret lair that was mine and mine alone and no others would ever be allowed to walk there. Then the doors opened and hundreds of art lovers wandered in.

It was easier to sustain the fantasy in a basement gallery at the Tate, where few people came, and where I was guarding a sculpture by Richard Long called *Slate Circle*. It consisted of 214 rough, largish, unworked pieces of Welsh slate, arranged on the floor in a precise circle about twenty feet in diameter. Guarding it wasn't much of a challenge. It was unlikely that anyone was going to slip a large lump of Welsh slate under their coat. Few visitors came to that particular room, and when they did, they had a tendency to ask, "Is this the bricks?" meaning Carl Andre's *Equivalent VIII*, made from, and consisting of, 120 firebricks, which to this day remains an exciting touchstone for art skeptics and philistines everywhere. I was delighted to be able to say, "No, it's not the bricks. It's the stones."

Long's *Slate Circle* explores a tension between art and nature, the indoors and the outdoors, between the created and the found object, between the making of art and the claiming of what's there. It was undoubtedly a sculpture, but the slate had not been "sculpted" in any conventional sense; it had simply been arranged. Two hundred fourteen lumps of slate had been extracted from the ground and carefully, artfully placed on the floor in the warm glow of an art gallery, where I could see and walk around them. They made my days of pacing very happy.

There were certain ironies in the artwork that I only became aware of later. The slate, I discovered, came from a quarry that Richard Long had gone past while walking, "From the source of the River Severn to the summit of Snowdon, 60 miles." That was the description of his walk and also the title of one of his works of art. Long is a sculptor and a conceptual artist, and has said that walking is the real medium of his art.

His first walking piece was made in 1967, a straight line in a field of grass, created by his pacing up and down until the grass was flattened and the line was made visible: one of those works of art that any damn fool could make if the damn fool were a conceptual artist. Later, Long's works became larger and more ambitious. Sometimes they involved the stamping out of patterns in earth or ash, sometimes the rearrangement of rocks along the way, sometimes "painting" with water in the course of the walk. Long even collected mud from the area where he'd been walking and used it to create works on the walls or floors of art galleries.

Some of his walks have been lengthy and arduous, across the

Sierra Nevada, through the Sahara. The works have titles such as *Walking a Circle in Mist, A Walking and Running Circle, A Cloudless Walk, A Walk Across Ireland, A Line of 33 Stones, A Walk of 33 Days.* He documents the walks with maps, drawings, photographs, texts, or a combination of these things. Some of these works are wonderfully inscrutable, consisting of no more than a few words. Here, in its entirety, is a piece called *A FIVE DAY WALK*:

FIRST DAY TEN MILES
SECOND DAY TWENTY MILES
THIRD DAY THIRTY MILES
FOURTH DAY FORTY MILES
FIFTH DAY FIFTY MILES

In a 2006 article and interview with Long in *Art and Auction*, the writer Roger Tatley admits to some skepticism about the "provenance of some of Long's walks," suggesting that maybe they didn't really take place and were artistic inventions. He puts this to Long and describes the artist's response as "gracious."

"My work," says Long in the interview, "has to work on all levels, for unbelievers as well. It is of course possible that I don't do any of these walks, and in some ways, if I didn't, they would have to work on the level of true conceptual art, like Lawrence Weiner's. He's a great artist in that his use of language means it doesn't matter whether the work exists or not. But the difference for me is that while ideas are important, it's crucial that I do make my art—that these are real walks, real stones, real mud."

When I walk through wild places, especially in the desert, I often see that people have been there before me and stamped out patterns on the earth or arranged stones or debris into shapes and designs, with greater or lesser degrees of skill and ingenuity, with apparently a greater knowledge of the conventions of art. The best of them look like fake Richard Longs, although of course there's always the possibility that some of them may be real Richard Longs.


One of Long's earliest works, created in 1974, was a drawing and text piece called *A Thousand Miles, a Thousand Hours*. Perhaps Long is invoking Lao-tzu and his remark about the journey of a thousand miles, but if you're at all familiar with the history of sustained eccentric walking, those words invoke a quite different character: Captain Barclay.

Captain Robert Barclay Allardice (1779–1854) was a Scot, a sportsman, an athlete, a soldier, a fan of horse racing, a gambler, a landowner, and a "gentleman." Sometimes these roles sat uneasily together. For instance, one of the rules of the English class system decreed that as a gentleman he was allowed to "spar" with professional boxers but he wasn't allowed to "box" against them. As a landowner he had no practical need to make money by performing athletic feats; he could have performed them as a gentleman amateur. However, he had the need to up the stakes and so bet heavily on himself. If he lost the bet, as he sometimes did, it could cost him the best part of a year's income.

On the other hand, some of Barclay's most impressive walking wasn't done in competition or for money. Often it seems to have been done for the sheer hell of it. In 1802, for example, he set off on a journey from his home in Ury to walk to Kirkmichael and back again. He took the low road on the way out, then decided to return by the more difficult highland route, and even so clocked 180 miles in two and a half days. This could possibly be construed as part of a training regimen, but it surely also involved a considerable degree of showing off. Barclay had a reputation, undoubtedly well deserved but buffed by rumor and fantasy, like the story, certainly untrue, that he trained by carrying a load of butter and cheese on his back.

Barclay's self-promotion paid off. History has remembered him as one of the very greatest walkers, or at least pedestrians. The two words were not quite synonymous in Barclay's time. To be a pedestrian in the early nineteenth century simply meant that you raced on foot, as opposed to on horseback or in a carriage. "Go as you please" races were popular, sometimes lasting several days, in which competitors were free to walk or run, or indeed hop, skip, and jump and certainly to rest, as and when they saw fit throughout the event. At the end the winner was simply the one who'd gone farthest around a predetermined route.

As a spectator sport, long pedestrian races must have been lacking in all sorts of ways: the competitors weren't necessarily on the track at the same time, if they were they certainly weren't likely to be on the same lap, and you might easily turn up to watch the event during a prolonged rest period and see nothing at all. But large crowds did gather at them, and large amounts of money were staked on the outcomes.

Young blades of the Regency period would bet on just about anything, so of course they bet on sporting events. But the rules of many sports were at that time unfixed. Every new contest was therefore an opportunity for invention, variation, and sometimes bizarrely complicated constraints to make the event, and the betting, that much more of a challenge.

Peter Radford, in his book *The Celebrated Captain Barclay*, recounts some gloriously eccentric pedestrian contests. One was devised by "an unnamed Duke" who wagered a thousand guineas that he could find a man to walk the ten miles from Piccadilly to Hounslow within three hours, taking three steps forward and one step back. He wasn't wagering on his own ability to do it, but on his ability to find a man who could, though Radford tells us the contest never actually took place

Barclay first performed as a competitive pedestrian while still at school. At the age of seventeen he wagered that he could walk six miles "heel and toe" (the standard definition of racewalking, with one part of one foot touching the ground at all times) on the Brixton to Croydon road within an hour. He succeeded, and won a hundred guineas, a good payday for anyone and a nice feat for a schoolboy, but not really so very impressive by Barclay's later standards.

His career as a pedestrian began in earnest in 1801. The bet was that he could cover ninety miles in less than twenty-one and a half hours. The contest took place on the Roman Road at Barmby Moor in Yorkshire, and Barclay went back and forth on a one-mile stretch and completed the distance with over an hour to spare. Radford says, "He mostly walked but broke into an easy run each time he came to one of the slightly uphill sections."

Barclay's success in that event wasn't completely unexpected. He'd been training fiercely and had done a trial at the nearby Newborough Priory, where he'd walked a hundred miles within eighteen hours through the toughest conditions. He walked in the rain, in the cold, in the dark, throughout the night. By day-break he'd created an ankle-deep circular track in the mud. Richard Long would have loved it.

Barclay performed other impressive feats in this period. In 1803 he wagered that he could cover the sixty-four miles from his quarters in Porridge Island (an alleyway near St. Martin's Church in central London) to Newmarket in Suffolk in twelve hours. He did it in ten, and this again must have been a pedestrian race rather than strictly a walking race, and some running or at least jogging must have been involved. In 1807 he challenged Abraham Wood, one of the best known competitive walkers of the day, to a twenty-four-hour race, the winner simply being the one who'd walked farthest in that time. Out of what can only have been sheer arrogance, Wood gave Barclay a twenty-mile head start, but then got into physical difficulties, resigned after six and a half hours, and subsequently died.

There was no shortage of other well-known pedestrians, such as a Lieutenant Halifax, who walked six hundred miles in twenty days at thirty miles a day, and then two hundred miles in one hundred hours. There was a pedestrian known as "Child, the miller of Wandsworth," who walked forty-five miles in seven hours and fifty-seven minutes. Foster Powell, in 1790, for a bet of "20 guineas to 13," wagered that he could walk from London to York and back in five days and eighteen hours; he did it with one hour and fifty minutes to spare. In 1808, a Mr. Downs walked four hundred miles in ten days, then thirty-five miles a day for twenty successive days.

The combination of speed and endurance was what made a great walker, but Barclay's greatest challenge and success, the walk that was to make his name forever, involved only the latter. In 1809, Barclay went for the big one, the one that Richard Long's 1974 art piece alluded to, and wagered that he could walk a mile in each of a thousand successive hours, for a prize of one thousand guineas. The event started on June 1 on Newmarket Heath and, if all went well, was due to end on the afternoon of July 12.

There's something elegant and elemental about those grand, high, rounded numbers, but paradoxically there's also something that sounds quite simple and straightforward. An average speed of one mile per hour is insultingly slow, and walking twenty-four miles in a day is not much of a problem for anyone who considers himself a serious walker. Even walking a thousand miles in just less than six weeks is well within the range of the possible. The problem is having to walk just a mile in every single hour. Think about it.

If you go at four miles per hour, that means that in each hour you're walking for fifteen minutes, and at rest for forty-five. If you join two miles together, the last fifteen minutes of one hour leading straight into the first fifteen of the next, that still only gives you a maximum of an hour and a half's rest before you have to start walking again. And naturally enough you slow down as the event goes on. The challenge is all about endurance, but over the course of the six weeks it seems to have as much to do with enduring sleep deprivation as it does with being able to walk a vast distance.

Barclay, of course, succeeded. Once per hour every hour for one thousand hours he walked a single mile on a set course in Newmarket, in Suffolk. He actually changed the course partway through the event when he changed his lodgings, on day sixteen, but the rules remained the same. Barclay struggled, he endured, he succeeded. If his stride was a yard long, then he made 1,760,000 strides.

It was, by all accounts, a huge public event. Vast crowds gathered to see Barclay, though most of them must have seen very little, and I imagine many came for the freak-show element rather than to witness a great sporting achievement. To a modern sensibility the sight of a man walking briskly for fifteen to twenty minutes at a time doesn't sound like rich entertainment, so surely the crowds must have come to see his suffering and agony, perhaps to see him collapse, or even expire like Abraham Wood. Partway through the event the *Edinburgh Advertiser* gleefully reported, "Captain Barclay was pursuing his extraordinary undertaking yesterday, but as he proceeds, the hopes of accomplishing it become ever more feeble." Perhaps they were disappointed that he succeeded, that he lived. Barclay showed them all. He did the deed, won his money, slept for some, not too many, hours, and then joined his regiment, based outside Deal, and went off to fight Napoleon.

Barclay's walking expressed something singular and profound about himself and about the human condition, demonstrating what the human body and the human spirit are capable of. His walking was something in the world and of the world, something natural but also something created and willed. Money was part of his motivation, fame and glory, too, but there was surely something inexplicable and irreducible about his obsessive walking, something that remains compelling and admirable, and ultimately mysterious, to this day.

Barclay didn't do drawings or text pieces or mud sculptures as part of his walk, but he did contribute to a book. Its full title is *Pedestrianism; or, an account of the performances of celebrated pedestrians during the last and present century; with a full narrative of Captain Barclay's public and private matches; and an essay on training*, and it's attributed to Walter Thom. Barclay appears as the book's hero rather than its author, but he provided a good deal of inside information about himself and about walking in general. The third person allows the singing of his praises in ways that would have appeared boastful or arrogant if he'd put his own name on it.

Half the book is an anecdotal history of walking, but the main section describes Barclay's walk, how he looked while he walked, with "a sort of lounging gait, without apparently making any extraordinary exertion, scarcely raising his feet more than two or three inches above the ground. . . . His style of walking is to bend forward the body, and to throw its weight on the knees. . . . Any person who will try this plan will find, that his pace will be quickened, at the same time he will walk with more ease to himself, and be better able to endure the fatigue of a long journey, than by walking in a posture perfectly erect, which throws too much of the weight of the body on the ancle-joints [sic]."

It describes his diet: roasted fowl (hot and cold), strong ale, tea, bread and butter, beefsteaks, mutton chops, porter, wine, and "such vegetables as were in season." And above all it describes his difficulties and his pain. "The spasmodic affections in his legs were particularly distressing," we're told. They started on day twelve in his calves, thighs, and feet, and got worse until he was in "great pain" by day twenty. By day thirty-three "he could not rise up without assistance." On day thirty-four he couldn't move without crying out. By day thirty-six, says Thom, he was walking so slowly it significantly reduced the amount of time he had to rest, though this is scarcely borne out by another part of the book.

A section at the end gives "box scores" for Barclay's walk, the statistics of his times, speeds, totals, averages, and so on. His first mile, for example, was done in a brisk twelve minutes, and although he gradually slowed down, he was still moving along very nicely. On day eighteen he was still averaging under seventeen minutes per mile; on day thirty-six, after he'd covered well over eight hundred miles, he was still averaging only a tad over twenty minutes; and his slowest mile in the whole event was only twenty-five minutes. His thousandth mile was walked in just twenty-two minutes and would have been quicker, but there were so many spectators crowding around and cheering him on, he could barely find room to walk.

About fifty years later an Australian called Allan McKean performed a similar thousand-mile, thousand-hour walk. He completed the feat in late 1858 in Ballarat, in Victoria, then incredibly did it again a few weeks later in Melbourne, ending this second walk in early 1859. The *Melbourne Argus* reported that "he completed his thousandth mile (actually his two thousandth) in fifteen minutes thirty-nine seconds, and appeared to be as little fatigued as when he had accomplished one-half of his allotted distance."

I'm sure I ought to be doubly impressed by McKean's feat, and nobody could possibly belittle it, and yet in the end Captain

Barclay remains the man that I, and history, have more respect and affection for. To be the first to do something is inevitably going to be a lot more impressive than to be the first to do it twice.

Twenty years later, two women in America did something that I sometimes feel is more impressive still, certainly more difficult, I think. In 1879, in Brooklyn, an Englishwoman named Ada Anderson walked 2,700 quarter miles in 2,700 consecutive quarter hours. Two years later this record was broken by the exotically named Exilda La Chapelle at the Folly Theatre in Chicago, who completed 3,000 quarter miles in 3,000 quarter hours.

Clearly both these women walked considerably shorter distances than Barclay or McKean, but what makes their walks so compelling, and so much more difficult, is the severe reduction in the periods allowed for rest and recovery. These can never have been more than a little over twenty minutes each. The poor women must have been hallucinating by the end. The *Washington Post* reported that watching La Chapelle's walk was like watching the Spanish Inquisition. Naturally, there was no shortage of spectators.

Anderson and La Chapelle were members of a small group of professional "pedestriennes." La Chapelle had turned pro at the age of thirteen. For a brief period in the nineteenth century female walking was a serious sport and a serious business. Large crowds turned out to watch, and successful women earned a great deal of money. Even so, it was an activity that had something sleazy and daring about it: pedestriennes weren't much better than actresses. It was only a passing fad, however. It was superseded in due course by the more exciting, and even more daring, sport of female bicycle riding, and some of the successful female walkers made an easy transition from two feet to two wheels.

In the interests of research, I decided to do an extended one-mile-per-hour walk. It took place in England, in Suffolk, the county where Captain Barclay walked his thousand miles, but instead of Newmarket, I would be walking in the village of Yox-ford, where I sometimes go to write. Suffolk has the great advantage of being flat.

My emulation of the captain was never going to be absolute. For one thing, I would be doing my walking on public paths and streets, not along a designated track. There would be no cheering crowds, nobody timing me, nobody wishing me well or ill, nobody providing me with roasted fowl and porter, nobody betting on my success or failure. Perhaps these things would have spurred me on.

Equally, I wouldn't be walking a thousand miles, but I did want a taste of how it might feel to do even a fraction of what Barclay had done. I decided to start, with infinite modesty, by doing fifteen miles in fifteen hours. I knew I could complete a fifteen-mile walk easily enough. It was spreading those miles out over the day, with all the gaps and the waiting, the stopping and the starting, that I thought would be interesting and difficult. And I was dead right about that.

Walking slightly more slowly than the good captain, at more or less three miles per hour, twenty minutes per mile, doing the miles in pairs at the end and beginning of two consecutive hours, I would create a pattern of walking for forty minutes and resting for eighty. That didn't seem too arduous. In fact I thought I could use those rest periods to do some writing, make phone calls, read a book, and so on. I was dead wrong about that.

Yoxford is an interesting little village—peaceful, picturesque, population less than seven hundred. There's a former country house, now a hotel-cum–Malaysian restaurant called Satis House, where Charles Dickens almost certainly stayed, and he used the name Satis House for Miss Havisham's home in *Great Expectations*. Since Dickens was a manic walker there's every reason to believe he walked in the very places that I did.

Yoxford is also where W. G. Sebald begins one of the cosmically melancholy walks in his book *The Rings of Saturn*. He writes, "I set out on foot...along the old Roman road, into the thinly populated countryside....I walked for nearly four hours, and in all that time I saw nothing apart from harvested cornfields stretching away into the distance under a sky heavy with clouds, and dark islands of trees." I'm pretty sure he's wrong about the Roman road starting at Yoxford. There *is* a good, straight Roman road nearby, but it's some way to the west of the village. However, the gloom he describes, which seems to be internal as much as external, sounds accurate enough.

A walk around Yoxford, therefore, has its historical and literary pleasures, but when you're following in Captain Barclay's footsteps, you're not very appreciative of such things. I simply set off from the house, walked briskly but aimlessly for a mile, as measured by my GPS, then stopped and went right back. This felt peculiar and arrhythmic, and frankly I was worried about what the neighbors might think.

Fortunately I didn't see many neighbors; the cold, damp rain and occasional snow flurries kept them indoors. I varied my routes as much as I could: to the station and back, round the cricket pitch and the bowling green, up to the end of the village as far as the closed-down fish-and-chips shop. At one point I found myself at the end of a mile taking shelter under the trees in the local graveyard as the sleet lashed down on me from an ash gray sky, and I heard the sound of a farmer's shotgun being repeatedly fired in the distance, at least I hoped it was the distance. This felt surprisingly good. There's nothing like bleak, adverse conditions for raising a walker's self-esteem.

As it got colder and wetter I walked more quickly, tensed up, head down, shoulders raised, hands shoved into pockets—very much not the Barclay style. Before long I was chilled through and my back was aching, but I carried on.

It soon became apparent that my plan to do something in the nonwalking periods wasn't going to work. It became impossible to think about anything except the next walk. I also discovered that waiting to walk is far more arduous than walking.

I did my fifteen miles in fifteen hours without any physical difficulty, and with some satisfaction, but the real satisfaction came from conquering the difficulties imposed by the frustrating stop-start pattern that Barclay's walk had imposed on him, and on me. Walking at a set pace, making sure each mile was completed inside each designated hour, then stopping, then waiting, then getting ready to walk again, required a discipline and an attention to detail that was quite at odds with the way I (or I imagine anybody else) usually walk. In that sense it was some of the hardest walking I'd ever done.

I did another similar walk in midsummer, and it was a little easier than the one done in winter, but not much. There were pleasures, but they weren't much like the ones that normally go with a good walk, and the fact is, notions of walking pleasure really didn't mean much to Captain Barclay. For him a walk was all about testing himself, and others, to the limit. He wanted to demonstrate his strength and stamina. He wanted to beat his competitors, and ultimately he had none. This undoubtedly made him a great walker, and an admirable one, but a walker who was sui generis and one that few mortals can imitate.

One thing that helped me to get through my Captain Barclay walks was making a record of my progress. It loosely resembled the one in the book *Pedestrianism*. I made a table that charted the time I set off for each walk, the time it took me to walk each mile, the speed, the total time spent walking, and the overall average speed. For instance, it took me four hours, thirty-four minutes, and eighteen seconds to walk the fifteen miles, which by my calculation averages 3.34 mph. Filling in this table, seeing the lines and columns gradually fill up, then doing the calculations, was a great source of enjoyment, at least as much as the walk itself.

There's surely something contradictory, though not unnatural, about the desire to document and memorialize walking. What could be more transitory and ephemeral than a walk? In one sense, the best you might hope for would be to leave some footsteps, and the current environmental wisdom might suggest that footsteps are precisely all you should leave. No doubt there are those who think the "interventions" that Richard Long makes in the landscape as he walks are a sacrilege.

The rest of us take photographs, shoot video, make drawings, write about it, fill in walking logs, and so on, and I've spent a certain amount of time wondering whether this is eccentric or not. Maybe all walking is eccentric; maybe none of it is.

One of the most unlikely reasons I can think of for walking is because the president, any president, advocates it. In 1962, John F. Kennedy, recently come to office, discovered an executive order issued by Theodore Roosevelt in 1956, stating that any self-respecting U.S. Marine ought to be able to walk fifty miles in twenty hours with full pack. Kennedy reckoned that his marines should certainly be able to do anything Roosevelt's marines could do, and asked his marine commandant to check on this. Kennedy also suggested that his White House staff ought to be able to do it, too.

This, evidently, was a joke; some of his staff couldn't walk any farther than the watercooler. But, as a publicity stunt, a fifty-mile walk was duly set up for White House staffers. Robert Kennedy, then attorney general, did the walk wearing oxfords.

As is the nature with stunts, there were unforeseen consequences. Such was the Kennedy charisma and popularity that fifty-mile walks suddenly became a national craze. A lot of very ordinary, very unfit civilians took it into their heads to walk fifty miles, often in large groups. Boy Scout troops did it. School groups and seniors did it. An eight-year-old girl named Judy Aylwin failed to do it on her first attempt but succeeded in doing it two weeks later, accompanied by her brother.

The administration was understandably alarmed. A lot of money and energy was being put into the President's Council on Physical Fitness and Sports to improve the nation's health. It was clear that if people who had never walked seriously in their lives suddenly walked fifty miles the results were likely to be anything but healthful, and so attempts were made to distance the White House from the madness.

Like all crazes, this one, perhaps fortunately, wore off pretty quickly. America returned to its sedentary ways. But not before a man by the name of Jim McNutt, from San Carlos, California, demonstrated that he could do it faster than anybody else, having walked fifty miles in seven hours, fifty minutes. Was he an eccentric?

Was the filmmaker Werner Herzog demonstrating eccentricity in November 1974, when he heard that Lotte Eisner was seriously ill and likely to die and said to himself "This must not be," that German cinema couldn't do without her, and set off on a walk from Munich to Paris in the depths of winter, trudging through ice and snow, sleeping outdoors, experiencing pain in his ankle and in his left thigh "around the groin," journeying "in full faith believing that she would stay alive if I came on foot"?

It certainly doesn't sound like a conventional reason for walking, or a conventional way of keeping someone alive, but it worked. Lotte Eisner didn't die until 1983. Wim Wenders's 1984 movie *Paris, Texas* is dedicated to her. So maybe Herzog's walk wasn't eccentric at all.

Herzog is also the man who wrote, in a manifesto called the "Minnesota Declaration," that "tourism is sin, and travel on foot virtue." He currently lives in the Hollywood Hills, not a million miles from where I do, though we've yet to encounter each other while walking.

At much the same time that Herzog was making his journey to Paris, the English traveler and writer Sebastian Snow was walking the length of South America, 8,700 miles from Tierra del Fuego to the Panama Canal. It took him nineteen months. Fellow writer and explorer Eric Newby reckons this is one of the longest uninterrupted walks ever accomplished. The explorer Chris Bonington accompanied him for part of the trip and "was reduced to wreckage after a few days."

Snow is one of my favorite walkers. He was an Englishman of the old school, droll, debonair, tough as granite, and an eccentric by any conventional standard. He was an old Etonian who (this is almost too good to be true) had broken his leg while playing football and had thereby avoided being drafted into the army for national service. They were worried about his ability to march.

Perhaps the greatest show of Snow's resolve and toughness was his ability to turn down lifts from passing motorists, however hard the going got. Often his refusal caused incomprehension, alarm, and sometimes anger in the spurned drivers. In the Peruvian desert a "young and very animated" Peruvian woman stopped her car and began chatting with him, complaining that desert driving is very monotonous.

"Desert marching is no sinecure," Snow replied, quick as a flash, but then he didn't want it to be. "By some transcendental process," he writes, "I seemed to take on the characteristics of a Shire (horse), my head lowered, resolute, I just plunked one foot in front of t'other, mentally munching nothingness."

. . .

Snow's rejections bring to mind John Francis, otherwise known as Planetwalker. In 1971, Francis saw a catastrophic oil spill in San Francisco Bay, and decided that from that moment he'd stop using motorized transport. It caused him certain problems, not least the loss of his job as manager of "a struggling avant-garde music group" called Spectrum of Sight and Sound, but he obviously believed he'd done the right thing, and for the next five years he spread the word. This in itself caused more problems. Certain people said he'd adopted a holier-than-thou attitude and that the way he talked about walking was designed to make them feel bad. So Francis stopped talking. The blurb on his autobiography reads "22 years of walking, 17 years of silence."

This sounds like pretty odd stuff, and Francis was clearly a man who couldn't operate very successfully in the "ordinary" world. But from his point of view, his actions weren't eccentric, they were natural and inevitable. He didn't do them in order to make people think he was a wild and crazy guy; he did them because he wanted to "make a difference."

Sometimes it seems the world is packed with such people. One currently in the process of making life difficult for himself is Arthur Blessit, who is walking round the world carrying a forty-pound cross. When I last checked his website he'd walked 37,352 miles in 307 nations in 38 years. That distance is equivalent to circling the earth one and a half times. Elsewhere on the website there's a calculation of how far Jesus walked in his lifetime: far enough to circle the globe precisely once.

And who can forget the two American Buddhist monks walking for peace who took a two-year, nine-month pilgrimage from Los Angeles to their home monastery in Ukiah, Oregon, an eight-hundred-mile trip in all, taking three steps forward, then making a full prostration, for the entire length of the journey. Peter Radford's "unnamed Duke" would have been impressed and hired them on the spot.

Another peace walker was Mildred Norman Ryder, known as Peace Pilgrim. In 1952 she became the first woman to hike the Appalachian Trail in one season, and then had a vision: "I saw, in my mind's eye, myself walking along and wearing the garb of my mission.... I saw a map of the United States with the large cities marked...as though someone had taken a colored crayon and marked a zigzag line across, coast to coast and border to border, from Los Angeles to New York City. I knew what I was to do. And that was a vision of my first year's pilgrimage route in 1953!"

The garb of her mission consisted of "one pair of slacks and shorts, one blouse and sweater, a lightweight blanket, and two double plastic sheets, into which I sometimes stuffed leaves." I had expected something more robelike.

Walking for peace may certainly strike you and me as futile and useless, but if a person believes it works, then it's the most logical and rational thing in the world. To walk for a reason, any reason, however personal or obscure, is surely a mark of rationality. Money, art, self-knowledge, world peace, these are not eccentric motivations for walking; they're damn good ones, regardless of whether or not they succeed. I find myself coming to the conclusion that perhaps the only truly eccentric walker is the one who walks for no reason whatsoever. However, I'm no longer sure if that's even possible.

# NICHOLSON'S LONDON, YOUR
# LONDON, ANYBODY'S LONDON

*Worst street to walk? The Rotherhithe Tunnel. Not really a street, but a
pedestrian way (or euthanasia path). West India Avenue & Cabot Square
(by Canary Wharf) would be right up there as an anti-street, high level
surveillance, suspended liberties, drone crowds, comic book architecture.*

—Iain Sinclair

One wet Sunday afternoon in the autumn of 1804,
Thomas De Quincey, age nineteen, and later to become
the author of *Confessions of an English Opium Eater*, was walking
along London's Oxford Street and finding it every bit as bleak
and depressing then as many still do to this day. In order to
cheer himself up he went into a druggist's shop ("The druggist,
unconscious minister of celestial pleasure") and bought himself a
tincture of opium. That brightened up his day no end. It was the
beginning of De Quincey's love affair with opium and a continu-
ing part of his love affair with walking the streets of London.

Later he would write, "And sometimes in my attempts to steer
homewards...I came suddenly upon such knotty problems of
alleys, such enigmatic entries, and such sphinx's riddles of streets

without thoroughfares, as must, I conceive, baffle the audacity of porters, and confound the intellects of hackney-coachmen. I could almost have believed, at times, that I must be the first discoverer of some of these *terrae incognitae,* and doubted whether they had yet been laid down in the modern charts of London."

Of course, opium is generally not a big help when it comes to finding your way home, but he may be speaking metaphorically here. It seems impossible that he was the very first person ever to have set foot in any given location, although it remains perfectly possible that he was walking in a place for which a map hadn't yet been drawn.

De Quincey's fantasy of an unknown London is an attractive one, since London is, in every sense I can think of, well-trodden territory: a place of walkers, with a two-thousand-year-long history of pedestrianism. I've trodden it as widely and as well as I know how, but like every London walker, I realize that I'm always walking in somebody else's footsteps. No part of London is genuinely unknown. However obscure or hidden the place, somebody has already discovered it, walked it, staked a claim on it. Your own exploration therefore has to be personalized; you're doing it for yourself, increasing your own store of particular knowledge, walking your own eccentric version of the city.

The first London walkers had to be the Romans, since before them there was no London (or Londinium), just expanses of marsh and swamp, thinly inhabited by surly, saturnine Iron Age Brits. Maybe the Brits walked, but they didn't walk in anything called London. The Romans invaded Britain for the first time in A.D. 43, probably used a pontoon bridge to cross what was to become the river Thames, then a few years later built the first permanent bridge across it, thought to have been just east of the present-day London Bridge. People could then walk from one side of the river to the other, if they chose, though then as now quite a few probably chose not to. North and South London continue to be inhabited by very different tribes.

The Romans weren't meanderers. Their walking was straight and direct, taking the shortest distance between two points. One of the first things English schoolkids learn is that the presence of a long straight road means the Romans were here. You don't need a highly developed sense of history to enjoy knowing that you're walking the same route that some legionnaire or proconsul walked nearly two thousand years ago.

Inevitably the growth of London, the change, the decay, plus a certain amount of bombing and urban redevelopment, has tended to obscure the Roman origins of the city, but even in central areas it's not so hard to walk along what was once a Roman road. De Quincey's Oxford Street, now a major shopping artery, and by many accounts a crass, soulless, overcommercialized place (but more of that later), was once part of a Roman route connecting Hampshire to Suffolk.

At this very moment somebody is out there walking the streets of London, consciously following in ancient Roman footsteps, trying to make a connection with some imagined Roman imperial past. I say this without much fear of contradiction, because I know that London's streets contain walkers of every description, each of them pursuing separate destinies, pacing out routes of personal need and desire, some based on history or literature or on more private obsessions. At least one of them must style himself as a Roman London walker.

The mayor's office tells us that seven million walking journeys are made in London every day, and although the majority of these will no doubt be short and mundane (and I do wonder what percentage involve going to or from the pub), that still leaves plenty of more programmatic walking expeditions. At the most modest level, these walks will be done by tourists. Showing the city to visitors is good business, and doing it on foot is a great way to reduce overheads. You see them all over London, walking tours being conducted by rather theatrical guides, who look like would-be or failed or maybe just unemployed actors, heading a gaggle of lost-looking walkers, showing them Dickens's London, Sherlock Holmes's London, Jack the Ripper's London, or the Beatles' London. Some more serious walks will have you tracing routes of plague, fire, riot, and terrorism.

In the interests of research—thinking I wasn't going to enjoy it very much—I went on one of these walking tours, called "The Blitz: London at War." It happens every Thursday afternoon at two-fifteen, rain or shine: meet at exit 2 outside St. Paul's tube station. The guide, a skinny, intense, blond woman with one of the more determined strides I'd ever seen—rushed, urgent, leaning forward into some fierce wind of her own imagining—led me and twenty or so others on a tight circuit that had St. Paul's Cathedral at its center. We looked at the shrapnel marks preserved in the cathedral's masonry, visited a bombed-out church that's been left in a semiruined state as a memorial garden, saw a monument to the Blitz firemen, and as we walked we spotted various incidental pleasures: the preserved ruins of the Roman Temple of Mithras, for instance, as well as an ice cream seller without a street trading license who was being collared by the law.

"I haven't got my license with me," the ice cream seller said shiftily.

"Now that *does* surprise me," said the arresting copper.

Inevitably there wasn't much Blitz to see. The German bombings ended well over sixty years ago, and so we had to rely on our guide, her anecdotes, and some photographs she had with her in an album. Her anecdotes weren't bad at all. One was about two old ladies who were walking down a London street in the middle of an air raid. This wasn't so unusual; a lot of people simply didn't bother to head for the shelters. As they walked, a bomb landed near the old ladies, not too close or they'd have been killed instantly, but near enough that they felt the tail end of the blast, which left their bodies unscathed but blew off all their clothes and left them standing in the street, alive, well, and completely naked.

We also heard the story of a young soldier whose job was to deal with an unexploded bomb that had landed close to St. Paul's Cathedral and vanished into the earth. Dealing with it involved digging down, finding the bomb, then defusing it. Of course the very act of digging might have been enough to make the bomb go off, but the young soldier was evidently a gentle shoveler and he successfully uncovered the bomb, at which point he saw that it was booby-trapped. Trying to dismantle the fuse was the very thing that would detonate it. The British army boffins were familiar with the type but hadn't yet worked out a method of disarming it. A controlled explosion on-site was recommended, but that would have brought down half the cathedral.

So a crane was brought and the bomb was painstakingly winched out of its hole, put on the back of a truck, and covered with sandbags. It was then very carefully driven the six miles from central London to the Hackney marshes, where it could be safely blown up, but to get there they had to take a main road, evacuating houses and clearing pedestrians as they went.

Suddenly I found myself tearing up at this story of unimaginable courage set against the familiar backdrop of a grubby, everyday city. I suppose courage is to be found everywhere, and especially in cities under attack. Courage seems to be unattached to ideology, though naturally we want it to belong to the one we support. To be walking in a London street where men had taken such terrible risks was both chilling and infinitely moving. I thought I was going to weep.

Thank God I managed to hold it in. Being reduced to tears on a walking tour would really not have shown the Blitz spirit at all. We walked on, not very far and not very fast. It gradually became obvious, and it was not exactly a surprise, that two hours of standing around listening to stories, interspersed with rather short walks, of no more than a couple of hundred yards each, was actually very hard work, much harder than walking continuously for two hours. As the tour ended twenty people were rubbing their backs, complaining about their feet, and saying they needed to sit down. I checked my GPS: in those two hours we'd walked just under a mile.

In the end no serious London walker allows himself to be guided around the city by anything other than his own instincts and internal compass. The real enterprise is to make the city "yours" as opposed to Dickens's or Sherlock Holmes's or the Beatles'.

This is perhaps what that fine London walker William Blake (or at least his hero, Los) meant when he said, "I must Create a System, or be enslaved by another Man's."

To devise your own system of walking in London isn't easy; it requires resolve and perversity. The true London walker avoids the obvious by pursuing some grand, if quixotic, agenda. He (it usually is a he) walks in search of lines of force, unrecognized symbols, secret bunkers, evidence of conspiracy, seeking the Land of Cockayne or a new Jerusalem. Personally, I blame the author Iain Sinclair for a lot of this.

Iain Sinclair is a poet, novelist, memoirist, and occasional filmmaker, who dwelled in pretty thorough obscurity until 1985 or so when Peter Ackroyd wrote a book called *Hawksmoor*, a transhistorical detective novel with a plot that involves the discovery of human sacrifices in the crypts of certain seventeenth-century London churches built by an architect not entirely unlike the historical Nicholas Hawksmoor, although in the novel he's called Nicholas Dyer, and Hawksmoor is the name of a present-day detective.

Ackroyd fessed up—he'd have been a fool not to—that the novel had been partly inspired by Iain Sinclair's *Lud Heat*, a prose poem that also invokes pilgrim routes, municipal gardening, and the American avant-garde filmmaker Stan Brakhage.

Ackroyd's book was a commercial success, and although that didn't convince throngs of people to start reading Sinclair's work, he did become a contender, a gray eminence, a distant, brooding literary figure, and a sort of guru for London's hipper literary walkers. His own commercial success came chiefly from writing nonfiction accounts of his walks in and around London, and although the thick, dense allusive prose of these accounts isn't easy reading, it's a whole lot easier than the thick, dense, allusive prose of his fiction. My favorite of his books, and the most accessible, *Lights Out for the Territory*, is subtitled "9 Excursions in the Secret History of London."

Sinclair's project, pretty thoroughly realized, was to connect his personal experiences of walking around the more feral parts of the city (in general the parts where the tour guides don't take you, although Sinclair is a Jack the Ripper maven) with various overlapping historical traditions: the literary, the bohemian, the criminal, the mystical, the alchemical, not so much the sexual. He brings together the worlds of various Londoners, some living, many dead, many of them walkers, some permanent residents, some who just passed through: Daniel Defoe, William Blake, the Kray twins, Derek Raymond, William Burroughs, Alan Moore, Rachel Whiteread, to name very few. He's also spectacularly good at revealing and connecting historical characters you wish you knew more about: "Thomas Canry Caulker, son of Canrah Bah Caulker, King of Bompey in West Africa; William Hone, bookseller, prosecuted for blasphemy...Samuel Sharpe, banker and Egyptologist...John Swan, originator of the steamship's screw propeller and the self-acting chain messenger." The text has frequent exciting references to "secret mythologies," "psychic landscapes," and "mystical geographies."

All this makes Sinclair a psychogeographer, though frankly, these days, who isn't? In its modern form psychogeography (of which, more later) often seems to be a way for clever young men to mooch around cities doing nothing much, claiming that they're flâneurs who are doing something really, you know, significant, and often taking Iain Sinclair as their role model. To be fair to Sinclair he seems amused by all this, and at the very least skeptical about the craze he's started. He refers to psychogeography as a franchise, which seems to get it about right; it neatly turns the psychogeographer into the McFlâneur.

For anyone to compete with Sinclair on his own terms would be folly. He knows more than you do. He has read more widely, more deeply, more obscurely than you. He's also walked more and walked farther, more often, more observantly, more obsessively. And so, not being an absolute fool, I decided it would be a good idea to have Iain Sinclair (metaphorically at least) walk on the footpath with me rather than stand beside it observing my failings. I thought I'd better talk to him. I made contact. He said walk on over, so I did. For a literary gray eminence he was remarkably welcoming.

Sinclair, as his writings regularly tell us, has lived for decades in Hackney, in the all too appropriately named Albion Drive. I'd walked past his house years earlier on one of my own walking excursions, and noted that it seemed a good deal less the dark shamanic lair than you might have expected from reading Sinclair's books.

The only other thing I remembered from that walk was seeing a graffito at the end of the street. Painted in blue on a pale yellow brick wall were the words *No lips.* I took a photograph of it, and over the years I've regularly looked at it and wondered what, if anything, those words meant.

Photographing graffiti is a suitably Sinclairian thing to do. One of the essays in *Lights Out for the Territory* has him walking from Hackney to Greenwich Hill and back to Chingford Mount, recording all the graffiti he sees on the way. "These botched runes," he writes, "burnt into the script in the heat of creation, offer an alternative reading—a subterranean, preconscious text capable of divination and prophecy. A sorcerer's grimoire that would function as a curse or a blessing."

When I went back to Hackney this time, on my way to see Sinclair, I walked around trying to find the *No lips* graffito again, but either it had been removed or I was looking in the wrong place. So I looked for other clues instead. Sinclair the writer is so preternaturally aware of his surroundings and their real, imagined, or clandestine histories and meanings that just going to see him is enough to put you on your sensory mettle. Not far from Albion Drive, for instance, was a street called Vixen Mews; surely that was a name that bespoke a dark past and a labyrinthine narrative. Later Iain Sinclair would tell me he had no idea where the name came from, though he was intrigued by it, too, and I admit I was relieved to find that his knowledge of London wasn't utterly encyclopedic.

On the other hand, when I mentioned that the previous day I'd been wandering around London and had found myself walking through the Nonconformist graveyard known as Bunhill Fields (where quite a few people go at lunchtime to eat their sandwiches, I discovered), his eyes lit up like Roman candles.

"Oh yeah," he said, "the epicenter. Blake, Defoe, and Bunyan." (All three of them have memorials there, though current scholarship thinks none of them is buried there.) "My theory is that all lines of energy or intelligence move out from that particular cluster. Bunyan's *Pilgrim's Progress* is actually the ultimate English walking book, where the physical journey that he does then becomes fabulated into this Christian mythology, but all the places are actually mappable. And then Daniel Defoe, because he traveled around the whole of England as an intelligencer and spy and double man. And then Blake with his cosmic and imaginary journeys, with specific wonderful transits of London that are in the Jerusalem poem where he starts on Highgate Hill, through the narrows of the riverside, and he actually lists all these places. So I think any sense of a journey must begin on that spot, in this wonderful cross between the three of them." In *Lights Out*, he writes, "Bunhill Fields. Everything I believe in, everything London can do to you, starts there."

Sinclair's appearance is professorial, alert, a touch gaunt, unamused, with a very correct posture that might make you believe he'd had a spell in the army, which as far as I know he hasn't. There was none of the soft fleshiness that deskbound writers are heir to. Maybe it came from all the walking. His voice, however, was soft, gentle, of a higher pitch than you'd expect to hear coming from that severe face. He was friendly but reserved, and obviously accustomed to being interviewed, even though I insisted I wanted this to be a conversation rather than a Q and A.

"London," he said, "is the ultimate walking city, although it's a kind of battle—it has that mysterious labyrinthine quality that keeps it interesting. It's never the same twice, and you duck in and out of alleyways and there's so much *business* going on, and very soon you can negotiate into green spaces, rivers. It keeps it interesting."

This is what I had come to hear. I was still on my sensory derangement kick. In fact I was still popping opiates for my recovering broken arm, but I wanted to talk about more recreational forms of medication. I've only once done any walking while under the influence of LSD and it wasn't much fun. I was walking in a crowded street, not in London but in Cambridge, and I believed I could read the minds of the people walking toward me. They were all nightmarish minds that I'd have preferred not to have been able to read. I said I couldn't imagine walking around London on acid.

"Very wise," Sinclair said, "because underneath there's a monstrous aspect to it."

The people I know who support the idea of walking around on LSD say what's so great about it is the way you see all the minutiae and fine detail that a drug-free mind simply skims over.

"But," said Sinclair, "you can train yourself to log and sense those details anyway. Over the years you can come to recognize aspects and details, down to the smallest particulars, and incorporate them into a larger sense of the whole. That's really what walks are about. As well as hoovering up information, it's a way of actually shifting a state of consciousness, and you get into things you didn't know about, or you begin to find out about, and that's the interesting part. Otherwise, it's just reportage."

I sensed that he thought few things in the world were quite as pernicious and worthless as reportage.

In his books Sinclair is seldom a solitary walker. He has a loose posse of fellow obsessives, mostly male, who share a taste for walking, thinking, recording, talking; especially talking, he said.

"It's the only time you've got to have a long conversation, even though it contains a lot of silence. You stop to have breakfast in a greasy spoon, then later in the day you drop into a pub, and you can have different kinds of conversation from the kind you have as you're rambling along, when you're not quite together, or you come together and then you'll do a stretch where one person goes ahead, then you meet up and he notices something, you notice something, over the course of the whole day, and there it is, it's very, very civilized, a perfect philosophical dialogue."

I wondered if he had a series of set walks.

"Yes, because we've been in this house since 1969, so there are many set-piece walks that I do. I've got different walks for different questions or problems or ideas that I'm dealing with, a whole chain of maybe fifty different walks that you do for different things.

"One would be that short-story walk. If it was a more confused situation, if I was worrying away at something, I'd go down to the river—it would be one of two ways. If it was a seriously difficult thing that needed to be really thought out, I'd go down the canal to Limehouse, get on the river, then I could go down the river as far as the problem needed, and loop back. If it was something more straightforward, I'd go straight down Bethnal Green, through Brick Lane down to Wapping, and hit the river there, and that would be enough to resolve this one thing, and if it was something I was looking for still, I'd go up to Waltham Abbey or the New Forest or Tilbury or something serious."

So, I suggested, the size and nature of the problem determined the size and nature of the walk.

"But it needn't necessarily be a problem," he said. "It might just be recharging the batteries in a particular way, or I have an instinct that there's something interesting there and I take off in that territory."

Given that he's written so explicitly about where he lives and walks, and since he continues to live and walk in the same place, I wondered whether he was ever recognized by fellow walkers.

"For a period I kept bumping into people somewhere around Shoreditch," he said, "who were actually walking about with books of mine, doing various projects from the books, but I haven't of late seen any."

And did he reveal himself to them?

"A couple challenged me, and one I saw just reading the book and I talked to him and pointed something out that he was looking for, and a couple of times on the canal, too, I saw a guy on a bike who was cycling through one of the books and ticking things off. He practically ran into me. But I think there are huge numbers of people walking, not with my books, but walking and doing their own endlessly strange projects across London."

I mentioned that I'd been rereading D. H. Lawrence's *Sons and Lovers*, and was amazed by the huge distances the hero Paul Morel would walk in order to go and see his girlfriend Miriam. Sinclair's eyes lit up again. "Yes indeed," he said.

The fictional Miriam is closely based on Lawrence's own girlfriend, Jessie Chambers. Morel's mother says, "She must be wonderfully fascinating, that you can't get away from her, but must go trailing eight miles at this time of night."

And she's right, of course. Miriam is wonderfully fascinating. The evenings together—Paul and Miriam's, D.H. and Jessie's—were intense and passionate, and one of their passions was for literature. In Jessie Chambers's memoirs she mentions the books they discussed. Turgenev's *Fathers and Sons* was one of them, its title perhaps an inspiration for Lawrence's own novel.

Iain Sinclair got up, left the room, and came back a minute

or two later with a small blue hardback copy of *Fathers and Sons*.
He opened it up and held it out to me. There on the flyleaf was
the signature "Jessie Chambers." This was Jessie Chambers's own
copy of *Fathers and Sons*. This book had belonged to the woman
for whom Lawrence was prepared to do so much walking. Sinclair had been given the book by a dealer as a thank-you for
carrying a box of books.

It had occurred to me that Iain Sinclair might invite me to
go with him on one of his fifty or so routes. I thought it might
make for good, if again well-trodden, material. He didn't, but I
did do one short walk with Iain Sinclair. It wasn't arduous, and
as far as I can tell it was devoid of secret histories and alternate
mythologies, although you can never be sure about these things.
Our walk together was about twenty feet in length, the distance
from his front door to his front gate, from his house along his
garden path to the street. Being a good host, he saw me all the
way out, escorted me off the premises. This, unarguably, was a
walk through Iain Sinclair's London.

I was left wondering which particular endlessly strange walking project of my own I should be doing in London. I tried to
envisage a map that showed every step I'd ever taken in the
city—from my first visit with my parents when I was eleven years
old, then all the visits I'd made when I was a student, thinking
myself pretty cool to have friends, even a girlfriend, in London.

Then, as soon as I got out of college, I went to live in London, and began a period of twenty years or so living in one
grim, unsatisfactory place after another, all over the map: Not-

ting Hill, Shepherd's Bush, Stamford Hill, Hendon, Baker Street, Greenwich, Bloomsbury, West Hampstead, Earls Court, West Ham. Eventually, and for the longest time, I lived in a small flat in Maida Vale that I wanted to move out of the day I moved in, and managed it just over twelve years later. I contemplated doing a pilgrimage walk around all these places where I'd lived, but it would have taken forever, and why would I want to depress myself?

Like Iain Sinclair, I had a certain number of set London walks, and I liked to think that over the years these had got more eccentric and sophisticated, more full of the connoisseurship of walking and London. Some of them were straightforward enough, various walks along and across and under the Thames, various walks that enabled me to watch the endless, cyclical destruction and reconstruction of London. Some were more consciously obscure: a walk to the six-hundred-year-old Whitechapel Bell Foundry; a stroll along Lombard Street to see where Alexander Pope, Aubrey Beardsley, T. S. Eliot, and Charles Dickens's first love, Maria Beadnell, had all lived at one time or another; an expedition to see the King's Place Nunneries—exclusive, expensive, eighteenth-century brothels, the best of them run by a woman from Guinea known as Black Harriott.

Sometimes I just took a shot in the dark. An afternoon spent on the green, cheerless expanse that is Wanstead Flats wasn't one of the great walks, but it took me to a place I'd never been before, and will most likely never go again: the Hornimann Museum—the home of stuffed critters and primitive musical instruments—was wonderful, and I promised myself I'd definitely go back, but so far I never have.

I had a brief obsession with a book on architecture, written by Charles Jencks, called *Post-Modern Triumphs in London*. I spent quite a few Sunday afternoons walking around looking at new buildings that were all faux this and high-tech that, and saying to my walking pals, "Well yes, it *is* postmodern, but is it a triumph?"

I discovered that a high percentage of the buildings I liked were designed by a company called CZWG. These included The Circle, a curved block, finished in purple-and-blue-glazed bricks; Cascades, an apartment building on the Isle of Dogs, twenty stories high, one side of it stepped, providing a stack of "penthouses"; the Janet Street-Porter House in Smithfield, a conglomeration of odd-shaped windows, balconies, metal grids, and four colors of brick. Janet Street-Porter, incidentally, remains a famous English walker, and was for a while vice president of the Ramblers' Association.

The G in CZWG belongs to Piers Gough, a tall, skinny, angular Beardsleyesque character with quite a public profile in England as a champion of postmodern architecture. Newspapers and magazines describe him as "flamboyant" and note that he's an advisor to Frank Gehry.

I met Piers Gough at a party in London. By then I had become interested in people who had difficulty walking, but I had no idea that Gough fit into this category. None of the cuttings I'd read about him ever mentioned that he's seriously disabled.

At the party I saw that he had terrible trouble getting around. In order to cross the room he had to make a series of lurches using tables, sofas, sometimes the walls, to support and propel himself. His legs pointed inward asymmetrically, and his feet, which splayed outward, were encased in special black leather shoes that were oddly stylish and almost semicircular in plan.

We happened to be leaving at the same time, and he offered me a lift: his legs worked well enough to allow him to drive an automatic car. As we walked the couple of hundred yards to his Saab, I saw that he walked more easily in the street than he had indoors. The lurches I'd seen were his attempts to launch himself: once he was in motion he could keep going. He also used a walking stick, one specially made for him from transparent Perspex. With the long black raincoat he was wearing, he cut an elegantly ruined figure.

I said I was writing a book about walking, and would he mind if I asked him a few questions. He graciously said he didn't mind. He'd been on a building site, he told me, and had fallen, not very far, about ten feet, but it had been enough to break his spine. That had been thirty years ago, when he was thirty. He'd been living with the disability for half his life. His wasn't a typical spinal injury, he said. In some ways he'd been lucky. Most people with a broken spine are completely paralyzed below the point of the break, but he wasn't; otherwise, he wouldn't have been able to walk at all.

I asked whether the condition was stable, whether it was getting worse, whether it could be improved somehow. He said it was only getting worse in the way that everything gets worse with age. And he had to do exercises to prevent deterioration. He went to the gym and went swimming.

What about walking, I asked. I had the notion that this might be a man who could walk only with great difficulty but who needed to continue to walk in order to improve his condition.

My notion was quickly destroyed. Gough had done enough walking in his life, he said. When he was growing up, his father had taught at a school in the middle of the English countryside. There were no buses, and the train station was three miles away. The frequent six-mile round-trip to and from the station had spoiled his taste for walking long before he had his accident.

But worse than that, he said, walking was actually bad for his condition. The more walking he did now, the less walking he would be able to do in the future. It was as though he had only a certain number of miles in him: every one he used up meant there was one mile less to use. He would eventually walk himself to a standstill.

I returned to imagining that cosmic map of Nicholsonian walks in London. There'd be thin spidery traces all over the city, some just a single line indicating a route I'd taken only once. There'd be some slight thickening around the places where I'd gone a few times to visit friends—the better the friends, the greater the thickening—and even more thickening in the places where I'd lived: the longer I lived there, the denser the markings. The decade spent in Maida Vale would result in the map being positively clotted and embossed along the route from the tube station to my front door. After that I suspected Oxford Street was the place I'd walked the most—the street that so many people hated.

I know plenty of Londoners who will go out of their way to avoid setting foot on Oxford Street. I'd taken to asking people what they thought was the worst London street for walking, and many said Oxford Street. It's not that it's notoriously dangerous or ugly or mean, it's just that it's full of people that a lot of Londoners don't want to mix with: tourists, out-of-towners, spivs, pickpockets, kids cutting school, mad shoppers. The real objection is that it's too popular, too full of ordinary miscellaneous humanity. It's unpopular with one set of people precisely because it's so popular with another.

Oxford Street is a thoroughfare running more or less east–west. The big department stores are on the north side, the sunny side of the street; De Quincey's druggist was on the sunless south side. It's the street where William Blake walked on his way to and from his house on Poland Street. It was the subject of a movie by Malcolm McLaren, and the site of one of the Sex Pistols gigs, at the Hundred Club. It's also a street where I once saw Bob Geldof walking along weighed down with his Christmas shopping.

It became Oxford Street only after 1713. Until then it was variously known as the Road from Uxbridge, the King's Highway, the Acton Road, Tyburn Way—the Tyburn being a river that still runs not so very deep beneath the street surface. In 1941 a German bomb made a crater that briefly exposed it.

Tyburn was also the place of public executions, at the very western end of Oxford Street, nearly but not quite where Marble Arch now stands. Hangings were regular, communal, celebratory activities. Prisoners were brought on horse-drawn cart from Newgate Prison a few miles away in the City of London, and eventually along the length of the street while large crowds followed on foot. To walk along Oxford Street is to walk the route of fifty thousand convicted criminals who were executed at Tyburn and those who liked to watch.

Tom Waits mentions the Tyburn Jig, the "dance" of the flailing legs of the hanged who won't be walking anywhere ever again. In fact a small paper could be written on Tom Waits and walking. In the song "Whistle Down the Wind" he refers to something called the "Marley Bone Coach"—that's how it's spelled on his website. Now, Marylebone is a district of London, no distance from Oxford Street, and I don't doubt there was once, probably still is, a coach that goes there, but the phrase "taking the marrow bone coach" is, or was, slang for walking, i.e., using the marrow bones in the legs. I'd like to think Waits is aware of this. In another song he warns that when you walk in the garden you'd better watch your back.

Most of my walking on Oxford Street was not done entirely by choice. I'd worked two jobs on the street and two more close by. Consequently, when I went out for a walk at lunchtime I found myself on Oxford Street. My bank was there. I bought food there. I bought clothes, books, records, spectacles. The truth was, despite everything, I rather enjoyed walking there, and yet I could see there was something troubling and paradoxical in having done so much walking in a place that was held in such contempt by so many. I felt that Oxford Street needed to be redeemed. I thought it might be a good place to do my particular strange walking project.

I came to a decision. I would make six transits of Oxford Street, there and back, from Tottenham Court Road tube station at the east end of the street to Marble Arch at the west, and back again. I would spread them out over the course of the day. I would see how the street and my walking changed.

The Oxford Street Shopping Association claims the street is a mile and a half long (though I suspect this is an optimistically high figure), so each round-trip would theoretically be three miles, for a total of eighteen. A few unexpected detours and diversions, plus the short distances between the start and finish of the walks, would surely make it add up to twenty miles. That seemed satisfyingly like hard work.

Why six transits? Partly because I was trying to work up a pun about "sic transit Gloria," but mostly because I was doing the walk on the sixth day of the sixth month of 2006. There were reports in the papers about this date having some relation to the number of the beast, 666, but I couldn't see that. No reasonable way of writing the date could be made to give you that bestial number. In any case, one of the notions being bandied about was that this would be the day the Anti-Christ was born, which in itself didn't seem to threaten much, at least for the time being. Even the Anti-Christ surely wouldn't hit his stride on the very day he was born.

During the course of the day I duly walked the length of Oxford Street six times in each direction and did my eighteen to twenty miles. I set off for the first walk at six in the morning, in bright sunlight, and I completed my last walk a little before midnight.

I walked the street when it was all but empty and when it was so packed that I could scarcely walk at all. Chiefly I saw other people: first the workers, then the shoppers, and finally the carousers and drunks and lovebirds.

At times there was something festive about it all. The weather was as good as English weather ever gets. The people on the street looked as though they were enjoying themselves. Many looked like tourists, and many of them seemed lost. A lot of maps were being consulted, and lots of photographs were being taken. I saw one man scanning the street with binoculars. A woman in full, engulfing Arab dress was wielding a video camera. The crowd was diverse in terms of race, age, and class. They wouldn't all be going to the same shops or buying the same things or spending the same amount of money, but they were all there to buy *something*, whether designer clothes or cheap T-shirts with a map of the London underground on them. They were united, made homogenous by the great equalizer of trade, and they all looked essentially happy about it.

I was hassled occasionally, once by a young man in a red T-shirt, smiling far too broadly, who stepped in front of me and demanded, "Do you have love in your heart?" I couldn't stop myself guffawing at the question. "I think you know I haven't," I said. That made him lose a lot of his charm. "This is a very serious issue," he said very seriously, which I didn't dispute. He was raising funds for a children's charity, a worthy cause as far as I know, and no doubt there is some research proving that asking dumb questions of people who are walking down Oxford Street is a good way to suck in money, but I was the wrong demographic.

"Does this ever work?" I asked as I walked away.

"Yes," the young man called after me earnestly. "Yes, it does."

Later, outside Marble Arch tube station two young Muslim men were standing behind a stall decked out with leaflets and hand-labeled DVDs. One asked me, "Now, what's your understanding of Islam?" He had the winning smile and the steady, open gaze favored by the more appealing sort of zealot, and I said I didn't really have any understanding of it at all. He asked me if I had a DVD player, and offered me a DVD. I said I'd rather have something written. "Ah," he said, "you want the *original*."

I ended up with two publications, one called "Jesus, peace be upon him, a concise Islamic Belief," and a booklet titled "Muhammad's Prophethood: an analytical view," by Jamal A. Badawi, professor of business management at St. Mary's University, Halifax, Canada. Badawi is very insistent that Muhammad was not an epileptic, nor did he suffer from "the falling down disease that was known to his contemporaries."

A minute after I'd left the Islamic boys, I encountered a Christian preacher, an American from his accent, shouting through a megaphone, asking whether I, or anyone else, wanted to know about heaven. He certainly hadn't perfected the winning smile and the steady gaze. I, and everyone else, looked away and walked on.

Halfway through the afternoon I noticed a fragmentation, people displaying tribal affiliations: retro punks, a pair of Japanese women in kimonos, some Hare Krishna celebrants, and a group of four particularly nasty-looking young skinheads. Not quite skinheads, actually; they'd left odd patches of velvety hair here and there on their skulls and had them razored into hard-edged geometrical patterns. This wasn't the style of authentic English skinheads I was familiar with, and when I heard the boys' German accents I was relieved. It seemed to explain something. And even if the prospect of German skinheads was ultimately no more reassuring than that of English skinheads, I felt some consolation in knowing they were no part of any tribe I remotely belonged to.

During the busiest part of the day I wasn't so much looking

at people as looking out for them, trying to avoid being bumped into, knocked aside, trampled underfoot. This, of course, applied to everyone else, too, and resulted in some general bad temper. People around me were getting annoyed because walking was becoming so difficult. It was becoming so difficult because of all the other people who were there, also walking, also having difficulties, also becoming annoyed.

You couldn't have called it chaos exactly, since there was no slide toward entropy, no heading toward a state of lesser organization. In fact, there was a great deal of steely purpose about many of the walkers, and there wasn't anything random about it. Everyone looked determined, like they were on a mission, like they had to get somewhere fast. They wished they were already there, and yet they were thwarted and frustrated by their fellow pedestrians.

As the day ended and the stores closed, garbage bags filled with commercial waste had been built into slack pyramids at intervals along Oxford Street. Each pyramid had its own scavenging homeless person. The bags were semi-transparent, which made it easier to see the contents and determine which bags needed to be ripped open.

The London rush hour came and went. It was a thing I was well familiar with from my days working on and off Oxford Street: a frantic, but not quite genuine, desire to get away, to go home, to draw a line across the day. But this was regularly undercut by a reluctance to engage with the rush at all; and so people chose not to go home but to find a pub or bar instead, to hang out with people from work and complain about work and delay the inevitable. At eight o' clock there were plenty of people on the street who'd spent a couple of hours in the pub and were now going home a bit drunk, a bit late, dashing along, working up excuses for when they got there, chasing after buses and missing them, cursing as though this was the worst thing that had ever happened to them in their whole lives.

I set out for my last transit at a little before eleven o'clock at night. Oxford Street was still well populated with people coming out of pubs, restaurants, burger bars; some finally heading home and walking to bus stops and tube stations or trying to flag down taxis. Others were looking for somewhere to carry on partying.

A few people were the worse for drink, but most seemed better for it, mellowed and easygoing, strolling, enjoying the warm night air, a lot of couples holding hands, one or two kissing in shop doorways. A lone, lanky, big-eyed bookish girl was coming out of a Borders bookstore just as it was closing, the kind of girl who gives hope, and then disappointment, to lone bookish boys everywhere. Two excited Italian gay boys had their digital cameras out and were photographing the window displays in some of the clothes shops; they looked deliriously happy.

It could have made you feel melancholy if you were that way inclined—walking alone and seeing all these people with significant others—and usually that's very much the way I am inclined, but the fact that I had a reason to be walking alone, that I was involved in my own endlessly strange project, made all the difference in the world. It made it all right. I was a walker, I was a writer; I had a double purpose, and no need, now at least, to feel lonely in my solitary walking.

The irony of all this, not lost on me even then, was that I had done the transits, completed my self-imposed mission, walked the journey of twenty or so miles, and I was right back where I'd started. Essentially I had got nowhere.

Had I made Oxford Street my own? Had I redeemed or reclaimed anything? Well, yes and no. Oxford Street remains unpossessed and unclaimed, but that means it's still available. It's yours for the taking. It's promiscuous. It's anybody's. In the course of the day I'd walked with and in the footsteps of a multitude of people, but I knew that I must be one of the very few who had ever walked twenty miles back and forth on Oxford Street in a single day. The perversity of this pleased me no end.


At the time when I made my Oxford Street transits, and indeed when I first wrote the above, I was unaware that Virginia Woolf had written an article called "Oxford Street Tide." It was one of six essays she wrote for *Good Housekeeping* magazine in 1931: they're collected in a very thin volume called *The London Scene*.

Now, Virginia Woolf is not exactly an open book to me. In the past I've forced myself to read her novels, including *Mrs. Dalloway*, which some regard as a great London walking novel, though not me. Mrs. Dalloway is so little of a walker that the very idea of having to walk to the florist is an incredible excitement that sets her off thinking, "What a lark! What a plunge!" You'd slap her, wouldn't you? The critic John Sutherland is similarly unimpressed and, devastatingly, calculates that to get round her circuit in the allotted time she must have taken a taxi.

In "Oxford Street Tide," Woolf knows she shouldn't like Oxford Street; it's so cheap and gaudy and full of plebs, awash with people "tripping, mincing, in black coats, in satin dresses," so downright vulgar. But then suddenly, to her great credit, she realizes she can't sneer at it completely. She notices something appealing in the energy and vulgarity of the place. She detects something Shakespearean about it and that makes it all right.

Then, on a street corner, she writes, "Tortoises repose on litters of grass. The slowest and most contemplative of creatures display their mild activities on a foot or two of pavement. . . . One infers that the desire of man for the tortoise, like the desire of the moth for the star, is a constant element in human nature."

Well, I think I saw a few elements of human nature in the course of my six Oxford Street transits, but I had not inferred that the desire for a tortoise was one of them. I'm pretty certain I wouldn't want to spend too much time in Virginia Woolf's Oxford Street, but for the sake of seeing the tortoises, I wish I could walk down it just once. They, as much as a tincture of opium, might be a cure for melancholy.

# AS I TRIPPED OUT ONE MORNING:

## Music, Movement, Movies

*They tell me, "Son, we want you, be elusive but don't walk far."*
—DAVID BOWIE, "We Are the Dead"

How many roads must a man walk down before you call him a man? It's a good question, and who better to ask it than Bob Dylan, who devoted a whole episode of his radio show to the topic of walking. I was asked it myself while in Manhattan, walking on 135th Street in Harlem. I had walked all the way uptown from 24th Street, along Madison Avenue. I was following a songline, investigating the way in which certain songs can act as self-guided walking tours.

Bruce Chatwin, one of the great "sacramental walkers" (his term), describes the "songlines" in his book of the same name. They are part of the belief system of the Australian Aboriginals, who of necessity were walkers since they never invented the wheel or domesticated a rideable animal. They believed the world was sung into being by ancient spirits; consequently, if you knew enough songs you would know the whole world. Chatwin writes, "A song... was both map and direction finder. Providing you knew the song, you could always find your way across country." I wanted to see if something similar might work in New York City.

I had a song in my head: "Walking Down Madison," words by Kirsty MacColl, music by Johnny Marr. It's one of those catalog songs ("Streets of London" is probably the most famous example of the genre) that describes the horrors of the big city; in the MacColl song it's homelessness, poverty, knife attacks, and hypothermia. She rhymes Madison with gun, fun, bums, nuns, and "philosophizing some," which neatly lays out the territory she's dealing with.

Whether people who live in large cities actually need any reminding of the horrors of the urban environment is debatable, but MacColl's song is better than many. It says that a single street, or avenue in this case, can connect high and low, rich and poor, the hopeful and the hopeless. The distance, physical and metaphoric, between the penthouse and the basement is "not that far," with sharks in the penthouse and rats in the basement. It isn't a subtle song.

I sang the song to myself as a sound track for 110 blocks or so of the avenue, from Madison Square Park, where it starts, up to where it becomes the on-ramp of the Madison Avenue Bridge. True, I was walking up rather than down, which was not precisely what the song describes, but it seemed more interesting to walk from an area I knew to one that I didn't. By the time I got to the end, through Spanish Harlem, then East Harlem, I'd be in extremely unfamiliar territory.

The song is political in its way, and since Madison Avenue is the home of the New York advertising industry, political targets are comfortably at hand, but advertising isn't mentioned in the song; perhaps that would have been too easy. I, for one, didn't know there was any such thing as the Madison Avenue Advertising Walk of Fame. It runs along Madison from 42nd to 50th streets. There's a plaque set right there in the sidewalk to prove it that reads, all in capitals—and the dots are theirs, not mine—"IN REC-OGNITION OF THE CONTRIBUTIONS OF ADVERTISING TO POP CULTURE AND ITS MOST ENDURING AND BELOVED ICONS AND SLOGANS . . . THE AMERICAN ASSOCIATION OF ADVERTISING AGENCIES DEDICATES THE MADISON AVENUE ADVERTISING WALK OF FAME AS A PERMANENT TRIBUTE TO THE MOST CREATIVE OF ALL INDUSTRIES . . . ADVERTISING."

Evidence of this creativity was available right there. Famous advertising icons and slogans, beloved no doubt, had been printed on banners that were hanging from the lampposts: the Aflac duck, Juan Valdez, "A mind is a terrible thing to waste," "Sometimes you feel like a nut, sometimes you don't."

It was no surprise that the home of American advertising was pretty swank, but around about 60th Street things became even swanker, with shops selling designer clothes and high-end luxury goods, elegant restaurants, a store with a chrome ejector seat in the window, a chauffeur-driven pork-colored Rolls-Royce waiting at the curb. But it wasn't so swank that a few blocks later it couldn't accommodate a young black man standing on the corner saying repeatedly to passersby, "Help me out, please," and then to himself, "Let it go."

Then at about 100th Street things changed with a bang. There were medical buildings, some project tower blocks, more people walking, street traders, crowds on the sidewalk, and it became a good deal less white. In a schoolyard at 104th Street a lone white teenager was sitting on a wall by the chain-link fence trying not to look nervous, and failing. He wasn't within a hundred yards of any other kid in the schoolyard, none of whom shared his skin color. If this were a movie you knew he'd integrate and ingratiate himself in some novel manner; as it was it looked like he was just sitting there praying for his school days to be over.

At 117th Street a group of forlorn but surprisingly good-natured people was blocking the sidewalk, including one man on crutches, one woman in a wheelchair, and a black kid who was saying loudly to nobody in particular and certainly not to me, "Gimme a bottle of Cleeko, eighty dollars, I'm ready to go." I don't think he seriously thought anybody was going to give him anything.

When I got to 120th Street and Marcus Garvey Park, still called Mount Morris Park on the map I had with me, I was reminded of another song, Joe South's "Walk a Mile in My Shoes." The fact is, walking a single mile in anybody's shoes really isn't very hard. You could walk that distance in shoes that really didn't fit you at all. Walking a mile, even several miles, in the boots I was wearing that day was fine. They were pain-free and really quite comfortable for about four and a half miles, but then they started to feel really uncomfortable, and after about five miles they became absolutely excruciating.

Suddenly I felt a terrible twinge and wrench in my right pinkie toe, as though all the skin had been abruptly ripped from the toe in one sharp slice. I limped into the park, found a bench, took off my boot and sock, and saw that, yes, all the skin had indeed been abruptly ripped from the toe in one sharp slice. It hurt and it didn't look pretty.

I thought about ending my walk, and hobbling to the 125th Street subway station. I'd already walked over a hundred blocks; there'd be no great shame in retiring injured. But I looked around the park at all the people who were sitting there killing time. Most looked as though they had a lot of troubles, and although I didn't presume to guess what those troubles were, I thought they were probably a whole lot worse than a toe with the skin stripped off. I sat for a while but then I put my boot back on and decided that—like Felix in a different song—I would keep on walking.

Given people's capacity to write songs about anything at all, it's hardly surprising that there are any number of songs about walking. The earliest form I know is the chanson d'aventure, devised by the Provençal troubadours in the twelfth century. Traditionally these songs often begin with the line "As I walked out one morning," and they go on to describe a troubling or surprising meeting or some unusual sight encountered while out walking. Compare and contrast with Bob Dylan when he goes out "to smell the air around Tom Paine" in the song "Tom Paine" on *John Wesley Harding*.

There's evidently something contradictory here. The moment you use those opening words, the listener knows something surprising is about to happen, which means that it's not really so surprising after all, which is an issue at the very heart of the idea of "going for a walk." We may not want our walks to be "adventures" in the most extreme sense—we can do without pirates, gunplay, caverns measureless to man—but we do hope to see something new on our walks, even in the most familiar surroundings.

"Walking out" in the troubadours' sense sounds like an everyday activity, something close to home, not necessarily part of some great thousand-mile journey, and the implication is that adventures and wonders are to be found wherever we are, if not in our own backyard, then within walking distance of it.

The trope "as I walked out one morning" is thrillingly close to the traditional blues opening line "I woke up this morning." And if you're trying to write a simple blues lyric it's very tempting to rhyme blues with shoes, and before you know it, you're writing a song about walking.

Robert Johnson didn't resist the temptation and wrote "Walkin' Blues." Johnson's words aren't easy to understand at the best of times, and attempts to nail them down in lyric sheets and songbooks don't make things much clearer. In a book of sheet music called *Robert Johnson at the Crossroads: The Authoritative Guitar Transcriptions*, the words are presented thus:

I woke-up this morning—feelin' 'round for my shoes
Know 'bout 'at I got these old walkin' blues.

Which isn't exactly what I hear when I listen to the song, and is any case inscrutable, but it seems he has the walking blues because his "little Bernice" has gone. She's walked out on him, and rather than stay at home moping, he's hitting the road again on foot. Alternate interpretations are no doubt possible. A whole bunch of fellow blues walkers, including Bonnie Raitt, Eric Clapton, and the Grateful Dead, have followed in Johnson's footsteps and done cover versions.

Johnson's plan to hit the road might not solve all his problems. In another of his songs, "Stop Breaking Down," he says that every time he walks down the street some pretty mama starts "breaking down" with him, and he wishes she'd stop.

Johnson, like most blues players, frequently uses the rhythm known as the "blues shuffle," the very basic "dum da dum da, dum da dum da" pattern at the heart of the classic twelve-bar blues. It's always struck me as a misnomer. The blues shuffle sounds more sprightly and purposeful than I expect a shuffle to be, especially if it's combined with a "walking bass" line.

The walking bass isn't confined to the blues; it's in all kinds of pop and jazz music. Since one note is played for every beat of a 4/4 bar it's certainly a rhythm you can walk to, as opposed to, say, the 3/4 time of the waltz that makes you want to dance, or Stravinsky's polyrhythms that make you want to celebrate the rite of spring. Karlheinz Stockhausen claimed to hear the march of the jackboot in any recognizable time signature.

Walking bass has something in common with "stride piano," the style of jazz playing where the player's left hand "strides" up and down the piano, alternating bass lines and chords. Some of these lines may "walk" regularly at the pace of a basic beat, but this being jazz, there'll be arpeggios, syncopation, and the intro-duction of mixed time signatures. You might be able to walk to this but you'd look darned odd.

One of the greatest stride pianists is Fats Domino, a man who's written at least three songs with the word *walking* in the title. The best known of them, called simply "I'm Walking," was, according to legend, written after his car broke down and a fan saw him making his way on foot to the nearest garage and yelled, "Look, it's Fats Domino walking." Fats went home and turned his misfortune into a song. I so want this story to be true.

In song, as in life, there are a lot of people who'd much rather be riding than walking. And you might think that country-and-western music, with its fondness for pickup trucks and eighteen-wheelers, would find walking a particular humiliation, but it appears not. Here walking is often synonymous with honesty and plain dealing, whether it's Faron Young's "Walk Tall," Keith Urban's "Walkin' the Country," or Johnny Cash's "I Walk the Line."

Rodney Crowell sings a song called "I Walk the Line (Revisited)," which is about the joys of hearing Johnny Cash sing "I Walk the Line" on the radio, but it's a car radio and Crowell is driving in his '49 Ford, an irony the song seems not to notice. But it wouldn't be country music at all if there wasn't some mawkish sentiment attached to walking, as in Wayne Newton's "Daddy Don't Walk So Fast," which is what the kid says as his daddy abandons him and walks away.

Some people reckon that Patsy Cline's "Walkin' After Midnight," written by Alan Block and Don Hecht, is a great song of female independence and empowerment, but it strikes me as deeply problematic. On the surface it appears to be about a female protagonist who has, we don't know how, lost her lover, and so she wanders the streets after midnight looking for him. Why she chooses this method and this time of night is left for the listener to guess, but earlier, more prudish sensibilities than ours couldn't imagine what any woman would be doing in the streets after midnight unless she'd become a hooker, a streetwalker. Another possibility might be that having been abandoned, she'd simply lost her wits, à la Ophelia, and is walking around in a daze, looking for love in all the wrong places, but this doesn't seem even remotely empowered.

When men sing "Walkin' After Midnight," as they often do, the streetwalker possibility seems much more likely. The guy searches the night for his lost love, trying to save her from a life of vice. Of course you could conceivably reverse the sexes on this scenario, too: the woman's searching the streets because she thinks the guy's become a hustler, but this is probably trying too hard.

Sexual role reversal plays a part in another great walking song, "These Boots Are Made for Walkin'." As sung by Nancy Sinatra this does indeed sound like a song of empowerment. She's walking over the guy and striding on to freedom. When you hear the original male version, as sung by the song's composer, Lee Hazelwood, it becomes a particularly nasty piece of vindictive masculine domination. Hazelwood, it always seemed, was perfectly happy with that interpretation. His other compositions included "Rebel Walk" and "The Walker" for Duane Eddy, and "'She Don't Walk on Water" for himself and Anna Hanski.

You might think that walking is in itself too tame a subject for the full-on, balls-out, hard-rock song, and writers of rock songs seem to agree. Not wishing to appear pedestrian, they envisage fancy or extreme walking that takes place in unusual or downright impossible circumstances: on the moon (the Police), on thin ice (Elvis Costello and Yoko Ono), through walls (Steve Hackett), on locusts (John Cale), on broken glass (Annie Lennox), on sunshine (Katrina and the Waves), and, in a particularly obscure favorite of mine, through syrup (Ned's Atomic Dustbin).

The most rock-and-roll walking song, or at least the rockingest song with the word *walking* in its title and lyrics, is surely Aerosmith's "Walk This Way." Supposedly it was inspired by the movie *Young Frankenstein*, in which Marty Feldman, as Igor, invites visitors to the castle to "walk this way," which they do by copying his shambling, hump-backed gait. In the context of the movie it's very funny, the silliness of the pun only adding to the comic mayhem. By the time of the Aerosmith song the pun has pretty much disappeared. It becomes a song about being sexually initiated at the hands of a cheerleader, and the lyrics don't require a very close reading, but the gist of it is that the girl is telling the guy to follow her round to the back of the bleachers, not to imitate her cheerleader moves. Either way, it doesn't sound like a very long or challenging walk.

The fact that Run-DMC did a fantastic hit version of "Walk This Way" is enough to make us realize that rappers can be walkers, too, though not very far or very fast, that would scuff up their immaculate sneakers, but whenever you have a lot of pimps you're likely to have a lot of people doing Tom Wolfe's "pimp roll." There's Snoop Dogg "walking down the street, smoking, smoking, sipping on gin and juice," Cypress Hill's "Stoned Is the Way of the Walk," Lil Wayne's "Walk It Off," Xzibit's "Get Your Walk On."

The walk Xzibit is referring to here is the Crip Walk, originally part of gang culture. Back in the day Crips would make heel-and-toe or V-shaped movements with their feet to spell out letters and words on the ground, often after they'd committed a crime. One word they tended to spell out was *Blood*, the name of their gang rivals, and then they'd "erase" the word by scrubbing their feet all over it. This does sound wonderfully baroque. It's not a walk that would get you from A to B, but it was certainly a walk that could get you into a lot of trouble if you did it in front of the wrong people: Crips believed it was for Crips only. But eventually it became mainstream. Ice-T Crip-walked on TV, and since then all and sundry have been at it. You can find tutorial videos on YouTube, a lot of dance moves have been added, and it's now often known as Clown Walking. It's also been said that it looks like hopscotch on crack.

References to walking are more at home in the apparently safer territory of the show tune and the standard. Walking here tends to be an innocent activity from an earlier, gentler, less sexualized age. And so we have songs like "Walkin' My Baby Back Home," "Winter Wonderland," or "You'll Never Walk Alone."

The oddest walking-related show tune I know is Irving Berlin's "My Walking Stick" of 1938, written for the movie *Alexander's Ragtime Band*, which is about how very attached the protagonist is to his walking stick. I say "he" because it's quite evidently a man's song even though in the movie it's sung by Ethel Merman, who performs it as a male impersonator. The lyrics say you can take his hat, his tie, his spats, and he can get by just fine, but take away his walking stick (which for the sake of a rhyme sometimes becomes a cane) and he'll go insane. If he's down lovers' lane and he's caught, then without it he's nought. It was a different age.

In October 1938 the *Times* of London ran a headline that read "While dictators rage and statesmen talk, all Europe dances—to The Lambeth Walk." It was referring to a song of that name, part of the hit stage show *Me and My Girl*, book and lyrics by Douglas Furber and L. Arthur Rose and music by Noel Gay.

To be fair, the Lambeth Walk is as much a dance as it is a way of walking, a jaunty strut that involves linked arms and raised knees, and occasionally shouting "Oi!" Traditionally it's been done by lovable, heart-of-gold, salt-of-the-earth Londoners. The song says "any time you're Lambeth way, any evening, any day, you'll find them all doing the Lambeth Walk," though this information is inevitably out-of-date.

The song rapidly became a hit and a political cause. King George VI and Queen Elizabeth went to see the show and loved it, and the song was even popular with some people in Germany, so popular that Noel Gay was asked to sign a document declaring that he had no Jewish blood in him. He declined. In 1939 this led to the Lambeth Walk being denounced by the Nazi Party as "Jewish mischief and animalistic hopping," though to a rational person it looks like none of these things. In due course, in 1941, a short English newsreel propaganda film appeared that went by various names including *Lambeth Walk—Nazi Style*. It filched footage from Leni Riefenstahl's *Triumph of the Will* and edited it so that Hitler and his troops appeared to be doing their own ridiculous, militaristic version of the Lambeth Walk. The film's provenance is mysterious, and it's most convincingly credited to Charles A. Ridley, though that's a name that's otherwise disappeared from film history. It's said that Goebbels was so infuriated when he saw the film that he ran out of the room literally kicking and screaming.

Lambeth Walk is the name of a street as well as a song, and I went there, following another songline. According to the lyric, everything there is free and easy, and it's a place where you can do as you darn well pleasey. The song asks:

Why don't you make your way there,
Go there, stay there?

I could think of several reasons. No doubt lovable, heart-of-gold, salt-of-the-earth Londoners still live in the area, but none of them was in evidence on the day I went walking there. In fact there were few people on the street at all.

Lambeth Walk was not thriving, and it seemed to be in trouble. A place by the name of Denby Court was a block of so-called sheltered housing. This is where the English authorities place the old, troubled, disabled, and generally vulnerable. The people in Denby Court weren't just sheltered, they were incarcerated, behind walls, bars, and metal fences, protected by metal spikes and closed-circuit TV cameras. No doubt it was a good thing that the inhabitants were protected, but to need so much protection suggested that they were permanently under siege, living in constant terror. What monsters walked this street?

On the day I was there, there didn't seem to be much to fear, unless you count the kid on a bike who did an aggressive wheelie a couple of feet in front of me, as if to say... well, I'm not sure what—that a kid on a bike owns these mean streets, that I was obviously a stranger there and I'd better watch myself, that I must be a sucker to be walking rather than riding a bike—who knows, but he was definitely saying something.

Perhaps he thought I had no reason to be there, and in a way he was right. There was nothing to see or do or buy. The Lambeth Walk Carpet Shop was boarded up, as was Lambeth Walk Seafoods, its sign smashed to pieces. Something called CORAS, the Colombian Refugee Association, seemed still to be in business, even though it was closed and there was a serious-looking metal blind rolled down over the front. Joy's Mini Market's (*sic*) was open for business, and a black woman, possibly Joy, was sitting on a box outside. I wasn't going to do anything so crass as ask her about the dance, but I did try to make eye contact, and she was having none of it.

In fact Lambeth Walk has some history of economic failure. In the nineteenth century there were two wells in Lambeth Walk, one called Nearer, one called Farther, trying to sell water for its medicinal properties. The wells hadn't lasted long and now there was no sign they'd ever been there. Finally I came to a bleak little courtyard where the owners of a couple of market stalls were just closing up for the day; one had been selling household products in industrial-sized packs, the other selling toys. And painted on the wall above them, high enough to deter all but the most determined taggers, was a faded mural showing a jolly man and woman with knees raised and arms linked doing, there was no doubt about it, the Lambeth Walk.


It might have been tempting, on these songline walks of mine, to wear a personal stereo and have the relevant song playing as I walked. For several reasons, I didn't. One was simply the issue of irritation: to have the same song playing over and over again might have driven a person insane. More crucially, as I walked I didn't want to be insulated from the sounds of the environment. The things you hear when you walk are every bit as important as the things you see, or for that matter touch, taste, and smell. There's also the safety issue. I wanted to be able to hear the approaching car, the ominous footsteps, the cries of "White man!" Perhaps I was being old-fashioned.

There's at least one generation, probably several, who can't imagine what it's like not to have music that's portable and always available, via the Walkman and its various higher-tech developments through to the iPod, known in some quarters as the "isolation Pod."

The name Walkman is one of those not quite English words belonging to some global tongue, devised by the people at Sony, who first marketed the personal stereo in 1979 in Japan. Toshiba had a rival product called the Walky. Walkman strikes me as a very unsexy word, and you'd think Sony might have called it the Runman or the Jogman, but the early versions were so sensitive that if you ran or jogged, or even walked too speedily, the playing mechanism faltered.

At the risk of sounding like an old fogey, I can not only remember a time before the personal stereo, I can remember the first one I ever saw. It was in London, and it was 1979, before the Walkman went on sale in England. I was working in a bookshop, behind the counter with a couple of other assistants who were big music fans, and a young Japanese man came into the store wearing a Walkman. It was as strange as seeing somebody with a jetpack on his shoulders. We had a halting conversation in which we tried to ask him what the Walkman was like. We couldn't believe that the sound quality could be very good, and the Japanese boy very definitely wasn't going to offer his earpieces for us to sample. We didn't blame him. We didn't expect it any more than we'd have expected him to offer us the use of his jetpack.

At least one of us said it would never catch on. Although it was easy enough to see the advantages of being able to take your music with you anywhere, the notion that life required a personalized, prerecorded sound track was a new and an unexplored one. We had no idea of the extent to which the personal stereo would subsequently be used to provide background music as a form of editing, something filmic, a way of combining sound and vision, manipulating what you see and hear, to make yourself believe you're living in a movie.

Absurd and unlikely juxtapositions are par for the course. They're expected and welcomed. By now we know that any sound and any image can be put together to create some sort of meaning. If you're walking, wandering lonely as a cloud, you might think that one of Erik Satie's *Gymnopédies* would do the job, but if your iPod randomly selects some Napalm Death, then that will create its own oblique and ironic resonances, too. These may be random, but they will not be meaningless. This is something we've all learned from watching so many movies.

Erik Satie, incidentally, as well as being a composer, pianist, Rosicrucian, and master ironist, was also a fine, determined, obsessive walker. Every day he left his home in the suburb of Arcueil and walked to his studio in the center of Paris, then at night he walked back again. It was a substantial journey, six miles in each direction, and some of it was potentially dangerous: Satie carried a hammer for protection.

Guillaume Apollinaire tells us that Satie did a lot of composing on his nocturnal homeward walks. He would create music in his head, then stop from time to time under a convenient streetlamp and write it down in a notebook. His productivity was greatly reduced during World War One when so many Parisian streetlamps were turned off. It's easy enough to believe that you hear the regular, repeated rhythm of the human footfall in much of Satie's work. He also said, "Before I compose a piece, I walk around it several times, accompanied by myself."

Satie's music, alas, has become something of a cliché of the less inventive movie sound track: an instant source of knee-jerk melancholy. Imdb.com would lead you to believe that he's one of Hollywood's most in-demand composers. His work has appeared in movies and TV shows as diverse as *The X-Files, Chocolat, The Man Who Fell to Earth, My Dinner with Andre, The Royal Tenenbaums,* and *The Benny Hill Show.*

There is one cinematic moment, however, where Satie's music is forever welded to an image of walking, and that is in the Hal Ashby/Jerzy Kosinski movie *Being There.* It's the last scene, when the hero, Chance the gardener, played by Peter Sellers, walks on water, across a lake, to the accompaniment of a version of Satie's *Gnossiennes.* The movie credits say "Rearranged by Johnny Mandel," though surely "arranged" would have been enough.

The scene was a spur-of-the moment invention. The script they were shooting from ended with Peter Sellers and Shirley MacLaine simply meeting each other while walking in the woods. Compared with seeing the hero walk on water, this was obviously tame stuff. Ashby found walking on water was a surprisingly easy movie effect to pull off. He got the technical details from Robert Downey Sr., who'd done something similar in his movie *Greaser's Palace.*

All you need is a certain kind of mobile platform that can be found at airports; you sink it below the surface of the water so that it can't be seen, and then any actor can take a short straight walk along it and appear to be doing some miraculous aquatic pedestrianism. In *Being There* the narrowness of the track also allowed Sellers to poke an umbrella into the water just a few inches away from his feet and have it sink deep below the surface, giving the impression there was no platform at all.

Another of Sellers's great walking scenes is one in which he scarcely walks at all, as Dr. Strangelove, who having been in a wheelchair throughout, suddenly leaps up, stoked by the prospect of nuclear attack, and yells, "Mein Fuhrer, I can walk!"

Sellers insisted he was an actor who had no "true self." He disappeared into his roles and became invisible. There is, therefore, no such thing as a "Peter Sellers walk." Certain other actors are far more inclined to have a trademark stride. A few who immediately spring to mind are Charlie Chaplin, Groucho Marx, Pee-wee Herman, Arnold Schwarzenegger, John Wayne. All of these might be construed as comical: by the time a walking style has become recognizable it has also become absurd. It also seems to be a particularly male trait. The only genuinely distinctive "female walk" I can think of is Marilyn Monroe's stylized wiggle. Sometimes this is attributed to her weak ankles, but that sounds like an explanation for something that needs no explaining.

I'm one of those people who finds Charlie Chaplin largely unwatchable these days, and his walk is certainly part of what I can't bear, its cuteness, its faux humility, its feverish attempt at ingratiation. If this sounds like too contemporary an opinion, Wyndham Lewis felt much the same about Chaplin back in 1928. His novel *The Childermass* is set in the afterlife, a world overseen by a character known as The Bailiff, who sometimes appears in the form of Chaplin. Characters in the afterlife are then forced to perform routines from Chaplin movies; it isn't hell exactly, but it's near enough. For Lewis this represents all that's wrong with popular culture; it's become no more than repetition and imitation at the expense of authenticity.

Certainly Chaplin is anything but inimitable. It's said he based his on-screen walk on that of a real tramp, a man rejoicing in the name of Rummy Binks, who drank in a pub belonging to Chaplin's uncle. There's also a story, maybe an urban myth, that Chaplin once entered a Charlie Chaplin look-alike contest, and lost. One version has him saying to a reporter that he was tempted to give the contestants lessons in the Chaplin walk, "out of pity as well as in the desire to see the thing done correctly."

Chaplin's high regard for his own trademark walk was confirmed—indeed, turned into a publicity stunt—in the 1920s, when he had his feet insured for $150,000. Is there any recorded case of anybody ever collecting on these Hollywood body-part insurance policies?

By the time of his movie *Limelight*, in 1952, Chaplin had transferred some of his concerns about walking onto another character. Chaplin plays Calvero, a fading comedian, and Claire Bloom plays Terry, a ballerina suffering from hysterical paralysis. There's nothing physically wrong with her, but she can't walk. It comes as no surprise to anybody when, late in the movie, she finds her feet again and yells, "Calvero! I'm walking! I'm walking!" One must have a heart of stone to watch this scene without laughing.

The main thing that makes *Limelight* endurable is the brief presence of Buster Keaton. Now there's a man who knew how to walk across the screen (as well as fall, tumble, slide, leap, swing, etc.). In *Limelight* he plays another fading comedian, and one who gets far, far less screen time than Chaplin. The two of them perform a creaky musical routine, with Keaton on piano, Chaplin on violin. The act is filmed very straight, very deadpan. There's a long period at the start of the scene (two minutes or so out of a total of seven) where Keaton fumbles with his sheet music while Chaplin shows off a series of "funny walks" based on the idea of having one leg shorter than the other. These are skillfully done as far as they go, but they point up a fundamental difference between the two comedians. Keaton could be funny when he walked, but he didn't do funny walks.

For Keaton, like any good actor, the walk was not a trademark but a part of characterization. In *Sherlock Jr.*, for instance, he plays a would-be detective following a suspect by walking about a foot behind him, their strides interlocking. Typically Keaton's gait is a combination of the stoic, the hesitant, the noble. He walks on, not in expectation of joy or success, certainly not in expectation of being loved like Chaplin's "Little Fellow," and yet for all the abuse and misfortune that gets heaped on him, Keaton's walk remains brave and optimistic.

According to legend, Keaton, while a child actor, was performing onstage and was required to walk down a flight of stairs, but he tripped and fell all the way to the bottom, then immediately got up, walked across the stage, and carried on as though it had never happened. Harry Houdini was supposedly in the audience and is credited as having said something along the lines of "Ain't he the little buster," but surely this is apocryphal.

It appears that Keaton may also have got something from the cartoon character Felix the Cat. According to Mark Newgarden, an illustrator and animator, who got it straight from the mouth of Otto Messmer, Felix's creator, there was a time in the 1920s when

Keaton paid the producer of the Felix cartoons (Pat Sullivan) so that he could use an approximation of Felix's walk: a backward-and-forward pace, head down, arms clenched behind the back. Newgarden, as do I, finds it amazing that Keaton thought he needed to make such a payment. What court would ever have found Keaton guilty of stealing a walk from a cartoon character? Still, these were Keaton's golden years; perhaps he had enough money that he thought it was a good investment to spend a little then and head off legal trouble later.

Like Felix, Keaton kept on walking, through TV specials, commercials, industrial training films, and even, in 1965, *How to Stuff a Wild Bikini.* That was the year before his death, and also the year he starred in *The Railrodder,* in which he's seen jumping into the River Thames in London, then seconds later emerging out of the water on the Canadian coast, having walked across, or along the floor of, the Atlantic Ocean.

It was also the year that he appeared in Samuel Beckett's *Film.* Keaton wasn't the first choice for the movie, and he seems to have had some trouble figuring out what he was doing in the part; even so, the casting now seems inevitable. Imagine the horror of Chaplin mawkishly puttering his way through the part. When we first see Keaton in the movie he's scuttling along beside a vast, tall, mythically featureless brick wall. He's moving quickly, hurriedly, with a frantic daintiness, trying hard, according to Beckett, not to be "perceived." He's definitely walking, there's no doubt about that, but if he were moving even the slightest bit faster it would definitely be running.

Samuel Beckett, interviewed by Kevin Brownlow, said, "The heat was terrible—while I was staggering in the humidity Keaton was galloping up and down and doing whatever was asked of him. He had great endurance, he was very tough and, yes, reliable."

Moviemakers may in general be happier depicting the rapid motion of actors: dancing, running, diving, swinging from jungle creepers, jumping off buildings, but there's no shortage of great movie walking.

Errol Flynn is Jim Corbett in *Gentleman Jim*, walking through the packed streets of New York City and using his fancy footwork to avoid bumping into passersby.

Fred Astaire walks down the Champs-Élysées in *Funny Face*, and because Astaire is Astaire even his walking looks like dancing.

The characters in Luis Buñuel's *The Discreet Charm of the Bourgeoisie* repeatedly find themselves transported from their bourgeois homes to a country road, where they walk along briskly, though without any obvious purpose, dressed for a dinner party rather than a country walk.

Kevin Spacey in *The Usual Suspects* limps along when he's playing the crippled, nerdy Verbal Kint, but then when he's free and clear, not a suspect anymore, he walks along the street and his limp disappears and he strides out as his true self, the cosmically evil Keyser Söze.

There's Michael Douglas as the crazed, disgruntled defense engineer in *Falling Down*. You know the guy's insane because he abandons his car and walks all the way across Los Angeles for his daughter's birthday. The most satisfying scene is when he crosses a golf course, and the mere presence of a pedestrian encroaching on their precious turf is enough to give one of the members a heart attack.

Cary Grant's last screen appearance is in the movie *Walk, Don't Run*, set at the 1964 Tokyo Olympics. Because of the accommodation shortage he has to share an apartment with Samantha Eggar and a guy who's an Olympic athlete. The guy's too embarrassed to say what event he's competing in, but given the title of the movie this really isn't hard to work out. Racewalking as a source of social embarrassment—now there's a topic not much explored in cinema. There is, however, a Harry Langdon movie called *Tramp, Tramp, Tramp* (1926), in which the hero enters a cross-country walking race in order to pay his father's mortgage. Then he falls for the sponsor's daughter and starts walking in earnest, determined to win the race and the girl. The girl is played by Joan Crawford.

Naturally, in any movie, choices will have been made about what sound track should go with any walking scene. Even those movies that were originally "silent" will be shown with a musical accompaniment of greater or lesser appropriateness. However, there are certain movies where music and walking fuse together in a magically cinematic way.

Admittedly, some of these fusions may take place in the brain as much as in the movie itself. I often think of Dustin Hoffman's walk as Ratzo Rizzo in *Midnight Cowboy* (a real limp—he put a stone in his shoe so that he wouldn't have to "act"), and I hear the song "Everybody's Talkin'," even though I know that's the music that plays when he's on the bus.

And of course I think of John Travolta, as Tony Manero, strutting his way through *Saturday Night Fever* while the Bee Gees sing, "You can tell by the way I use my walk I'm a woman's man, no time to talk." But the scene I remember best is from the ludicrous sequel, *Staying Alive*, where the conversation goes, "You know what I wanna do?" "What?" "Strut." And Travolta goes striding off across the Brooklyn Bridge, or is it the Verrazano-Narrows?

All this, I know, is just scratching the celluloid. However, when I began writing this book there was no doubt in my mind about what I thought was the perfect coming together of music, walking, and film: the opening scene from Wim Wenders's *Paris, Texas*. The camera, up in a helicopter, makes a long swoop across the pale, jagged Texas desert, and finally rises over a long, sharp, horizontal ridge to reveal Harry Dean Stanton, playing the part of Travis, in a suit, tie, and baseball cap, walking along, floppy and swift-moving, in the middle of the harshest of landscapes, not on any recognizable track, coming from nowhere, going nowhere.

The accompanying music has a perfection about it. The scene, in fact the whole movie, is unimaginable without Ry Cooder's slide guitar–driven score, based on Blind Willie Johnson's "Dark Was the Night," which in turn was based on a nineteenth-century hymn. It's "mood music" all right, but it's hard to define the mood. It's deeply ambiguous desert music, with a floating, swaying, self-renewing sadness. You wouldn't necessarily think of it as music to accompany walking, though it does have a forward movement, a restlessness, a rise and fall, tension and release, as it struggles with and then descends into melancholy. It's a cinematic moment that could make you fall in love with a director, an actor, a musician, a cinematographer, a desert. It's a perfect start to a movie, a huge visual statement that asks an even bigger question. It's a moment so strong and enigmatic that the rest of the film sometimes seems to exist simply in order to explain and justify that image.

The scene had long been etched firmly in my mind, and there was another scene, or at least a shot, that I remembered. Still quite early in the movie, Travis is trying to escape from the brother who has come to rescue him, and he begins to walk along an endless, dead-straight railroad track into an empty, pale blue, featureless desert landscape.

I decided I'd better see the movie again. These two scenes were there, largely as I remembered them, but there were a couple of other walking scenes that I'd forgotten about. One has Stanton walking across a freeway bridge, where he encounters a madman screaming at the traffic below. He gives the screaming man a sympathetic pat on the back as he walks on.

The other scene shows Travis trying to make amends to the son he abandoned four years earlier; the boy is now eight. He asks his brother's maid how he should walk in order to look like a "rich father." She tells him he must walk with his head up, his body stiff, and with dignity. We can see that Travis isn't quite able to pull this off, but he and the maid are happy enough with the effect.

He then meets his son after school and they walk home together, but instead of sharing the same sidewalk, they walk along on opposite sides of the street, doing little comic walking routines for each other's amusement. It's a scene of enormous warmth and charm. It's hard to think of Harry Dean Stanton as a purveyor of funny walks, and that's precisely why these walks work so well, because they belong to the character rather than the actor.

But that's pretty much it for walking in the movie. Sure, people walk across rooms and across parking lots, but there are no more genuine walking scenes. *Paris, Texas* turns into what it was threatening to be all along: a road movie.

Travis buys a 1959 Ford Ranchero, and father and son drive off in search of Mom, played by Nastassja Kinski. They find her, mother and son reunite, and Travis, knowing that he's the problem rather than the solution, drives off with an ambiguous smile on his face. It has become a Sam Shepard story of love, loss, alienation, and manly men driving alone in pickup trucks, which is to say it has become rather unsurprising.

Within the scheme of the film Travis has redeemed himself. He's become part of something. In the beginning he was a lost, crazy man walking alone through the Texas desert. In the end he's a sane man, integrated, driving along highways in his incredibly cool twenty-five-year-old classic Ranchero.

There is a moral here that I'm not very comfortable with. Naturally, one has sympathy for Travis. We don't want him to be a lonely, miserable outsider, and yet I can't see why a man driving along in a Ranchero is necessarily any better off than a man walking alone in the desert. It would have been crass for the end of the movie to have him returning to the desert on foot, yet the vision of the smiling man driving his pickup into the American night feels like too easy a resolution.

There was also something about one of those earlier scenes that worried me. In the beginning Travis walks in straight lines, without regard for topography or established paths. He doesn't walk down any actual roads. When his brother sees him walking along the railroad tracks he stops him, peers into the distance, in the direction Travis is heading, and says, "What's out there? There's nothing out there." It rings hollow, because there *is* something out there and maybe it's something that can be better found on foot than in a pickup truck.

So what's the answer to the question: How many roads must a man walk down before you call him a man? In an episode of *The Simpsons* called "When Grandma Simpson Returns," Homer first says it's eight, and then when he's told the question is rhetorical he corrects himself and says it's seven. Douglas Adams in *The Hitchhiker's Guide to the Galaxy* says it's forty-two. But the answer surely has to be none. A man's still a man even if he walks down no roads at all. It's just that he's likely to be more interesting company if he's walked and sung his way down a few more than that, and if he doesn't rely too much on his pickup truck.

Meanwhile, back on Madison Avenue, I walked from Marcus Garvey Park to 135th Street, where the on-ramp for the Madison Avenue Bridge starts. I then started heading west toward the subway station. For most of the time I'd been in East Harlem I hadn't been the only white man on the street. There had been one or two others along the way. But now as I walked along 135th Street, I was certainly the only one, and apparently a rarity, rare enough for someone to shout out in my direction for the benefit of the guys he was with, "White man! White man!" I wished he hadn't, for all sorts of reasons. He wasn't, I'm pretty sure, saying, "Hail fellow well met." He was saying it more in the tone of someone who'd seen some exotic or threatened species, the way you might have called out, "Look, a spotted owl!" though no doubt there was some disconnect between what he said and what he meant. In fact, I don't really know what he meant, and I certainly didn't know how to respond. "Why yes, you're right. I *am* a white man, aren't I?" In any event I pretended not to hear.

I had some of that feeling of being in a movie, though not an especially original one. You know the kind: where the white guy strolls into the wrong part of town and terrible things happen to him. I was also reminded of a couplet from Kirsty MacColl's song:

When you get to the corner don't look at those freaks
Keep your head down low and stay quick on your feet,
  oh yeah.

I don't know that the guy yelling at me was a freak, but I did keep my head down and continued walking at a brisk New York pace all the way to the subway entrance. And as I walked I was reminded of one last song, Lou Reed's "I'm Waiting for the Man," which asks another question: "Hey, white boy what you doin' uptown?" Walking a songline is not the answer anybody would expect or, I'm sure, accept.

## A MAN WALKS INTO A BAR:

### New York, the Shape of the City, Down Among the Psychogeographers and Mixologists

*Provincial American cities evoke in me a terrible feeling of desolation as evening falls and the citizenry retires to home, hearth, peevish wife and importunate children. Whereas in Manhattan at any hour of the night one can step into the street and encounter a werewolf or at least a derelict who will vomit on one's shoes.*

—THOMAS BERGER

If anyone can claim to be "America's most famous pedestrian" it is probably Edward Payson Weston (1839–1929), always accepting that fame can be both local and transitory. He began his career in 1861 as the result of losing a bet, though no money was involved. The wager was that if Abraham Lincoln won the presidential election, Weston would walk the five hundred or so miles from Boston to Washington in ten days to get there in time for the inauguration. Lincoln won the election and Weston started walking, though he didn't quite manage to do the walk in ten days. He was a couple of hours late and missed the inauguration ceremony, though he arrived in time to attend the ball that evening.

Weston's walk was a grueling one. Walking fifty miles a day is no easy ride for anyone. He walked through rain and snow, was chased by dogs, was arrested once, fell down several times, and on one occasion sprained his ankle. There were compensations, however. Along the way he became a celebrity, cheered on by crowds, kissed by local girls, given free food and lodging, and he also had a sponsorship deal from the Grover & Baker Sewing Machine Company. At the inauguration ball the new president was happy to shake his hand.

Before long Weston turned pro. In 1867 he walked 1,300 miles from Portland, Maine, to Chicago in twenty-six days and won $10,000. In 1869 he walked 5,000 miles for $25,000. In 1871, in St. Louis, he walked backward for 200 miles. He spent eight years in Europe, competing against the best walkers there, and in England in 1879 he challenged "Blower" Brown to walk over 500 miles, and won by covering the distance in a little under 142 hours.

Weston was a public figure and a showman. Postcards from the time show him to have been a flamboyant, barrel-chested dandy. He wore kid gloves, black velvet knee britches, and a cap with a plume. Sometimes he would deliver lectures along the way: "Tea Versus Beer" was one.

Weston seemed only to get better as he got older. When he was seventy years old he planned to walk from New York to San Francisco in 100 days, but got delayed (he had to crawl through parts of the Rockies on his hands and knees), and it took him 104 days. This is the kind of failure most of us could live with, but Weston was bitterly disappointed, and to make amends he walked the return route (starting in Santa Monica) in 76 days.

Ultimately, New York was not kind to Weston. In his lectures he encouraged people to walk rather than drive, and in 1927, at age eighty-eight, he was run down by a New York taxicab—the automobile's revenge. He was seriously injured, and had to spend the last two years of his life in a wheelchair.

It's to be assumed that Weston was sober when he was run down. In 1884 in England he'd undertaken something called the Great Temperance Tour: 5,000 miles in one hundred days, with Sundays off, and the occasional performance of a temperance lecture titled "Struggling." On the other hand, we do know that in 1871 he wagered $2,500 that he could walk a hundred miles in twenty-two hours with champagne as his only sustenance: a bet he won. Certainly after the accident he managed to find some patronage, and one can only hope it was enough to keep him in champagne, if that was what he wanted, since the pleasure of walking was no longer available to him.

In Paul Auster's novel *City of Glass* a detective named Quinn follows a character named Stillman as he wanders around New York's Upper West Side. Eventually Quinn realizes that these wanderings, when plotted on a map, have a shape to them and are spelling out the phrase "Tower of Babel." In fact he never does spell out the last two letters, EL, which Auster explains for the benefit of Gentiles is "the ancient Hebrew for God."

Stillman's wanderings make for a fine literary conceit, but even as you read the book, and look at Auster's doodles that illustrate the walks, you realize that on the ground things wouldn't be nearly so clear. Walking the shape of an O for instance is exceptionally difficult on a grid: Auster's badly drawn O could be a badly drawn D, and the W in *tower* is so shapeless it might have been a V or a U, or a roller coaster, or as Quinn himself says, "a bird of prey perhaps, with its wings spread, hovering aloft in the air." This is a big perhaps.

The walking of a shape, symbol, or word is one of the basic practices of psychogeography, what is called a "constrained walk," exploring a city on foot while following a restrictive or perverse logic, which might include tossing a coin at each street corner to determine the route, walking so as to avoid all security cameras, walking in a dead straight line without regard to actual geography, and so on.

Psychogeography was a subject that had been exercising me, because I was about to go to New York for something called the Conflux psychogeography festival. With this in mind I'd been spending a lot of time staring at maps of the city, looking for patterns, hoping that the layout of streets might reveal some symbol or logo that could form the basis of my own constrained walk: a nuclear disarmament symbol, a Volkswagen trademark, a muted post horn. The only two I could make out on New York's grid pattern were the cross and the swastika, and I didn't feel much like walking either of those.

I was grateful to Auster's book because it told me about the Roeblings, father and son, the men who built the Brooklyn Bridge. After Roebling Senior's death, the son, Washington Augustus Roebling, took over the job and spent long periods working underwater supervising the building of the bridge's caissons. He was down there so long he developed decompression sickness, the bends, and eventually became so disabled that he couldn't walk and was confined to his home and had to watch the construction of the bridge from his window.

The psychogeography festival, it turned out, was to be based in Roebling Street in Williamsburg, Brooklyn, at the McCaig-Welles art gallery. The event was, and I'm quoting now, "the annual New York City festival where visual and sound artists, writers, urban adventurers, researchers and the public gather for four days to explore the physical and psychological landscape of the city. Say hello to Brooklyn!"

In truth I wasn't only going to New York for the festival. I was going because I love the city, because I love walking there, and I intended to do plenty of walking under my own steam outside the festival. New York is a city where you end up doing a great deal of walking even when you don't consciously decide to go walking at all. When I arrived I had no specific walking project in mind, but I hoped something would present itself.


There are plenty of people who will tell you that walking in New York is a universally difficult and painful business. They cite the lack of flow and rhythm, the stopping and starting as each block presents you with a traffic signal and the instruction to walk or not walk. Of course, New York pedestrians try their damnedest not to obey instructions, to walk when they're told not to, but self-preservation demands that once in a while you need to stop and let the traffic have its way. Walking in New York involves a lot of waiting to walk.

I lived in New York between 1996 and 2003, an interesting time, not least because it involved the removal of the Walk/Don't Walk signs from crossings, and the arrival of signs featuring images of a pedestrian (white) and a hand (red). The change must have cost millions, and like any good, cynical New Yorker I thought I detected a scam, a payoff. Precisely for whose benefit did the city abandon the English language in favor of the signifier? Who in New York is so illiterate or so foreign as not to be able to recognize the words "Walk" and "Don't"?

The city fathers who designed the grid pattern of Manhattan's streets claimed it would bring "beauty, order and convenience" to the city, and to some practical extent that's obviously true. The pattern does exert control, on both drivers and walkers, and the numerical arrangement means it's hard to get thoroughly lost in Manhattan. However, within that structure people's eccentricity, waywardness, hostility, and madness are free to manifest themselves and run wild. Perhaps a more random or "organic" structure would create, indeed necessitate, more self-control. I know that's another big perhaps.


I first visited New York in the late 1970s, when the city's reputation for Darwinian, perhaps Malthusian, selection was part of its dangerous charm. You had to be "fit" in certain specific ways. If you couldn't take it, you didn't belong there. If you failed to survive, you didn't deserve to. The locals I knew offered a lot of wisdom on how you should walk the streets in order to remain unmolested. You should stride along, head down, showing you were aware of what was going on around you but weren't too interested because there was somewhere really important you had to get to in a hurry. The other part of the equation was that you should never look like the most vulnerable person on the street. The bad guys were cowards: they only went after stragglers. As long as there was somebody nearby who looked more like a victim than you did, you were OK, comparatively.

It made for a particular and peculiar walking style, alert yet cocooned, and always hoping there was some wimpy college student or feeble old person within striking distance to divert attention from you. It was easy to get this wrong. I did my best but even so I got hassled: not mugged, not robbed, not attacked, not raped, but messed with. Maybe I was trying too hard, or maybe my attempt to look like a tough guy in a hurry was so unconvincing that it became the very thing that marked me out. In those days I stayed clean and sober as I walked the streets of New York. I'd have no more wandered drunkenly through Manhattan than I'd have worn a sign saying "Please Kill Me."

When I started going back to New York in the mid-1990s, and eventually living there, things were different. For one thing I was older, a little tougher, more substantial. I looked less like prey. But the city had changed, too. It was no longer bankrupt, for example, and there weren't hookers in hot pants on every street corner. And many things about the culture had also changed. If you wanted drugs or pornography you didn't have to make the trek to Times Square to get them; they were available in any and every neighborhood. People, of course, complained about the Disneyfication of Times Square, bemoaning the fact that the mean spirit and the dark heart of New York had become soft. Any fool could now walk safely in New York, and that just didn't seem right.

A case can still be made, however, using accident statistics, that walking in New York is a thrillingly dangerous activity, as risky and reckless as playing Russian roulette. Of the 70,000 or so pedestrians who are injured by cars in America every year, 15,000 of them are New Yorkers, a staggering proportion. With 2.7 percent of the nation's population the city has 21 percent of the injuries. Nearly three-quarters of these occur on crosswalks, and quite a few of them occur while the pedestrian is actually on the sidewalk. That makes for some edgy walking, surely.

In recent years, the figures have improved a little, and although this may owe something to better road design and increased public-safety awareness, it's also because people are simply walking less, because they're scared of being run over.

Alcohol plays a surprising part in those statistics. It's not usually the driver who's been drinking. Drunken driving accounts for just a few percent of pedestrian deaths, but in 1998 one-third of pedestrians killed by a motor vehicle were legally drunk. Over the years 1998–2001 the proportion had increased to 40 percent. It will surprise nobody to learn that considerably more drunken pedestrian deaths occur at night than in the daytime. Careening around New York City at night with a snootful of booze is such a high-risk activity, it's a surprise that anybody survives at all.


You could be forgiven for not knowing what a psychogeography festival in Brooklyn might be like. I had little idea myself.

Indeed, you could be forgiven for not knowing what psychoge-ography is, period, but with that I can help. Psychogeography is described rather elegantly by the author Merlin Coverley as "what happens when psychology meets geography." It's a French invention, the brainchild of Guy Debord (1931–94), a Lettrist, then a Situationist, who defined it, in 1955, in a paper called "Introduction to a Critique of Urban Geography" as "the study of the precise laws and specific effects of the geographical environ-ment, consciously organized or not, on the emotions and behav-iour of individuals." This is fine as far as it goes, but it doesn't go very far, and Debord himself didn't go very much further.

The chief, glaring objection to Debord's definition is that it's hard to see that there are any "laws" whatsoever about the way we experience environments as we walk. Rather, there is a clus-ter of imprecise and frequently conflicting personal impressions and preferences. There is a general consensus that walking in the Tivoli Gardens is preferable to wandering along a street filled with dangerous crackheads, but it wouldn't be hard to find some urban explorer who took the opposite view. You and I walk down the street together and come to the opening of a dark alleyway; I think it's intriguing, you think it's scary. Some people think that Disneyland's Main Street, U.S.A. is a walkway of charm and winsome nostalgia; others don't.

These different reactions obviously say something about indi-vidual psychologies, preferences, and previous experiences in dark alleyways or main streets, but surely nobody is experiencing the effect of anything as hard and fast as a "law." In which case psy-chogeography seems to be concerned with a minor statute like the prohibition of jaywalking rather than a universal law like gravity.

Walking was, and remains, psychogeography's main mode of operation; specifically, in French, the "*dérive*," in English the "drift," which Debord defined as "locomotion without a goal," abandoning your usual walking habits and letting the environment draw you in, letting your feet take you where they will and where the city dictates. By drifting, he believes, we detect the "ambiance" of different parts of the city, their special feeling and psychic atmospheres. If we let ourselves drift we are drawn by the "unities of ambiance." Naturally he accepts that these ambiances may not be unified at all, and may change abruptly from one street to the next. All this strikes me as perfectly, unarguably true, but also patently obvious to anyone who's walked though a city, and not quite worth the effort of whipping up into a theory.

Where Debord becomes insufferable is in his insistence that the drift should be a group activity. Yes, he says, you could drift by yourself, but "all the indications are that the most fruitful numerical arrangement consists of several small groups of two or three people who have reached the same awakening of consciousness, since the cross-checking of these groups' impressions makes it possible to arrive at objective conclusions." This is obviously twaddle. If they've all reached the same level of consciousness, then what kind of cross-checking can possibly go on, let alone objectivity? But the real objection is to that very phrase "awakening of consciousness." It sounds, at best, doctrinaire, at worst Stalinist, with a broad hint of the clique and the school playground. "You can't come walking with us because you haven't reached the required level of awakened consciousness."

But perhaps I am taking Debord too seriously. Other members of the Situationist International mockingly referred to him as "The Bore," although coming from a member of the Situationist International this is a bit rich. Then again, the group remained small, because of Debord's practice, as David Bellos puts it in his biography of Georges Perec, of "excommunicating members one by one, until he was in fact the only one left."

Debord did insist that "the *dérive* entails playfully constructive behavior," and the idea that the city can be a place of elaborate fun and games is an appealing one, and it sounded as though there would be plenty of that sort of thing on offer at the Conflux festival. For instance, there was "The World Is My Studio," in which an artist named Sitka was giving "a narrated tour in which she talks about everyday objects and spaces as if they were her work, contextualizing things like moving cars, people's pets and social gestures as the products of her artistic practice."

There was Paul Harley's "Pansy Project," in which he revisited "city streets planting pansies where he has received verbal homophobic abuse. These self-seeding pansies act as a living memorial to this abuse and operate as an antidote to it; each pansy's location is named after the abuse received then posted on his website."

Things were scheduled to start at ten o'clock on Thursday morning at Conflux headquarters in the art gallery on Roebling Street. I got up in good time to discover that New York was caught in the fierce tail of a hurricane. It had never crossed my mind that it might rain in New York in September, and I had no idea what effect it would have on the festivities. I'd thought I might get to the gallery by walking over the Williamsburg Bridge, but that now seemed unnecessarily challenging. I told myself that walking in the rain had a long, respectable, and bittersweet history; even so, I took the subway from Manhattan to Williamsburg.

When I got to the gallery, just a little before ten, it was closed, and two hassled young women were struggling hopelessly with the lock on the front door. It looked like they had enough on their plates without answering questions from me. There was a café next door where a few would-be psychogeographers were sheltering from the rain and waiting for something to happen. I joined them.

Only very gradually did it become apparent that the start had been delayed, not because of some organizational glitch, but because of sabotage. The gallery wasn't simply locked, it was sealed. Someone, a disgruntled artist it was assumed, had come along in the night with a caulking gun, glued the gallery door shut, and squirted more of the caulk into the lock. Then, on the concrete in front of the gallery, he (it was surely a he) had painted the sentences "Mr. Gorbachev, open this gate! Mr. Gorbachev, tear down this wall!"

The gallery walls were not torn down, but a locksmith duly arrived and opened the door so that the group of us, twenty-five or so by now, who'd gathered in the café were belatedly able to get into the gallery. Eventually some opening remarks were made by Christina Ray, the curator of the festival. This was the fourth Conflux, she said, and over the years the festival's events had become more technologically based and less "analog." A lot was now happening online, a lot of the psychogeography was now virtual. I found this disappointing. There are few activities more analog than walking. And she said that whereas in previous years Conflux had often featured maps to help you find your way around, this year there would be maps to help you get lost.

I looked out the window and saw that in front of the gallery, in the rain, there was a young woman sweeping the street. This, I knew, was a walking art project entitled "Sweeping (Sidewalk Performances #1)" by an artist named D. Jean Hester. By her own account, "I will sweep the sidewalks near the gallery. Based on a daily activity of shop owners and residents in my urban LA neighborhood, sweeping the public sidewalk is an expression of pride in one's place, as well as a gift given to others who use the area. While sweeping and engaged in a 'helpful' activity for the neighborhood, I may greet people who pass by with a 'Good morning!' Will the activity of sweeping make me more approachable, allowing people to interact with me in a less guarded fashion?"

I didn't have an absolute answer for her question. True, I did approach her, but the interaction was guarded on both sides. By the time I got out to the street she'd stopped sweeping. She'd been at it for all of ten minutes, and that was another disappointment. I'd imagined she'd be sweeping throughout the festival, for the whole four days, for a hundred hours or so of continuous endurance sweeping and walking. I liked the sound of that. But no.

She told me it was really hard to sweep in the rain, what with holding her umbrella and all. I asked her how large an area she was planning to cover, and she said that given the rain, she was just going to do the small stretch in front of the gallery, but maybe when the rain stopped she'd do the whole block. Again, I had been overambitious on her behalf. I'd thought she might try to sweep the whole zip code.

Then I asked whether she was sweeping the road as well as the sidewalk, since I could see there was a lot of garbage lying there in the street. No, she said, just the sidewalk. We agreed it was good to set yourself limits.

The first event in the gallery was a "discussion session" with an artist named Sue Huang, about her ongoing project "Street Cut Ups." It involved walking the streets of wherever she happened to be, looking for bits of text on signs, posters, ads, and so on, which she would cut out, take away, and then stick together to reveal other, more subversive meanings. It came as no surprise that she claimed to be influenced by the "cut up" method, and by the "literary play" of Oulipo. It was more surprising, and disappointing, that her press release referred to someone by the name of William S. Borroughs (*sic*).

The discussion session consisted of the artist sitting at a table in the gallery with a laptop in front of her, like a nervous vendor at a trade show, as people milled around her, and occasionally someone would stop and ask, metaphorically at least, "What are you selling?" Again I had unreasonable expectations. I'd thought the artist might lead a tour, and we'd walk through the streets of Brooklyn, slashing at posters, snatching words, liberating them, performing a specialized form of anti-logorrhea, sucking words in rather than squirting them out. But we looked out through the window at the rain, and it became all too clear that nobody was going anywhere. Except me. This session was due to last an hour to be followed by a session with a different artist, which I suspected might be all too similar. I couldn't face that. I left the gallery, went back to Manhattan, and kept my powder dry.

The next day I was signed up for something called "Public Parking," a walking tour of certain Brooklyn parking lots, organized by the Temporary Travel Office, the brainchild of one Ryan Griffis.

I'm a big fan of walking in parking lots, partly because it's simply a perverse thing to do, but also because it's a small act of reclamation and defiance. Taking a walk, even just a shortcut, through a parking lot is a way of saying that this open space, and sometimes it can be the only open space for miles around, isn't the sole province of cars and drivers. And if there's a chance of being run down by cars maneuvering into or out of parking bays, then so be it.

I felt there had to be some ironies in a walking tour of parking lots, but I wasn't sure that the Temporary Travel Office's ironic fault line was in the same place as my own. Certainly the professed purpose of the walk was po-faced enough, which didn't mean that it was easy to take it entirely seriously.

"Public Parking," said the Temporary Tourist Office, "is an investigation into the realities of utopian thought as materialized in the mundane and pragmatic spaces of parking lots. Parking lots, one of the most visible, yet overlooked, artifacts of American mobility reveal the concrete space required to store the supposed tools of utopian ideals." There was quite a bit more of this stuff, including a reference to "participatory mapping of personal utopias upon the topography of property development." I tried to remain optimistic.

The tour started at four in the afternoon. It was still raining hard. A dozen or so of us packed into the Temporary Travel Office's rented van, dripping and steaming, and for forty-five minutes Ryan Griffis, a pleasant, friendly, nervous, enthusiastic man, drove us through Friday afternoon rush-hour traffic, heading eastward for the first of the parking lots.

As we drove through a Brooklyn of factories, workshops, warehouses, and self-storage units, we heard a recorded commentary, interspersed with music, telling us facts and figures about parking. This was perfectly unironic as far as I could tell, and it sounded like urban studies research rather than art, but this suited many of the people in the van, since it appeared there were some genuine parking lot scholars and enthusiasts onboard.

The traffic was impenetrable, the drive was slow, and the recorded commentary had ended long before we arrived at the first lot. This was the Grant Avenue Municipal Parking Lot adjacent to the Grant Avenue subway stop on the A line in deepest eastern Brooklyn. It had been chosen precisely because it was so far from anywhere.

It was a nice enough parking lot in its way, spacious, not full, a place you could leave your car without fearing it would be stolen or stripped down, and it had a surface that was smoother and better maintained than anything we'd driven over on the way there. There were signs telling you how to park: at 90 degrees to the retaining wall, and inside the parking bay, and to reverse into the spot so that leaving was made easier. Our van pulled in and parked.

Rain was sluicing down, hard as ever, but some of us, though by no means all, felt a duty to get out of the van and set foot on the lot. But none of us walked very far. We huddled under umbrellas, walked maybe a hundred yards from one corner of the lot to another, making the kind of conversation you might make on a tour of parking lots with people you didn't know.

Then we all returned to the van and drove a very long way back west to see two other lots, one private rather than municipal, and one that was no longer a parking lot at all but was now "developed" into the construction site for a theater designed by Frank Gehry. Nobody left the van at these sites; in fact the van didn't even stop. As a professed walking tour it was a bust, and we were running late because of the traffic. By now we were a van full of restless, fidgety, full-bladdered tourists.

As we drove back to the art gallery, we lost the traffic and eventually passed through an amazing landscape of gorgeous industrial ruin. I had, and still have, only a sketchy idea of exactly where we were, somewhere near the water and in sight of the Williamsburg Bridge, an area of big, blank, formidable buildings interspersed with empty and ruined lots. There was nobody visible on the streets, certainly nobody walking, and you couldn't have said there was any *activity* as such, and yet there was evidence of inscrutable things going on: anonymous trucks parked in front of loading bays, Dumpsters full of intriguing waste, barred and bolted doors and windows suggesting something precious or forbidden on the other side. I'd have been happy to walk around there on my own, and the next day I tried.

The rain had finally stopped by then and I returned to Conflux, this time for a lecture by Denis Wood called "Lynch Debord! About Two Psychogeographies," but I gave myself a couple of hours to take a walk before it started. Denis Wood is the author of a fine and light-footed book called *The Power of Maps*, which discusses the ways in which maps serve all sorts of purposes, very few of them having much to do with getting from A to B. Every map, he says, is made in somebody's interest, and that interest is very unlikely to coincide with yours. I was hoping he'd say a few droll and irreverent things about Debord and psychogeography.

In truth I never got back to the exact streets we'd driven through the previous day, and I told myself it didn't matter much. A walk was still a walk even if it didn't take you exactly where you wanted it to. The area I found myself walking in wasn't quite as rough or blighted as the one I'd seen through the van windows, but it was rough and blighted nevertheless. And at one moment I found myself under the roaring expressway, quite alone, standing on the forecourt of a garage next to a wrecked, rusted, and very beautiful 1950s Cadillac, which I think always gives class to a neighborhood.

But the best thing I saw, by far, was a huge factory built of red brick, a manufacturer of rubber goods, with a sign outside that said "If it's made of Rubber we have it." This was good in itself, but then I saw the name of the company (and I would still have some trouble believing it if I hadn't taken a photograph): it was called the Auster Rubber Co. Inc. I walked all the way around the block that contained it, aware that I was tracing a rectangle that couldn't seriously be mistaken for any letter, however misshapen.


The Conflux lectures were being held in the back room of a nearby bar, the Lucky Cat. I got there five minutes before the Denis Wood lecture was due to start and I just about managed to get in the door. The crowd was spilling out of the back room into the front. There was standing room only and not much of that, and although I could see someone far away in the back, standing beside a screen and talking, I couldn't hear anything he said.

This lecturer, it turned out, wasn't Denis Wood, but the guy delivering the preceding lecture. There was no sign that this event was about to end, and even when it did, it seemed unlikely that the crowd would clear out and free up any seats. Denis Wood was going to be a hot ticket; if you were in possession of a chair down at the front you weren't going to give it up.

The Lucky Cat was as hot, humid, and packed as a New York subway platform in highest summer. Sweat dripped off me and off everyone else. There was a dense, cloying smell of fried food and ketchup in the air. Maybe if I could have got to the bar and bought myself a drink it would have been different, but there was no way I could get through. I thought I might fall down or throw up. Suddenly I realized there was no way in the world I could bear to be in that space for another second, much less to stand there for the amount of time it would take to watch someone deliver a lecture on Debord and psychogeography.

I staggered out to the street. The evening was a warm one, but compared to the bar it offered a blast of cool, bracing air. I stood for a minute or two watching as more people arrived for the lecture; at first I thought I should join them, go back in, and tough it out. Then I thought, no, I don't have to do that. I don't have to do that at all. There was no duty, no obligation, nobody checking up on me. I was perfectly free to miss the lecture, to abandon my plan, to walk away; and that's exactly what I did.

And as I went, I realized that walking away is one of life's greatest pleasures, whether it's walking away from a bad job, a bad relationship, a bad educational course, or a bad psychogeography festival. There was an extraordinary sunset over Williamsburg that night. The clouds looked like orange lizard skin and there were people on the street photographing it. The sky was putting on a show to celebrate my decision. I felt fantastic: I'd escaped. I was giddy with relief.

I had no complaints with anyone at Conflux. They were what they were. They did what they did. My needs and expectations weren't their responsibility. I blamed myself. I was too cynical, too unhip, too much of a sourpuss, a loner, a solitary walker. And perhaps it's absurd to call yourself a loner and a solitary walker when your chief walking pleasure involves exploring the streets of major metropolitan cities, but that was how I felt about New York, that it was a city crammed with solitary walkers, just like me. I didn't need a guide or a map. I'd find my own damned way of walking this city. I would find my own version of a "constrained walk."


By then, it seemed to me that all walks are constrained walks one way or another. They're inevitably constrained by time, by our imagination, by our physical limitations, and by the special character of the terrain we're walking. One way to deal with the whole notion of constraint is simply to walk down every street in a given area or zone. This is certainly programmatic, but it does create a kind of pedestrian democracy, and makes all streets, all routes, equal. It also certainly avoids all the unities of ambiance.

The annals of pedestrianism are littered with people who have walked down every street of major cities. The queen is

Phyllis Pearsall, the creator of the *London A–Z*. Starting in 1935, she walked 3,000 miles, mapping 23,000 streets, and working (though not necessarily walking) for eighteen hours a day. As far as I'm aware, nobody has attempted the same thing in the five boroughs of New York, but I know of three people who have systematically walked down every street in Manhattan, and there are surely more.

Thomas J. Keane, a naval officer, did it in the early fifties, and according to the *New York Times*, finished on December 15, 1954. Caleb Smith, a librarian at Columbia University, did it between 2002 and 2004, and on his website says he "walked over 700 miles," which is very different from the mileage claimed by another Manhattan completist, Joseph D. Terwilliger, also connected to Columbia University, as an associate professor of neuroscience. He claims to have covered 1,279 miles, and he is certainly willing to enter into a debate about what constitutes a street, and indeed what constitutes Manhattan. He first did it in 2002, but it took him the whole year. And then he did it again in eighty days, between October 28, 2004, and January 14, 2005.

Terwilliger said his least favorite neighborhoods were SoHo and the Upper East Side because there were "too many tourists, 'suits,' and folks who would be scared to death by the thought of walking around Mott Haven or Crotona Park East after dark." Terwilliger also claimed that the most dangerous zip code was "10039 (South of the Polo Grounds Projects around the 150s and Frederick Douglass)." Even he didn't walk there at night. He writes, "When walking here at 3 PM a group of men hanging out on the corner turned to me and said 'Good afternoon, Officer.'...Nice to know I looked like an undercover cop—

being a big tall guy with short hair is a good thing sometimes."
But only sometimes, I think.

Clearly, on this brief New York trip of mine I wasn't going
to be able to complete anything of any great substance. Nevertheless I was still keen, edging toward desperate, to undertake
a walk that would mean something and have some psychogeographic resonance to me, if nobody else.


When I lived in New York in the 1990s I learned to drink
martinis, and I also learned that sometimes it was better not to
drink martinis. I often thought the Manhattan cocktail would
have been more appropriate, given its name, but for me it never
addressed the pleasure and pain receptors in quite the way a
martini did. A martini felt more like a drug than a drink. It had
my name on it. It hit hard: it wasn't for wimps.

After a martini or two I would walk the dark streets of Manhattan
feeling a little "bagged," a bit "lit up," with a new sense of power and
possibility, and as I found out later, risk being run down. I wouldn't
have cared. Certain edges were taken off and certain others (the
ones to do with feelings of invulnerability and inflated self-esteem)
were sharpened up in their place. It wasn't quite sensory derangement à la De Quincey, but it was definitely an altered state, and that
was good enough. Sometimes it felt like flying as much as walking.

I was two martinis to the good when I first proposed to the
woman who's now my wife, but who was then more or less a complete stranger. We were walking down Crosby Street, an access
street parallel to lower Broadway, and I had spent a total of one
hour in her company. She didn't say no.

Later, once we were an item, there were many nights when we walked through Terwilliger's hated SoHo, where her office was, heading north up Thompson or Sullivan Street, and ahead of us was the illuminated Empire State Building and behind us the illuminated Twin Towers, and we said that one of these days we'd have to go up to Windows on the World, the swank bar and restaurant in the north tower, and have a martini or two. It never happened. We didn't know there was any reason to rush.

I wasn't in New York on September 11, 2001. I was three thousand miles away in England. My wife was two and a half thousand miles away in the opposite direction visiting her sister in Washington State. After the event I spent some time wondering whether we should consider ourselves lucky, or if we should regret having been absent at such a crucial and calamitous moment in history. There was some guilt, too, because by then I felt like a New Yorker and it seemed only right that I should have to go through what other New Yorkers had gone through.

As soon as I could, I got on a plane and went back to New York. Once there I walked the streets, and saw that dust and shreds of paper were still falling all over the city, and there was a strange smell in the air that was reported to be horrifying, a combination of jet fuel and incinerated human flesh, they said, but it really wasn't so bad.

And I did what everybody else was doing. I walked to Ground Zero, to see what there was to be seen. I joined the procession of people a mile or more from the zone, on lower Broadway, a long stream of walkers that got broader and flowed less freely as it neared its destination. It was a solemn crowd but not a quiet one. This was New York. There was some yelling, some bad temper, and at least half the crowd was shooting stills or video, though I don't know what they were seeing.

We were kept at bay, behind barriers. The viewpoint we were allowed was a distant one, and even the most powerful telephoto lens wouldn't have got you in very close. We could see rubble, a spout of water being hosed from a great height, and we could just about make out the famous twisted, perforated façade, but it wasn't nearly so clear or so dramatic as the pictures we'd seen in newspapers and on TV.

In the end there was very little to see. As a place of pilgrimage, Ground Zero seemed inadequate. It was a walk without a goal, though not a psychogeographical drift. I had a sense of frustration and deflation. I wanted more from this walk. I noticed that all around me people were crying, and that seemed incomprehensible at first. There was nothing there to cry about, no relics, no triggers, nothing. I found myself unmoved.

And then, up against a barrier that was blocking our way, I saw a member of the National Guard, an older man, fat-faced, densely built, not looking much like a soldier. A stream of people kept walking up to him, and he handed something to each of them, a paper tissue that they could cry into. He did it quietly, undramatically, and the gentleness and dignity of the gesture moved me more than anything else I saw that day. It was as much comfort as anyone could offer, or had any right to receive. The tears started rolling down my own cheeks and I didn't try to stop them.

．　．　．

I walked down to Ground Zero again a little less than a year later, a week before the one-year anniversary. There were very few people there at that time, and the site had the windswept feel of a tourist attraction out of season. There was even less to see than there had been on that first visit, but now you could get right up to the wire fence and peer down into the vast excavated pit, six stories deep. It had all gone. The evidence had all been taken away. You had to be impressed by the sheer industry and determination that had been required to clear away all that horror and debris and chaos.

I went there again a week later, on the anniversary itself, when the crowds had returned, and only families and VIPs were allowed anywhere near the pit. The rest of us just milled about in the surrounding streets. The front page of the *New York Post* ran a photograph of the standing Twin Towers with the headline "Lest We Forget." I found myself infuriated, spitting with rage. What kind of attention-deficient rubes did they take us for? We were being entreated to remember something none of us could possibly have forgotten. Did they think it might somehow have slipped our minds?

And I walked to Ground Zero again the day after I abandoned my psychogeography festival, more or less five years after 9/11. As ever there was nothing much to see, although some work had been done to make the place more tourist-friendly: walkways, notice boards, signage. Still, there was a sense of lost purpose. The crowd was thin. The pilgrimage element had disappeared. You didn't need to join any stream of walkers. Tour buses were pulling up very close, you could hop off, take a quick stroll, take a few photographs, get back on the bus. And in order that the visitors might have something to look at, a series of large, iconic photographs had been mounted on the chain-link fences surrounding the site. In the absence of anything more tangible, people were taking photographs of the photographs.

I headed a little ways uptown. I needed a martini. I found myself on University Place, near Washington Square, an area where a man might reasonably find a bar to serve him what he needed. It was a busy night, everywhere was crowded, and when I saw a restaurant with a bar that opened onto the street and a couple of empty stools, I went in and sat down. I now saw that I was in an Indian fusion restaurant, not the obvious home for great cocktail making, but I tried to be positive. I asked the girl behind the bar for a martini and a look of panic flashed across her face. This was her first day, she told me. She'd never made a martini before. She turned to one of the waitresses for help and her friend talked her through the process. For a first try it really wasn't bad.

I'd picked up a free magazine on the way in, so that I'd have something to read as I drank, and now I saw there was an ad on the back page showing a map of Manhattan. I looked at it with a certain desperation. I was feeling more than ever the need to do a "good," "proper," "constrained" New York walk. I hoped that some walking route would leap up off the map and demand to be done.

And then—OK, I'd sunk most of a martini by then—as I stared at the pattern of streets near to where I was, I quite clearly saw the shape of a martini glass. Really. A stretch of University Place formed the base of the glass. Eighth and 9th streets heading west formed the uprights of the stem, while Christopher Street and Greenwich Avenue diverged at equal angles to form the two sides of the conical bowl. The triangle was completed by Hudson Street, not an absolutely straight line across the top since it contained a slight kink or rise about halfway along, but that was OK, and could be thought to resemble the meniscus of liquid that rises above the rim of a truly full martini glass.

I drew on the map, emphasizing the outline. What else was there to do but walk the streets that represented the shape of the glass, and at certain strategic points around the route find a bar and have another martini? There was something a bit dumb about it, but it didn't seem a whole lot dumber than some of the things the Conflux crowd had come up with. It featured walking, martinis, exploring the city, imposing a shape on the environment. What more could a psychogeographer want?

As a route for a walk, and a bar crawl, it had its attractions. It took me past and/or into some famous watering holes: the Cedar Tavern, home of the fighting abstract expressionists, and from where Jack Kerouac was supposedly ejected for peeing in an ashtray; the White Horse, where Bob Dylan went to hear the Clancy Brothers; the Stonewall, scene of gay resistance, though closed and available for rent when I walked by. And on Greenwich Avenue I saw, painted on a wall, the outline of a muted post horn; if you're in the right frame of mind a post horn can look a lot like a martini glass.

But you know what, all in all it was another bust. The overriding problem was that walking the streets gave no sense of following the shape of a martini glass. Even though I had it clearly enough in my head, it still didn't compute. You'd have had to be a bird or a tracking satellite or a god to see what I was doing down here. As Denis Wood says, "The map is not the territory."

It occurred to me, not exactly for the first time, that psychogeography didn't have much to do with the actual experience of walking. It was a nice idea, a clever idea, an art project, a conceit, but it had very little to do with any real walking, with any real experience of walking. And it confirmed for me what I'd really known all along, that walking isn't much good as a theoretical experience. You can dress it up any way you like, but walking remains resolutely simple, basic, analog. That's why I love it and love doing it. And in that respect—stay with me on this—it's not entirely unlike a martini. Sure you can add things to martinis, like chocolate or an olive stuffed with blue cheese or, God forbid, cotton candy, and similarly you can add things to your walks—constraints, shapes, notions of the mapping of utopian spaces—but you don't need to. And really, why would you? Why spoil a good drink? Why spoil a good walk?

I abandoned my own constrained walk with as much enthusiasm as I'd abandoned the psychogeography festival. I walked the city feeling remarkably free, a spring in my step and several much-needed martinis in my bloodstream.

Guy Debord was a serious drinker who enjoyed the derangement of the senses. He drank as he drifted, and had no shame about it. In his memoir *Panegyric* he writes, "I never for a moment dreamed of concealing this perhaps questionable side of my personality, and it was clearly evident for all those who met me more than once or twice. . . .

"At first, like everyone, I appreciated the effect of mild drunkenness, then very soon I grew to like what lies beyond violent drunkenness, once that stage is past: a terrible magnificent peace. . . . Although in the first decades I may have allowed only slight indications to appear once or twice a week, I was in fact continuously drunk for periods of several months."

He was undoubtedly drunk while conducting some of his psychogeographic drifts. He was probably drunk when he formulated some of the tenets of psychogeography. He adds, "I have wandered extensively in several great European cities, and I appreciated everything that deserved appreciation. The catalog on this subject could be vast. . . ." He then proceeds to catalog not great sights, much less unities of ambiance, but rather the joys of alcohol: first, beer—English, Irish, German, Czech, and Belgian—then he goes on to celebrate wines, spirits, cocktails, punches et al.

Debord ended his life as a scholarly recluse, living in his cottage in Champot, in the Upper Loire, with his second wife, Alice Becker-Ho. The photographs taken of him in the early 1990s show a plump, happy man, usually with a drink and a pipe in his hand. He doesn't look much like a walker, but we know that walkers come in all shapes and sizes. In any event, as he got older he did far more drinking than walking, and eventually he developed a form of polyneuritis brought on by alcohol. The pain was so intolerable that he committed suicide in 1994 by shooting himself in the heart.

Debord never visited New York, but in his article "Theory of the Dérive" he writes, "Within architecture itself, the taste for dériving tends to promote all sorts of new forms of labyrinths made possible by modern techniques of construction," and quotes from an uncited newspaper article describing a proposed New York apartment block.

"The apartments of the helicoidal building will be shaped like slices of cake. One will be able to enlarge or reduce them by shifting movable partitions. The half-floor gradations avoid limiting the number of rooms, since the tenant can request the use of the adjacent section on either upper or lower levels. With this setup three four-room apartments can be transformed into one twelve-room apartment in less than six hours."

Debord concludes that here, "One can see the first signs of an opportunity to *dérive* inside an apartment."

He was wrong about this, too. If he had ever been in one of the minute apartments where most New Yorkers actually live, he'd have seen just how limited the prospects are for the at-home drift. In fact, it's always seemed to me that one of the reasons New Yorkers spend so much time walking the streets is precisely because their apartments are so small. They need to get out and walk, to experience the city's "beauty, order and convenience" so that they don't go completely mad. This may also be why they need to walk to their nearest bar for a dry martini.

# SOME DESERT WALKERS, WALKING
# IN AND OUT OF NATURE, WITH
# AND WITHOUT GOD

*Holden: You're in a desert walking along in the sand when all of a sudden
    you look down—*
*Leon: What one?*
*Holden: What?*
*Leon: What desert?*
*Holden: It doesn't make any difference what desert, it's completely
    hypothetical.*

—screenplay of *Blade Runner*

I don't know much about gods, but it seems that they like
their believers to do a lot of walking, metaphoric and literal. A lot of people are keen to walk with God; a lot of people
insist that they already do.

In A.D. 341, St. Anthony, an Anchorite, one of the Desert
Fathers, sometimes known as St. Anthony of the Desert, then
age ninety, had a vision that told him Paul the Hermit, the very
first Desert Father, was "nearby," living in a cave in a different

part of the Egyptian desert. Prayer walking was part of the Desert Fathers' creed. They walked as they prayed, prayed as they walked. Anthony set out on foot to find Paul, although he had no idea where he was. According to St. Jerome, who is the only source for these events, a visionary centaur appeared to Anthony and pointed him in the right direction. After walking through the desert for three days he found Paul the Hermit, age 113, weak and close to death.

The two saints spent the night in prayer and the next morning, knowing he was about to die, Paul asked Anthony to walk back to the monastery from which he'd come to pick up a robe that had belonged to Athanasius the Great and bring it back. Paul wanted to be buried in the robe.

Anthony did what was asked of him, walked for three days back to his monastery, picked up the robe, and began the journey back to Paul's cave. On the third day of this walk, i.e., his ninth consecutive day of desert walking, Anthony had a vision of angels and prophets ascending to heaven with Paul the Hermit among them, a clear sign that Paul was already dead. And so it proved.

Finding Paul's dead body in the desert cave, Anthony wrapped it in the holy robe as preparation for burial, but then found he was too weak to dig the grave. Two lions came running out of the desert, knelt beside the body of Paul the Hermit, roared in lamentation, then dug a grave with their paws before disappearing into the desert again.

It's strange what you find yourself seeing when you're ninety years old and have been walking in the desert for nine consecutive days.

. . .

I was in the Mojave Desert, in Death Valley, in early November. I was there to do some walking, and I'd gone to the general store in Furnace Creek, bought some supplies, and was sitting on a bench outside the store drinking a soda before setting off again.

One of the guys who worked there, a large, heavy, slow-moving man, walked by and said to me, "So, where you from?"

I said, "L.A."

"L.A.," he repeated. "So how do you like walking in my desert? I bet you think it's all a big nothing."

Few things could have been further from what I actually thought about the desert, which I wasn't much inclined to think of as "his" or anyone else's, but in an attempt to keep things simple I said, "I love the desert."

The man grunted and softened a little, and told me that he was originally from the L.A. area, specifically Pasadena. Then he said, "If you walk on concrete for too long you start to think like a predator."

I thought this was a great line, but then he added, "'Cause everybody wants something from you," which I thought rather spoiled the effect.

The less simple thing I might have said to him was, first, that I don't think the desert is a big nothing at all, I actually think it's a beautiful, intense, profoundly moving "something," and then I'd have said that although by far the majority of my walking has been done in cities, and continues to be, I've also walked in a lot of places that are not cities. I've done my time walking in the great outdoors (not that cities are "indoors" exactly), in forests, woodlands, wetlands, seashores, hills, even mountains so long as they were the walkable rather than the climbable variety, but it's only in the desert that I've ever found anything that came close to giving a spiritual dimension to my walking, whereas others seem to find that spiritual dimension just about everywhere they look.

I've been trying to find where the phrase "walking in nature" came from. I'm guessing its first use must have been an ancient one, and in itself it's a perfectly harmless form of words. However, all too often it gets hijacked by what I might as well call New Agers. A quick browse among New Age walking sources will soon have you screaming for mercy as you're told that nature is an unalloyed source of goodness, purity, benign intention, spiritual insight, higher consciousness, and (oh spare me) healing.

Here's someone named Linda Leonard on the website livinglifefully.com: "I find nature so nourishing. I love to hike, especially in the mountains. When I'm walking in nature, I feel in awe of the wonder of creation. Nature is full of surprises, always changing, and we must change with it. In nature, the soul is renewed and called to open and grow."

Here's a blog entry from Stephen Altschuler, who calls himself the Mindful Hiker, which is also the title of a book he wrote: "Walking is not anything separate from life," he bleats. "It is integral to life, especially walking in nature. Yesterday, I encountered a rattlesnake on the trail—came quite close to it—and I marveled at its wildness, the ferocity of its rattle as I almost stepped on it."

Altschuler may not be the very worst of the New Age

walkers but he's certainly the worst I've found, and his sins are compounded because they're published in book form. *The Mindful Hiker* comes with spiritual exercises you can try for yourself. "What is your relationship to physical pain?" he asks. "The next time you feel physical or emotional pain, go to a soul place in nature and take a walk with that pain. Go slowly, because pain needs time to explain itself."

This is the kind of thing that gives walking, nature, and spirituality a bad name.

I know that mocking the jejune philosophizing of New Agers is like dynamiting New Agers in a barrel, but that doesn't mean it's not worth doing. I don't doubt that the Mindful Hiker and his ilk are sincere and well intentioned; it's just that their idea of nature comes weighed down with meanings, values, and assumptions that I neither share nor accept. Their ramblings make me wonder exactly which bit of nature they've been walking in. Frozen wastes? Disease-ridden jungle? Malarial swamp? Floodplains and tornado alleys? Or just the local park?

Personally, I blame Thoreau for a lot of this. In *Walking* he creates a hymn to walking and nature that expresses the idea that American nature is the very best nature.

"Some do not walk at all," he writes, "others walk in the highways; a few walk across lots. Roads are made for horses and men of business. I do not travel in them much comparatively, because I am not in a hurry to get to any tavern, or grocery, or livery stable, or depot to which they lead. I am a good horse to travel but not from choice a roadster. The landscape painter uses the figures of men to mark a road. He would not make that use of my figure. I walk out into a nature such as the old prophets and poets Menu, Moses, Homer, Chaucer, walked in. You may name it America, but it is not America. Neither Americus Vespucius, nor Columbus, nor the rest were the discoverers of it. There is a truer account of it in Mythology than in any history of America so called that I have seen."

These days most people who want to walk in nature want to walk in a very specific version of it, something that confirms their prejudices about spirituality-lite. What I'm sure of is that they want to walk in *managed* nature, which is probably just as well, since nothing else is currently available to us. At this point in history every American environment, for better or worse, is a man-made environment. Those places that are of "outstanding natural beauty" are not pristine, much less untouched; rather, they've been managed in very specific ways to create very specific effects and to give the walker a very specific experience. Death Valley, for example, is run by a company called Xanterra Parks & Resorts, which gets its name, the company says, from Samuel Coleridge's Xanadu. They'll also tell you that they're "proud stewards of the park," a formulation that makes me want to scream. However, this at least indicates an awareness that left to its own devices, nature just might not be the educative, compassionate, nurturing place that some would like it to be, and in fact insist that it is.


A description of nature that makes much more sense to me is to be found in a book called *The Desert*, written by the naturalist and art critic John C. Van Dyke in 1901. There's serious doubt these days about whether Van Dyke was really the intrepid desert explorer he made himself out to be, but his observations certainly ring true. He writes, "And yet in the fullness of time Nature designs that this waste and all of earth with it shall perish. Individual, type, and species, all shall pass away; and the globe itself become as desert sand blown hither and yon through space. She cares nothing for the individual man or bird or beast; can it be thought that she cares any more for the individual world?"

Is that a religious thought or an antireligious thought? Is it some notion of being at one? It's pretty much my version of nature that he's describing: rough, scary, utterly indifferent. In the face of this, a walk seems like exactly what it is: something but not much, certainly not a means of salvation. It may be pleasurable and worth doing, it may stop you getting depressed, but in the end it's just a walk. Why would you want it to be more?

I was born and brought up in England, so it was a long time before I ever set foot in a desert, though I was familiar with the concept. I'd seen it on-screen: in Road Runner cartoons, in cowboy movies, in Russ Meyer's *Faster, Pussycat! Kill! Kill!*, in any number of cheap science fiction movies, and in a few very expensive ones. The initial appeal was primarily visual. The desert appears in so many movies because it looks so good.

On the other hand, it never looked like a place you could actually go walking. It seemed too mythic, too otherworldly for that. When I eventually discovered you could drive a car out into the American desert, park at the side of a dirt road, and walk off into the distance, that was quite a moment, quite a realization, and I've been doing it ever since.

I know that some people find the desert frightening: all that space, all that isolation, all the terrible things that can happen to you. And of course I realize that terrible things really can and do happen out there, from dying of thirst to falling and breaking something to encountering Mansonite cults, but that's part of what I like about it. Charles Manson at his trial: "I am the biggest beast walking the face of the earth." Charles Manson at his 1992 parole hearing: "But there's a line that man walks. All men walk a line. And I walk that line in prison."

You have to be on your mettle when you're walking in the desert, you have to take charge of yourself, you have to know what you're doing. And to an extent the desert helps you. It sharpens up the senses, makes you more aware and more self-aware. I've never felt lonely in the desert.


I've only been really lost in the desert once and, of course, once might have been more than enough. Ultimately it lacked drama because I lived, and because it was brief, certainly no more than a couple of hours, but it was a long couple of hours, and for all I knew they could have been the first of my last hours.

It was in Western Australia, about twenty-two miles outside the mining town of Kalgoorlie. I was with my then girlfriend and we'd just picked up a Land Cruiser in which we planned to do some not-too-serious off-roading and some walking. But that was ahead of us. On that afternoon in question we were making a minor foray into the desert, to get the lay of the land and the feel of the vehicle.

We drove out to a ghost town called Kanowna, which even by ghost town standards was a big nothing. There really was nothing worth seeing. There had once been twelve thousand people living there, along with their churches, hotels, breweries, and railway station, but there was no sign of any of these now, and although a few signposts had been put up indicating where a post office and courthouse had once been, they weren't marking anything other than a few bits of rubble and piles of ancient tin cans.

Disappointed, we left the Land Cruiser and walked around. We didn't bother to take water or even sun hats with us. There seemed to be no need. We weren't even doing anything so definite as "going for a walk." We were just wandering about. We investigated some old tailings dumps, peered into a lethal-looking open mine shaft. If we went more than a mile I'd be surprised.

Before long we decided to head back to the Land Cruiser. After we'd walked for a while in what we felt sure was the direction of the vehicle, we realized we were mistaken. We didn't arrive at the vehicle. In fact, now that we looked around us more critically, we realized the Land Cruiser was nowhere to be seen. That didn't seem right; it scarcely seemed possible. We set off in another likely-looking direction, and that didn't take us to the Land Cruiser either. Above all, it seemed plain odd and incomprehensible, but it was frightening, too, and we realized it was perfectly possible that both our attempts to get back to the vehicle might in reality have taken us farther away.

We felt like idiots. If we'd been heading out to do some serious desert walking we'd have done all the right things: studied maps, carried a good supply of water, brought a compass. As it was, we had nothing.

It seemed absurd that we could get lost in territory like this. It was a tame, flat, unexceptional, unthreatening bit of desert, but that was a large part of the problem. It was a landscape without landmarks, and certainly without any high place you might climb up to in order to get your bearings. This terrain was featureless, with every bush and rock looking very much like every other bush and rock. Then we noticed a lot of stripped animal bones lying on the ground, and we saw a skull, the kind you see in cartoons that opens its jaw and says, "You'll be sorry." We realized just how bad and serious our situation was.

To cut a short story even shorter, we did, of course, eventually find our way back to the Land Cruiser. It had everything to do with good luck and nothing at all to do with good judgment, and I know that the story might very easily have turned out quite differently and that I'd be in no position to write it. Perhaps we didn't altogether deserve to survive.

We wandered aimlessly for what seemed an age, but which, as I said, was only a couple of hours, and suddenly we spotted the open mine shaft we'd seen before. From there we were able to find our way back to the Land Cruiser. In some ways it was an anticlimax, though not an unwelcome one. It taught me that simply walking off into the desert is a very stupid thing to do, but perhaps that's something I shouldn't have needed to learn. Walking lost in the desert was an entirely unspiritual experience. It did not make me feel at one with anything, least of all nature.

In retrospect I realize what I should have done was to choose a spot on the ground, any spot, and walk a spiral course moving outward in ever-expanding circles. That way I would inevitably have come to the Land Cruiser sooner or later.

If you had been watching this from the air you might possibly have thought that I was performing a labyrinth walk, the most ancient form of spiritual walking, and the New Agers have naturally picked up on it. Labyrinth walking has figured in rituals and religions from Iceland to Sri Lanka, from Tunisia to Sumatra, from India to Brazil.

In common parlance the words *maze* and *labyrinth* tend to be interchangeable; however, there's a significant difference. Whereas a maze contains multiple paths and dead ends, and therefore many opportunities for getting lost, the labyrinth contains just one path. By taking it you inevitably get to the center. In a maze you encounter high walls or hedges that conceal the path and the pattern. Labyrinths generally have no walls, no concealment. They're marked out on the ground in two dimensions, in earth, sand, or tile. If you chose, you could walk straight across to the center, avoiding the marked path completely, although naturally this is frowned upon by serious labyrinth walkers. Walking around a maze is a form of puzzle solving; walking around a labyrinth is a spiritual exercise. The notion that there's only one true path is of course attractive to believers. You cannot get lost in a true labyrinth.

Virginia Westbury, author of *Labyrinths: Ancient Paths of Wisdom and Peace,* asked the many labyrinth walkers she encountered what they thought labyrinths were "for." The replies she got included "meditation, celebration, spiritual connection, talking to God, talking to spirits, self-exploration, healing, sensing 'energy,' wisdom, worship, divination, inner peace, forgiveness, transformation and communicating with others." Is there nothing a labyrinth can't do?

There are Christian labyrinths inside the French cathedrals of Chartres, Reims, and Amiens. The one at Chartres is the oldest, dating from the early thirteenth century. These are pavement labyrinths, set into the cathedral floors, and the original symbolic intentions have largely been lost. It seems they may have been as much concerned with seasonal rituals as with prayer walking, but we do know that in the eighteenth century pilgrims would walk around these labyrinths on bended knee while praying, as a penance.

There are currently a number of prisons in the United States that have installed labyrinths in their exercise yards. A few years ago the authorities at Monterey County Jail in Salinas, California, spent three thousand dollars on a portable version, a purple labyrinth painted on canvas, ninety feet across. It was unrolled from time to time and prisoners walked its path.

Prisoners reported feeling calm and at peace having walked it, though Cynthia Montague, one of the jail's chaplains, reckoned its chief function was metaphoric. The labyrinth walk was about getting and staying on track, returning to the narrow if not the straight. Montague said, "If you accidentally step off the path and go onto a different part of the path, you might find yourself heading back out. But you're allowed to start over again and keep at it."

The most famous of all labyrinth walkers must surely be Theseus, who walked into the labyrinth in Crete to slay the minotaur. In order to avoid getting lost he used Ariadne's ball of golden thread to trace his steps. This means, of course, that he was actually in a maze rather than a true labyrinth.

Instead of a golden thread, Hansel and Gretel tried leaving a trail of bread crumbs to stop themselves from getting lost, although you could argue that they were not so much lost as abandoned by their father. And in fact they did perform considerable walking feats. The Grimms' fairy tale has them dumped in the middle of the forest and then "walking all day and all night" to get home.

The Death Valley '49ers, of 1849, the desert's most famous lost pioneers, had neither golden thread nor bread crumbs, but they did have a map promising a shortcut through the desert, via the Walker Pass, taking five hundred miles off their journey from Salt Lake City to California, where the Gold Rush was in full swing. The phrase "I know a shortcut" should strike fear in the heart of any serious walker.

The '49ers started out as part of an expedition led by Captain Jefferson Hunt, under the auspices of the Mojave San Joaquin Company, known as the Mojave Sand Walking Company, a name that gives me pleasure every time I think of it, although this started out as a wagon train rather than a walking expedition.

Hunt's progress was too slow for some, and there were various splits and regroupings, some temporary and some permanent, before a faction known as the Bennett-Arcane party, following the dubious shortcut map, at last found themselves lost, stranded, exhausted, and helpless in the heart of what is now Death Valley.

Two of the younger, fitter men—William Manly and John Rogers—decided they would simply walk out of the valley on foot, cross the Panamint Range, get help, and return to rescue the survivors, if any. This, incredibly, they did, although Manley confessed in print that it had crossed his mind never to return for the others.

In any case, Manly and Rogers did the right thing. They walked 250 miles from Death Valley to the San Fernando Valley, where they obtained supplies, along with two horses and a mule. They were intending to ride at least part of the way back, but both horses died en route, so it turned into another walking expedition. Once they'd saved the people left behind, they all had to walk the route once again.

Manly eventually wrote his account of events in a book titled *Death Valley in '49*. It is the story of his life as well as the story of the 49ers, and parts of it read like a primer on the pains of walking and adverse walking conditions. He writes: "Walking began to get pretty tiresome. Great blisters would come on our feet, and, tender as they were, it was a great relief to take off our boots and go barefoot for a while when the ground was favorable." "This valley was very sandy and hard to walk over." "All the way had been hill and very tiresome walking." "At times we walked in the bed of the stream in order to make more headway, but my lameness increased and we had to go very slow indeed."

Manly's book makes very little mention of God, or the Almighty's role in his enforced walking, though he does describe the desert as the "most God-forsaken country in the world." He's extremely skeptical about "God's purpose" in imposing the ordeal on him, although others on the expedition take a more high-minded view.

Undoubtedly, walking may be used as a form of divine punishment, as variations on the story of the Wandering Jew indicate. Although he was supposedly present at the crucifixion, the Wandering Jew does not appear in the Bible, and seems to have been an invention of the thirteenth century, though refined and made more widely significant in the seventeenth century thanks to a series of pamphlets published in Germany from 1602 onward.

He goes by many names—Buttadeus, Ahaseurus, and Isaac Lacquedem among them—and is variously a shoemaker or Pontius Pilate's doorman. What is central to the myth is his mocking of Christ. He sees Jesus carrying the cross and taunts him for walking too slowly. Jesus certainly received worse insults, but on this occasion he did not turn the other cheek. He condemned the Jew to walk the earth until the time of the Second Coming.

There is some resemblance here to Cain, the fratricide, to whom God says, "A fugitive and a vagabond shalt thou be in the earth." This isn't quite the same as condemning him to "walk the earth," but a fugitive and a vagabond no doubt ends up doing a good amount of walking.

There's also a resemblance to Jules Winnfield, played by Samuel L. Jackson in Quentin Tarantino's *Pulp Fiction*, who says, "Basically, I'm just gonna walk the earth. You know, like Caine in *Kung Fu*—walk from place to place, meet people, get in adventures." It must have been such a delight for Tarantino when he was writing the script to invoke the biblical Cain and then immediately ditch him in favor of David Carradine's TV character.

An Armenian bishop visiting England in 1228 not only asserted that the Wandering Jew was alive and walking, but that he'd met him. This was good news for Christians. To have someone around who had been an eyewitness at the crucifixion proved the historical basis of Christianity. It was also a myth that had its uses for Jews. The Wandering Jew dramatized and personified the diaspora, while also emphasizing the anti-Semitism and downright vindictiveness of certain Christians.

It is also an extremely rich and inventive myth of punishment. The sinner is punished not only by enforced walking but by joyless immortality. He must walk forever but he isn't going anywhere. There's no destination, no journey's end. He is walking with no purpose, just killing time. He must exist in a state of constant fatigue, never experiencing rest, nor even the possibility of rest. He approaches an exhaustion that will never arrive, because if it did, then he would stop walking, and the divine power will not allow that.

Following the sighting by the thirteenth-century bishop, the Wandering Jew was spotted all over Europe throughout the seventeenth and eighteenth centuries, and at least once in the nineteenth century in the United States. According to Alex Bein in *The Jewish Question: Biography of a World Problem*, the "*Desert News* reported on Sept. 23, 1868, that he had visited a Mormon named O'Grady." How and why the Wandering Jew traveled to the United States must remain a question for speculation, but if he came by boat he must surely have spent the entire voyage walking around the deck. Perhaps he is walking still.

An Italian folktale, known as "Malchus at the Column," is a variant on the story of the Wandering Jew, and devises an even worse and more inventive punishment. Malchus, by this legend, was one of the Jews responsible for the crucifixion of Jesus, and although all the others were forgiven, Malchus remained unforgivable because he'd physically struck the Virgin Mary. Consequently, he was confined inside a mountain, and forced to walk endlessly around a column until the end of the world.

As the story "opens" Malchus has been walking in circles for so long that his footsteps have dug a deep circular trench in the earth and only his head appears above ground. When the path is trodden lower still and his head finally disappears, the world will come to an end and he will be sent to a place that God has prepared for him. I can't decide whether this would be an incentive to walk more quickly or more slowly.

These stories seem to involve a myth more ancient than Christianity, more the stuff of Sisyphus or Tantalus, but the notion of a punishment without limit or motion, without hope of rest, is truly horrifying. We do want our walking to take us somehere: we want it to have an end.


Non-Christian gods and non-Christian believers can also be passionately concerned with walking. Taoism, for example, employs various walking meditations that function as exercise, as spiritual practice, and ultimately as martial arts. The best known is Baguazhang, which is based on the *I Ching* and essentially involves walking in circles, sometimes known as "Turning the Circle." The technique is four thousand years old and is based on the Taoist principle of seeking stillness in motion. It's a way of walking that doesn't in the practical sense take you anywhere, although as a martial art it does enable the initiate to walk in such a way that he can defend himself against attackers coming at him from eight different directions.

It was a Taoist, a Chinese woman named Guo Lin, who, in the middle of the twentieth century, developed a series of spiritual exercises known as Walking Qigong or Guolin Qigong. Qigong is the ancient Chinese art of balancing and strengthening the "life force." Walking was her version of it, and she used it as a cure for cancer.

Guo Lin had had several bouts of cancer over more than a decade, along with the operations to "cure" her, but finally in 1964 doctors declared that the cancer had won, and Guo Lin was given six months to live. Being full of fight and perhaps thinking she had nothing to lose, by relying on instinct and trial and error, and consulting some texts that had been left to her by her grandfather, a Taoist monk, she developed a method that worked for her. There were bending and stretching exercises, the control of breathing, the massaging of acupressure points, but the cornerstone was walking for two hours per day. At the end of her allotted six months the cancer had gone.

By the 1970s Guo Lin was a living, walking legend, traveling around China spreading the word, teaching her technique to classes that sometimes contained four hundred eager learners. She continued in this way, revered and idolized, until her death in 1984.

There has so far been no large-scale scientific investigation of Guolin Qigong either inside or outside China. However, the anecdotal evidence is sufficiently impressive that millions of people, by no means all of them in China, practice it every day to prevent cancer.

Posited explanations for how or why Guo Lin's method works are unlikely to convince nonbelievers. One theory is that it simply increases oxygen supply, and this kills cancer cells. If only.

Another suggestion is that it is balancing the yin and the yang, which is, of course, what all Chinese medicine professes to do. Still, if you had cancer and were able to exercise and walk for two hours a day (by no means a given), why wouldn't you try it? Nowhere can I find any evidence that Taoism ever uses walking as a punishment.

Walking meditations are also employed in Buddhist practice, sometimes called meditation in action. Walking is one of the four asanas, or postures, in which the Buddha is depicted. A practicing Buddhist I know says he finds walking meditation much easier than sitting meditation because the mind doesn't drift as much when you walk. Walking forces concentration. You become aware of your body, your breathing, the sun, the air, and so on and this all helps to create—he tells me—Mindfulness.

He also tells me that the Buddha encouraged something called the Development of Lovingkindness meditation. While walking, whether in the town or the countryside, in or out of nature, ancient Buddhists would try to exude benevolence. In the towns this went out to their fellow man; in the countryside it went out to wild animals and was considered a very good way to avoid being attacked by snakes.


And so we come to Islam, the only religion I'm aware of that insists its adherents must undertake an arduous walk in the desert. All Muslims are implored to make a journey to Mecca, to participate in the hadj. These pilgrims are not required to walk all the way there (though a few do), but they have to do some walking when they arrive.

Among other rituals, they are required to follow in the footsteps of Muhammad, walking seven times around the Kaaba, the cube-shaped shrine in the center of the Great Mosque in Mecca. The first three circuits are to be taken quickly, the last four slowly, because that's the way Muhammad circled it. And as they walk, the pilgrims must try to touch the sacred Black Stone, part of the Kaaba, on each circuit.

There is currently a quota system in place: only two million Muslims per year are allowed to make the visit at hadj—many more would do so if they could—but that still represents a staggering number of people crammed into the Great Mosque for these religious circumambulations. It sounds like a recipe for pedestrian chaos rather than spiritual harmony, and film of pilgrims at the Kaaba shows a great seething slow-moving mass, but for obvious reasons I have no personal experience of it.

Someone who did was the English explorer Sir Richard Burton, who visited in 1853, in disguise, and went to elaborate lengths to measure the dimensions of the Kaaba, spending a good many hours walking with the rest of the pilgrims. There was much cursing and pushing, he reports, especially when he monopolized the Black Stone in order to see what it was made of (aerolite, he thought). At last he emerged "thoroughly worn out with scorched feet and a burning head—both extremities, it must be remembered, were bare."

Burton also tells us, "Many pilgrims refuse to enter the Ka'aba for religious reasons. Those who tread the hallowed floor are bound never again to walk barefooted." Is that a religious reason? He was also surprised to find that the Muslim circumambulations went counterclockwise. As an old India hand he was more familiar with the Hindu Pradakshina, the clockwise circular walking performed in Hindu temples around the sanctum sanctorum.

Ziauddin Sardar, a contemporary Muslim academic and journalist, who has completed hadj five times, reports that things have got worse rather than better since Burton's time. When pilgrims arrive at the Great Mosque, he says, they encounter the mutawwa, the Saudi religious police. To ensure that the walkers keep moving, the mutawwa hit them with long sticks. Sardar writes, "Pilgrims performing the tawaf or praying by the Kaaba are constantly hit on the head and asked to move, and not infrequently beaten and 'shooed' as though they were cattle." He also says that he has witnessed "unreported numbers" of pedestrians on their way to the Great Mosque who suffocate, are crushed underfoot, or die of heat stroke. Personally I find it hard to see the spiritual dimension in this aspect of walking, but then I am, of course, an infidel.

I used to be a bit of a snob about walking in the desert. I wanted millions of acres of untrodden, untouched, and uninhabited desert. If there was a trail or a ranger station or an information board or if I met another walker, I thought this was a terrible defilement, and that my desert walking experience was being spoiled.

Well, that was precious and stupid of me, and I've lightened up a lot, for a number of reasons. First, because I know that there aren't millions of acres of untrodden, untouched, and uninhabited desert available. Second, because I now realize that trails, ranger stations, and information boards can be helpful, might even in certain circumstances save your life. Third, because if you meet someone walking in the desert they're likely to be, if not exactly a kindred soul, at least someone with a shared interest. The other part of this equation is that most visitors to the desert aren't very serious walkers, or walkers at all. They drive, stop their car, walk no more than a few yards, take a couple of photographs, and drive on. If you walk even a couple of hundred yards off the beaten track you can be very alone indeed.

Just as important, I've learned the pleasures of the undramatic desert. If you go wandering around some celebrated desert attraction, White Sands or Zabriskie Point or the Grand Canyon, well, of course you're going to run into crowds of people. But if you go walking in, let's say, the Big Morongo Canyon Preserve in California, which is only about forty miles from Palm Springs, you'll certainly find some information, some designated trails, and even a rest room, but on most days you can be pretty sure of being the only person there. A desert walk, I realized, doesn't have to involve rolling sand dunes, fields of cacti, Joshua trees, breathtaking gorges, rattlesnakes, and so forth. It certainly doesn't have to involve spiritual enlightenment.

The desert, naturally, as St. Anthony proved, is a place of mirages, of fata morgana. The desert walker "sees" all manner of things that may or may not be there, figures viewed through a heat haze appearing to move relentlessly toward you but never quite arriving, or large expanses of sparkling, glittering water that turn out to be nothing but sand.

There are, however, one or two places where the water is not a mirage at all. Badwater in Death Valley is one of these. Badwater is a long, wide salt flat that stretches to the distant blue mountains. At 280 feet below sea level it's the lowest point in the western hemisphere. When I first visited Badwater, a decade and a half ago, you pulled off the road, parked on the dirt, and went wandering across the scorched, salted surface. Some of us did, but not many. Now there's a big parking lot, so everybody thinks there must be something really worth seeing and masses of people park and walk.

Sometimes, especially in the winter, there's water on the flat, low desert bed standing perfectly, eerily still, reflecting the mountains and the sky like a mirror. From a distance you can't possibly guess how deep the water is—it's easy to imagine it profound and limitless—but in fact large stretches are no more than a couple of inches deep.

In these conditions hundreds of people walk out from the parking lot, drawn into the emptiness, like true believers, like earthlings going out to meet the mother ship. But since there is no mother ship, nothing to believe in, they just go and investigate the water, discover how shallow and smooth it is, then walk a few yards into it and have their friends and family take pictures of them so they look as though they're walking on water.

Abul Hasan al-Shadhili, a thirteenth-century Sufi master, warned would-be mystics to avoid performing miracles such as walking on water. He regarded it as a distraction and a form of showing off. Of course there is some anti-Christian sentiment at play here, but also the idea that walking on water is a perfectly achievable goal.

And so, at Badwater, hundreds of people appear to go walking on water. It's playful, good-natured, and as far as I can see, not remotely sacrilegious. Even so, you have to think that it wouldn't mean nearly as much if we weren't all familiar with Jesus' biblical example. I found it impossible to avoid singing Leonard Cohen's line from his song "Suzanne": "Jesus was a sailor when he walked upon the water." But obviously this is nonsense. If there was ever a moment when Jesus *wasn't* a sailor it was precisely when he walked on the Sea of Galilee—when he was absolutely a pedestrian.

I also found myself thinking about a line from Jack Kerouac, a born Catholic turned self-invented Buddhist, and a man who did his share of walking in nature. He had serious doubts about LSD, chiefly because it seemed to offer an instant religious experience. He thought this was a cheat. He thought religious enlightenment was something you had to work for, that couldn't be found at the drop of a hat. He summed it up perfectly for me when he said, "Walking on water wasn't built in a day."

# THE WALKING PHOTOGRAPH

*Consulting the rules of composition before taking a
photograph is like consulting the laws of gravity
before going for a walk.*
—EDWARD WESTON

Garry Winogrand, walking on the crowded streets of
New York in the 1970s, carrying a Leica M4 with a
28mm lens, the leather strap wound tightly round his hand, the
camera being constantly raised and lowered to and from his eye,
turning his head, refocusing his gaze, looking for visual triggers,
for subjects, endlessly, relentlessly pressing the shutter, shooting
pictures, sometimes just shooting.

Winogrand walks, but not at the same pace as the pedestrians
around him, and sometimes he stops completely so that the flow
of people splits and eddies past, and sometimes he sees something on the other side of the street, and pushes through the
crowd, dashes over there, dodging traffic or forcing the traffic to
dodge him. Then he continues taking photographs. You'd think
that New York's angry, purposeful walkers would knock him out
of the way, walk all over him; but he's found a way to avoid that.

Sometimes he smiles and nods at the people he's photographing, offers a word or two, chats, and in the main nobody minds. It's a technique he's developed, a way of presenting himself as just another eccentric on the streets of New York, crazy, self-absorbed, obsessive but essentially harmless—which is not a complete misrepresentation of Winogrand.

And then somebody perceives him as something else. A woman, irate, offended, full of righteous indignation, believes that in photographing her, Winogrand has stolen something from her. "Hey, you took my picture!" she protests, and Winogrand, in his rough, tough, amused New York voice, says, "Honey, it's *my* picture now." It's an old story, and another one that I very much want to be true.


Garry Winogrand (1928–1984) was from the Bronx. He told Tod Papageorge that when he was about ten years old he walked the streets of his neighborhood until midnight to avoid going home to the family apartment, because "his parents did not put a high priority on privacy." The idea that the streets offer more privacy than the family home is one that needs no explaining.

Winogrand was a street photographer, by most reckonings the ultimate street photographer. The term is a porous one: even the most studio-bound of photographers occasionally takes a photograph on the street. And paparazzi are certainly street photographers of a sort, along with their modern mutations, the stalkerazzi and the snapperazzi—members of the public who happen to see a celeb in the street and take their picture.

You might also think it's a term that doesn't require much definition: if you take a photograph in the street you're a street photographer. Well, not quite. Eddie Adams was certainly in the street in Saigon in 1968 when he photographed the Vietnamese chief of police, Nguyen Ngoc Loan, walking up to a suspected Vietcong collaborator and shooting him in the head, but he wasn't quite a street photographer in the way that Winogrand was.

A street photographer, as we generally conceive it, is someone who finds subject matter not in exotic locales or war zones, but in quotidian settings, in public, in the city. If, in the process, he or she manages to make that setting look like an exotic locale or a war zone, then so much the better. There was a time when these photographs were often referred to as "candids," but nobody seems to use that word anymore. Perhaps candidness is no longer considered something that a photograph can offer us.

All my favorite photographers are, in some sense or another, at least some of the time, street photographers: Henri Cartier-Bresson, Robert Frank, William Klein, Diane Arbus, Stephen Shore, William Eggleston, Martin Parr, Bruce Gilden, as well as Winogrand. Some of these people view the world with a comparatively benign eye; others are downright brutal in their gaze. In either case the streets offer them the kind of subjects they're looking for, that they and their art need.

There are ways in which street photography might seem very straightforward. There's no need for props, lights, assistants, paid models, stylists, or any of the other detritus that some photographers carry with them. You simply go out with your camera and take pictures of what's there. There may be some premeditation, but in the end it's an improvised form with an unpredictable outcome, a sort of visual free jazz.

And yet a moment's thought tells you that there's nothing

straightforward about it at all. Much of street life is actually quite banal. Even in a city as full of grotesques as New York, for every character there are thousands of ordinary Joes. People come and go rapidly, without arranging themselves into attractive or dramatic tableaux.

Conflict and awkwardness may be part of the deal; nevertheless, the best street photographers do demonstrate something that looks like ease. They're at home in their environment, they're able to operate confidently in public, among people. Street photographers share a space with their subjects, are on equal footing, in the same place at the same time.

What makes a great street photographer is the amount of walking he or she does. Street photographers inevitably take a lot of photographs of people walking. Just as inevitably they themselves spend a lot of time walking as they look for subjects. They are walkers who photograph other walkers.

Luck plays an enormous part in street photography, and the cliché remains true that the more work you put in, the luckier you get. There are times when Winogrand seems to have had the luck of the devil. Every time he walked down the street, dwarves, identical twins, and people cuddling monkeys would appear and pose themselves for his delight.

In 1978, Winogrand moved to Los Angeles. Some of the work he did there is wonderful. One of my favorite photographs—I have a poster of it in my office—was taken at LAX airport and shows two women in superbly stylish 1960s dresses, heels, and hairdos, backs to the camera, walking toward the futuristic Theme Building. However, the move to L.A. coincided with Winogrand's going shutter-crazy. In the eight or so years he was there he took more than a third of a million pictures, or at least that's how often he pressed his camera's shutter. But this was not picture making or photography as most of us understand it. The vast majority of the film he exposed was left unprocessed. Some rolls were developed but never printed. Even when contact sheets were made he gave them only the slightest attention, never engaging with them long enough or seriously enough to do anything resembling editing.

Some of these contact sheets have been displayed in exhibitions and published in magazines, and although no photographer should be judged by the quality of his contact sheets, it appears from these that Winogrand had not only lost his luck, he had lost his eye, too. Apparently he also lost some of his basic technical competence when it came to exposure, processing, and camera shake.

Most significant, a lot of them are taken from a moving car. Often in his L.A. period Winogrand sat in the passenger seat and was driven around the city by various friends and associates while he shot relentlessly through the windshield or the open side window. He had always done this to some extent—quite a few of the photographs of the road trip depicted in his book *1964* are taken from a car, but by no means most. Maybe he thought this modus operandi was appropriate to Los Angeles. All the same, there's something dispiriting about it.

Of course a photographer can do whatever he wants, use any method that occurs to him, but for Winogrand this method of working seemed to mark a profound dislocation and separation. The pictures have a perfunctory, stolen look. Once he had been a fellow walker, a fellow traveler, sharing the same street, the same sidewalk, as his subjects; now he was doing drive-bys. He still photographed people, including people walking, but he also endlessly pointed his camera at parked cars, empty intersections, and blank streets.

John Szarkowski has written, "Many of the last frames seem to have cut themselves free from the familiar claims of art," which is a thrillingly elegant and charitable way of saying that a lot of these photographs seem to be of nothing in particular, though not quite of nothing at all.

In London I went to see Martin Parr, one of my very favorite photographers, and a man who was quick to say, "I'm not the biggest street photographer, you realize. The *real* street photographer I know is Bruce Gilden. He really does work on the streets, still, and he's very religious about going out."

Bruce Gilden was just a name to me at that time, although I'd seen and admired his work. And frankly Martin Parr seemed to be enough of a street photographer for most purposes. He was also the only street photographer I happened to know.

Parr made his reputation in England in the 1970s, with photographs showing very English people doing very English things, some working class, some posh. His subjects were the English seaside, English garden parties, horse trials, empty rugby grounds, people trudging through terrible English weather.

International success has taken him around the world and broadened his subject matter—international tourism is a major interest—but the eye is much the same. A recent collection of his work is in *The Phone Book,* a series of close-ups of people talking on their cell phones, photographs snatched in public or on the streets, often taken just a couple of feet from the subject's face.

We met at Martin Parr's London office, just a stone's throw from Bunhill Fields, Iain Sinclair's walking "epicenter." Parr accepted my basic premise that being a street photographer involves doing a lot of walking.

"Yes. Basically you keep walking and you think, 'God, this is boring, it's going nowhere,' and suddenly something will happen. So really all you do is keep walking, because you know that sooner or later you're going to get something. You become a hunter, if you like, a hunter-gatherer.

"The thing you've got to remember is, most of the time there's nothing happening and suddenly it *will* happen, but you can't have the time when it happens without having all the dull time, so even though you're not taking good pictures, you're in the rhythm. You know, you have to take some bad pictures, because if you only saved yourself for one good one you'd never take one at all, and suddenly you're onto something, and you might take two or three frames of the same shot."

In fact, this describes my own experience of walking without a camera. A walk is never equally fascinating for its whole length. Certain stretches may seem dull or mundane, and then suddenly you see a number of amazing things that make it all worthwhile.

I wondered if Martin Parr had developed a sense for loitering in certain places that were likely to produce the shots he was looking for. Did he ever simply lurk rather than walk?

"Sure. You're looking for a place where you know things might reveal themselves, but generally on the street you don't get much background, people take up most of the action, but I certainly know in the case of Bruce Gilden, he returns to the same place, he knows exactly where, the time of the day, the traffic flow in terms of people, and he'll keep going back to those places. You can almost recognize people, you know. You [the photographer] become almost part of the street furniture."

I asked what reaction he got from people he photographed on the street.

"It varies," he said. "Occasionally people say, 'What on earth are you doing?' I'm not as aggressive as Bruce Gilden. He's aggressive. If you appear guilty, then people are going to get cross with you. If you appear confident in what you're doing, it helps enormously. That's why Gilden gets away with it. He thinks it's his absolute right to be on the street photographing, and he's absolutely correct, of course. Therefore there is no problem, there is no issue, whereas I get people who write to me or I meet people who say, 'How can you do that, photograph strangers walking on the street?'"

Did he ever encounter aggression?

"Occasionally. It's inevitable. And more and more of course these days as people know their rights and it gets more difficult to be a street photographer. It's a dying tradition because now everyone sets everything up, and there are problems with model releases. It feels like an outdated mode. Philip-Lorca diCorcia is the last really modern street photographer, and of course he's moved on from that as well."

DiCorcia was the photographer who set up cinematic lighting rigs on the street, waited for people to walk into the frame where they were perfectly lit, and then pressed the shutter. He got into a whole lot of trouble for it, too. He was sued by a Jewish Orthodox priest, of eye-catching appearance, named Emo Nussenzweig, under New York's right-to-privacy laws that forbid the use of a person's likeness for commercial purposes without the person's permission. The case went to the Manhattan State Supreme Court, where it came down to a definition of commerce, or more properly, of art.

Even though diCorcia made money from the photographs, it was declared they were first and foremost art, and therefore he was protected under the First Amendment. This is something else Garry Winogrand might have said to the woman who protested his taking her picture. It's good to know that street photography is a form of free speech, but having to go to the Manhattan Supreme Court to prove it is the kind of thing that must deter newcomers to the field.

Equally, this law may make pedestrians feel especially vulnerable. They are protected from commerce but not from art. It's illegal for a company, or its advertising agency, to take a picture of you in the street and print it with a headline that says "This Man Eats Hamburgers" or "This Man Needs Life Insurance." But if there's no headline, or if there's a caption indicating that this is a piece of street photography taken by a serious street photographer, then you have no recourse. Personally, on balance, I think it is as it should be, but then nobody's made a ton of money by taking my photograph while I was walking on the street.

Martin Parr and I discussed Winogrand. We talked about his taking photographs from cars, and I said that it didn't seem quite right to me. Parr was quick to say you could take pictures any way you like; for instance, there's a British photographer named Tom Wood who takes "street photographs" of a rather special sort—the subjects are often walking in the street, but he's on a public bus. However, Parr tended to agree there was something not quite right about Winogrand's method.

"That's when he was going bonkers," said Parr. "He knew he was going to die and he was shooting like there was no tomorrow, because for him there was no tomorrow."


At the time I saw Parr I'd been trying to work out who took the first photograph of somebody walking. It was a natural subject for early photographers, but at first it was an impossible one. The long exposure times required meant that only the stationary world could be recorded and celebrated.

The first photograph to show a person is thought to have been taken in 1839 by Louis-Jacques-Mandé Daguerre. It's called "Paris Boulevard" and it shows trees, what appears to be an empty street, and a solitary standing man. Samuel B. Morse said of it: "The boulevard so constantly filled with a moving throng of pedestrians and carriages was perfectly solitary, except for an individual who was having his boots brushed."

By "solitary" he means deserted. Even though, when the picture was taken, the boulevard was full of pedestrians, they were moving too fast to be fully recorded by the camera and so simply failed to register. To be in motion was to be invisible.

Even Eugène Atget's photographs of Paris, taken over fifty years later, are haunted by moving specters, blurred ghosts of walkers who pass through the scene too rapidly to be recorded. Atget himself was a determined walker, but to appear in one of his photographs his subjects had to adopt a posed stillness.

Consequently, the works of William Fox Talbot, Matthew Brady's Civil War pictures, and William Jackson and Timothy O'Sullivan's American West are all essentially still lifes. For his

1840 self-portrait Hippolyte Bayard found it useful to depict himself as a drowned man.

There's a photograph by Charles Nègre, dated 1852, that shows three chimney sweeps walking along a Parisian embankment. The pose looks natural enough, and was praised as such by Nègre's contemporaries, but it *is* a pose. There's a hint of motion blur, but it comes about because the subjects can't quite keep still, not because they're actually walking.

From 1859 onward George Washington Wilson, of Aberdeen, published a series of stereographs, some of which record street scenes. There are certain technical quirks of the stereographic process that help to freeze action. It's also a fact of photographic life that the farther the subject is from the camera, the slower the shutter speed required to freeze it. Washington Wilson's stereographs do indeed show people walking. A typical image depicts a crowded Princes Street in Edinburgh, with many pedestrians, but they're small and far away. You can tell that the people are really walking but you can't tell the identity of any individual walker.

It was Eadweard Muybridge, in the last quarter of the nineteenth century, with his "motion studies" and his battery of linked cameras, their shutters firing sequentially, who first photographed the process of human walking, although not until after he'd photographed the process of equine trotting. Muybridge had been asked by Leland Stanford to resolve the question of whether all four of a horse's hooves ever leave the ground at the same time as they move in a fast trot. As we all now know, they do.

Muybridge began considering the matter as early as 1872, but there were gaps in his work, caused by personal crises and professional commitments. A single negative from 1877, now lost, showed Stanford's horse Occident with all four feet off the ground, and the case was proved, but by then it was clear that Muybridge's methodology had other uses. In fact, he had photographed people in motion from the time he started his work, but his major investigations into the ways the human body moves were started in 1882 under the patronage of the University of Philadelphia. The results were published as a book titled *The Human Figure in Motion: An Electrophotographic Investigation of Consecutive Phases of Muscular Action.* (I tried to consult a first edition of this book and failed; a copy is listed in the catalog of the British Library but is declared "missing.") Walking was far from Muybridge's only concern. He showed men playing tennis, baseball, and cricket, and women dancing together or helping each other bathe. But for me the walking pictures remain the most fascinating because they reveal the magical nature of something we take so much for granted. The revelation is helped along by the fact that the people in the photographs are in most cases partially undressed, and sometimes completely naked.

When I first saw Muybridge's photographs, knowing little about their origins or purpose, I remember finding them highly charged sexually, not arousing exactly, but nevertheless fetishistic and genuinely odd. I can't believe I'm alone in this. Muybridge's figures exist in some strange, unspecified world, moving in front of a black background marked with a white grid. There's obviously something of an experimental nature going on here, but it doesn't look precisely or narrowly scientific. It looks more personal and obsessive than that.

Some of the most striking of Muybridge's images show a naked walking man who from the neck up looks like an ancient patriarch, with wild white hair and beard. From the neck down, however, he looks like a much younger man, with a strong muscular body, and in some of the photographs he's displaying extremely large testicles. The oblivious and irony-free Rebecca Solnit writes, "Halfway through his fifties, he was still straight-backed and strong, though age is apparent in the whiteness of his beard and the strained skin of his neck as he raises a tool." The model is Muybridge himself. Erwin Faber, who worked with Muybridge, reported that he looked so much like Santa Claus that when he went walking, children would often stop him in the street and ask for presents.

These days we're encouraged to see Muybridge's images as both high art and high science, and Muybridge's own Victorian public seems to have shown few signs of being shocked or offended by them, which frankly surprises me. Muybridge's work was available in popular as well as highly expensive limited editions, and he regularly gave public lectures in which he demonstrated his zoopraxiscope, a projector that enabled him to put the separate still images together again and create the illusion of movement.

Muybridge's zoopraxiscope makes him, by many accounts, the father of the motion picture, and for me this was one of those fall-off-the-chair moments: the point in history at which we could take a still photograph of a man walking was essentially the same moment at which we could also take a moving picture of a man walking.

I had always thought that Muybridge's work was the inspiration for Marcel Duchamp's *Nude Descending a Staircase*, but Duchamp himself rather vaguely claimed to have been inspired by the later work of Étienne-Jules Marey, a scientist first and a photographer second (the opposite of Muybridge). Marey was a physiologist, the inventor of chronophotography, who investigated the movements of birds and insects and a whole menagerie of animals before turning his attention to human locomotion. He was a contemporary of Muybridge's and they were aware of each other, but most of his work on human locomotion came after Muybridge's.

Marey did, however, pioneer the use of "motion capture" suits, with white stripes on the arms and legs to record motion, the kind of thing used today in computer animation and regarded as very high-tech.

Incidentally, the process Muybridge used to investigate equine trotting would pretty much destroy the human sport of racewalking. Historically, walking was defined as a form of locomotion in which a part of the foot always had to be in contact with the ground, giving rise to the bizarre and faintly ludicrous gait of the serious racewalker. But modern cameras are so rigorous in their gaze, they show that the vast majority of racewalkers, even the very best of them, fail this basic test. The naked eye can't pick up the airborne moment but a modern camera certainly can. Attempts have been made to redefine the sport in terms of what the naked eye can or can't detect, but that's clearly unsatisfactory. You either leave the ground or you don't. Once technology has determined that most of a sport's practitioners are breaking the sport's most basic rule, things are unlikely to go well.

And so I went to visit Bruce Gilden, the man Martin Parr considered the greatest pure street photographer and, as I discovered, one of New York's fiercest walkers. He specializes in gritty, grainy, black-and-white, flash-lit grotesques, the misshapen, the troubled, and the troubling. He's drawn to the ones with the bad skin and the bad teeth, with noses that jut and droop, mouths that hang slackly open or clench with tension or around fat cigars. He's a fan of bad makeup, bad hair, bad wigs, of clothes that are too big or too small, out of style or were never quite in style in the first place. Sometimes his characters look terrifying; sometimes they look terrified. They may be wild-eyed or dead-eyed, obese or skeletal, mad or maddening, scarred or deformed, hyperaware or utterly oblivious. If he can get a couple of these opposing types in the same frame, that's great, but often the frame is so tight it will only hold one person. Gilden operates at close range, Leica in one hand, flashgun in the other. There's nothing discreet or clandestine about the process. He's right in the faces of his sub-jects. They are in transit, in turmoil, and it's only the flash and the magic of the camera that freeze and hold them still for a moment before the chaos engulfs them again. Bruce Gilden and New York were made for each other.

I met him in the offices of the Magnum photo agency in Man-hattan. He was sixtyish, lean, balding, bearded, scruffy in a com-fortable way, alert, intense, big-eyed, a serious man who laughs a lot. A part of Gilden conforms to everybody's idea of what a New Yorker is or should be: motormouthed, tough, abrupt yet warm.

I tried to explain why I wanted to talk to him and gave him my spiel about street photographers having to do a lot of walk-ing and in the process photographing a lot of walkers.

"Sure," he said. "If you don't walk you're not gonna get the picture."

That might have been the end of it right there. Fortunately, Bruce Gilden is a man who likes to talk.

"My style," he said, "is very predatory, like Moriyama had a book called *The Hunter* years ago and I was always intrigued by the title. When I started, I liked these social-documentary-type photographs. Dorothea Lange, Henri Cartier-Bresson. I like the street. I like being around people. Well, I do and I don't, OK.

"Anyway, when I started I went to Coney Island and did work on Coney Island, because for me I don't like to talk to people, I mean I will if I have to in the street, but I'm basically shy and also I have a fear factor. I'm a physical guy, I'm quick-tempered, so what that means is that I'm afraid of violence but also I'm violent. I have a very good sense of where danger is, who can be dangerous, I'm streetwise, OK, so having said that, you know when you put your camera up and put it in someone's face and you come from a background like mine there could be fire, you know, it could be quite bad, so I've learned to have a very good bedside manner.

"In the early days I went to Coney Island because it's a meeting area, there were people there, interesting kinds of people. You didn't have to ask to photograph people. You could ask if you wanted to but you're in a freak zone, so why ask?

"The pictures I took were quite traditional, documentary pictures. Cartier-Bresson was an influence; well, I shouldn't say that. I liked his pictures OK, and I was able to do that type of picture, but then I said, 'Wait a second, who could do Cartier-Bresson better than Cartier-Bresson? Why would I want to be a little Bresson? What could I add to it?' So it evolved. I liked film noir. My influence is black-and-white television, and my father. My father was a film-noir character; he was about five foot seven, two hundred twenty pounds, gray hair, pinkie ring, smoked cigars, racketeer-looking. I idolized him when I was five years old. He was everything. He was the fireman, he was George Washington, you name it, it was him."

Had he ever photographed his father?

"No, because I don't photograph people I know, maybe because I am very ironic and very satirical and sarcastic, so I don't. People have said in the past, and in the present also, but it has been said that what Bruce does is really easy, he photographs characters. No. It's not easy."

And why so confrontational, so in your face?

"I don't want to be accused of sneaking something. 'Hey you, are you taking a picture of me? What are you? A sneak?' But sometimes I'm so close that people think, 'Oh yeah, he took a picture of something back there behind me because he can't be that close.' But when you use the flash people know you took a picture. You can't say, 'I didn't take a picture.' So I'm quite honest usually unless there's really a lot of danger.

"Since I'm quite an emotional type of guy, a physical type of guy, was a good athlete, and I like to be close to people 'cause I want to take their guts out, it evolved that I would get very close and use a flash.

"I used to have a schedule. No longer. I used to try to go out every day. Now I haven't been out for two months. I had jobs, my daughter was playing soccer in England, but generally I would go out about two, two-thirty in the afternoon and stay out till it gets almost dark, but the problem here for me is that I've been on the street so long, you know, I'm trotting over the same ground. And there aren't so many characters as there used to be, so you know the city is shifting, I'm getting older, things are changing, the world is smaller."

I'd heard that he had certain set daily routes that he'd walk constantly while looking for people to photograph.

"Sure. I'd go on Fifth Avenue from like Forty-ninth Street to Fifty-seventh, up and down, up and down, up and down, one side of the street, too, not the other, the west side. It's quite funny, you know. And Broadway between Forty-third and Forty-seventh, the west side, it'll be darker on that side of the street.

"I used to work Forty-second Street when it was a little bit of a hovel, but you had to be careful there, people really didn't want to be photographed. When I photographed there in the mid-eighties you had these young kids pickpocketing people, black kids, and one day, you know, I had my camera and they gave me a little shit, they were maybe thirteen but they weren't little, and I said to the guy, 'Listen, if you don't like it let's go round the corner.' That's the way I felt, OK, so we became friendly, OK, then about five, six years later I'm on the train, I must have been living in Brooklyn Heights, and I saw the kid. I didn't know him but I said, 'Hi, how you been?' and he said, 'Oh, I've been in prison, you know.' These were no good, these kids, so their whole life would be in and out of prison, so we talked a little bit and . . ."

So, I said, inviting him round the corner for a fight was enough to make a friend for life.

"Of course, because if they respect you they're fine. If they don't respect you they'll shit all over you. A cop once said to me, 'What the fuck are you doing taking these pictures?' And I'm an anti-police guy. He said, 'If you took a picture of my wife and me walking on the street like that, I'd knock you out.'

"I said, 'You could try.' Who was he to talk to me that way, you know? So we became friends. It's all about respect. If they respect you, it's fine. If they don't, then you have a problem.

"And, you know, I'm not the toughest guy in the world, but I'll stand up for my rights, within reason, though there are times when you have to put your tail between your legs and not take that picture.

"And if you're walking a lot, you can't walk as well when you get older, you don't react as fast and even some things mentally go through my head, like I'll say why should I slam the camera in that eighty-year-old's face, you know?

"Whereas before I'd only be deterred by the fear factor; the fear factor would say, 'You're going to get your ass kicked.' You know, I've challenged people in the street. I can be quite ferocious but I'm also not stupid.

"I walk hard in the streets, OK. Even when I'm not taking pictures. I was coming out of the subway the other day and I know when people are jerking with me, and there was this black guy, about thirty-five, solid, and he was going to get me, you know, I saw it, so I armed him, you know, with my elbow and he looked at me and said, 'What are you doing?' and I said, 'Well, you know, I didn't hear you say excuse me,' and I guess he knew that I wasn't just going to roll over, so he kept going. But you have to walk hard and if you walk hard and look people in the eye and I'm quite aggressive, I really don't want to fight because I already lost one camera in a fight and I lost the lens, too, so it was an expensive day for me.

"But if you walk hard here and you're smart, then people don't think you're weak. See, I find that if I'm strong and I tell people,

'If you don't like it, call a cop,' it discourages a lot of people. Once you show weakness, weak people take over. I want this and I want that and you're not going anywhere, and then it'll lead to more things and they'll start touching you, start grabbing your arm, 'Oh, I want the film.' So I think my mantra is I deal with it all the same way and the same attitude, that's it, I don't make an exception unless there are six guys, then I make an exception, you know, when I'm caught, then I try to look for the nearest exit. I never run. I walk. If you run, then you look like you're in the wrong.

"I'm very smart in the street, very streetwise. And I'll be the first person to give someone a hand. There was a lady a few years ago and a black kid was annoying her. I went over to the lady, she was crying, so I said, 'Don't worry,' took the kid, and I threw him into these bushes. I can be kind but I can also be nasty. So . . . I'm a good friend, I'm not a good enemy."

This sounded to me like the authentic voice of the New York walker. I thought it might be fun to be Bruce Gilden's friend but not easy. When I left him I felt invigorated. There was something exciting in the way he described walking in New York as a risky activity, a form of combat, a struggle for dominance, sometimes a contact sport. I thought there was something very familiar and accurate about it, too. New York is a city where the people not only enjoy getting in your way as you're walking down the street, they'll actually go out of their way to obstruct your progress. They'll inconvenience themselves for the greater pleasure of inconveniencing you.

But there's a certain kind of hard walker, or perhaps a certain kind of crazy bastard, that people, even on the streets of New York, do leave room for. He looks madder and more determined than most, with a walking style that says "Get out of my way," and most people do, because it's also saying more than that. It's saying "Get the *fuck* out of my way, get the fuck out of my face." It's saying "Fuck you. And if you've got a problem with that, then OK, let's take it round the corner." If you're looking for an argument when you're walking in New York, you can find one on every block.

As I walked away from the Magnum offices I started to move really fast and hard, my idea of the way Bruce Gilden walked, determined, fierce, kind of angry. It was only an act, only a pose that I was trying on for size, but I was serious about it, in some way I meant it, and it worked. It was strange and oddly gratifying because people really did start to move aside for me, to get out of my way. I don't know if they really thought I was a madman looking for trouble, but they were taking no chances and I didn't blame them. On most days I'd have done exactly the same. Most days you steer clear; you look at this poor bastard and see what New York has done to him, turned him into a furious walking monster. You have pity and contempt, a certain amount of fear, and maybe just a little sympathy. And then on other days you realize that the furious walking monster is you. What happens when you meet another of your own sort, when a Bruce Gilden walks into another Bruce Gilden, doesn't bear thinking about. You probably wouldn't want to be standing in the street next to it, but it'd be really interesting to see a photograph of it.

# WALKING HOME AND AWAY
# FROM HOME

*If you would attain to what you are not yet, you must*
*always be displeased by what you are. For where you*
*are pleased with yourself, there you have remained.*
*Keep adding, keep walking . . .*
—attributed to St. Augustine

My mother always said, in what at first might sound like an approving way, that as a toddler I'd been very eager to walk and had learned the skill early. Then, in a less approving way, she'd add that perhaps I'd walked *too* early, while the bones in my legs were still soft, and that's why I'd developed such terrible bowlegs. I'm not sure that I have bowlegs at all, but if I do, then the bowing is so slight that nobody except my mother has ever remarked on it. I always said to her it was because I was so eager to get away. Welcome to my childhood.

I was born on the kitchen table of my grandparents' house, literally in a dead-end street in northern England, in the steelmaking city of Sheffield, in a tough, poor, lively working-class suburb called Hillsborough. The majority of the family lived within walking distance of one another. For that matter they lived within walking distance of everything they needed: shops, pubs, dog track, football ground, betting shop, church. The steel factories my uncles worked in were equally nearby. Next to them were the candy and soda factories where my female relatives worked. Everybody walked to work. Everybody walked everywhere. Everything you could want was right there, unless you happened to want something else.

My parents and I lived in my grandparents' house until I was about five years old, when we moved into subsidized public housing, ending up in a "council estate" in a place called Longley. We had only gone a few miles, and we went back to Hillsborough at least once a week, but it was spoken of as though we'd moved to the outer fringes of the twilight zone.

An English council estate is similar to, but culturally very different from, an American housing project, and I think the name says a great deal. Both are places where the poor, underprivileged, and undereducated live, but Britain likes it to sound as though its poor people are on some grand country manor, while America prefers to think they're part of a science fair experiment.

Longley was regarded as one of the "good" council estates. "Good" meant low on crime, not bad schools, not too many problem families. These things are comparative and the gradations were very fine. Eventually my parents moved into the private sector and bought their own house, but that took some time. I was well into my adolescence before they made the move.

Longley was the place I grew up and the place I knew best. I'd walked all its streets endlessly, and it was a very long time since I'd set foot there.

Certain ironists like to say that Sheffield is just like Rome: it's built on seven hills. There, of course, the resemblance ends. And Roman citizens never had to cope with Sheffield winters, long, hard, with plenty of snow. Because I'd got into the "good school" over on the other side of the city I had to take two bus rides to get there, one downhill from home into the center of town, then a second one uphill to where the school was.

When the snow fell buses could get down the hills but not up. It wasn't unusual to find yourself stranded in the city center surrounded by hills that buses couldn't get up. You either walked to school or you walked home. Sometimes you did both. When I complained to my mother about the misery and downright unfairness of this state of affairs she said I should be like Felix the Cat, and keep on walking.

There's a persuasive theory that the hills of Sheffield are what keep the old people's hearts ticking and in good health. All over the city little old men and women struggle to walk up impossibly steep hills, often weighed down by shopping, and they struggle and stop for breath every now and again, but they keep going. They keep walking.

My oldest friend, Steve, who still lives in Sheffield, has in-laws who live on the flatlands of Hull, a city fifty miles away, and at one time they used to visit him in Sheffield, but they gave it up. The hills were too much for them. A lifetime's easy walking on level ground had left them without the right stuff to tackle Sheffield's hills.


There were many things my family didn't do very well, and holidays were the worst of them. Both my parents seemed to believe in holidays and think they were a good thing. They wanted to go away somewhere, and yet there was never anywhere they particularly wanted to go or anything they particularly wanted to do when they got there. By default, we more often than not went to Blackpool, a seaside town that's easy to praise for its gritty working-class vulgarity and energy, until you get there.

My mother always complained that there was nothing to *do* on holiday in Blackpool, that all people did all day was "mooch around"—walk up and down the seafront. She had a point. The boardinghouses we stayed in had a ridiculous and strictly enforced rule that "guests" had to be out of the premises from ten in the morning till five in the evening. You were paying for bed, breakfast, and an evening meal, nothing else. That was a lot of time to stay outside. Blackpool had a beach backing onto the Irish Sea, and both beach and sea were generally too cold and bleak to engage with, but it had a six-mile-long promenade known as the Prom. That was where you spent the day mooching.

Along the Prom there were fairground rides, a local version of the Eiffel Tower, bingo halls, souvenir shops, stalls selling fish and chips, seafood, sticks of rock candy, but we never went to these places. My parents regarded them as a frivolous and needless expense. Going to the seaside was holiday enough. Why gild the lily? Instead we joined all the other moochers, walking up and down the Prom, all day long, dragging their miserable kids behind them, not looking as though they were having the slightest bit of fun. The Nicholson family fit right in.

I can't swear that we really walked the full length of the Prom in both directions every day, but it certainly felt like it. Even though there was public transportation, and even though we weren't really going anywhere, my dad insisted we go there on foot. Today I wonder whether he was enjoying himself or punishing himself, or punishing my mother and me, or whether he was simply doing his best and really didn't know how to take or share pleasure.

The problem of what to do as a family was never solved. After my father died I did my best to be a good son to my widowed mother. I was living in London at the time and she would come to stay and I'd try to entertain her. It was never easy. There was still never anything she wanted to do, and my attempts to second-guess were hopeless. When I suggested once that we might have a walk round the London Zoo, she reacted as though I'd suggested she might like to watch the goings-on in a brothel. And so we did nothing much except wander round London's streets and shops. We covered miles, and she never complained, but I always had the terrible feeling that I was extending an unhappy family tradition.

My dad wasn't good at teaching me things. I was a slow learner and he was short of patience. When his first attempts to teach me how to operate, for instance, a yo-yo, a tenon saw, or eventually a motorcar didn't bring instant results, there generally wasn't a second attempt. He had fixed ideas about how things should be done, including walking.

I was happy to amble along, slouching, hands in pockets in a sloppy, uncoordinated way, which I think is normal for kids. In the course of writing this book I've spent time watching children walk, and they're all over the place, no rhythm, no balance, no sense of purpose. Maybe it's because they don't have anywhere to go.

My dad pointed out that if you swung your arms you made much better progress. Your arms acted like pendulums carrying you inexorably forward. I could see he was right. I tried it. It worked. This was one of the few things I managed to pick up at the first attempt. My father wasn't nearly as pleased as I'd have liked him to be.

There was nothing pretentious or aspirational about my father. In fact, it always seemed to me he put far too much energy into insisting on how ordinary he was. Nevertheless, he displayed a curiously aristocratic belief that the rules applying to other people didn't apply to him. So if we were out walking and saw signs that said "Private, Keep Out, No Trespassing," they made no impression on my dad. As far as he was concerned these notices were intended only for others.

It might have been nice to think my father was a socialist firebrand who refused to obey the rules imposed upon him by the landowning classes, and in the north of England there was a Bolshy local tradition of walking where you weren't supposed to walk: political walking. In 1932 five hundred or so walkers performed a famous and symbolic "mass trespass" on Kinder Scout in the nearby Peak District, trying to assert the right to walk across private open land that was used only twelve days a year for grouse shooting. There were clashes with police and game-keepers, some fights, some arrests, but eventually, many years later, a "right to roam" was established in England. It was, and still is, regarded as a mighty triumph for the working classes of northern England. My father, however, didn't quite belong to this tradition. He wasn't defiant, nor was he oblivious, but it was as though he believed that the makers of "No Trespassing" signs would surely regard him as a special case.

And so one Sunday morning, when I was about ten years old, we found ourselves tramping along a woodland path on the outskirts of Sheffield, and we were confronted by a "Keep Out" sign. Naturally my father ignored it and we kept on walking. We hadn't gone more than twenty or thirty steps before we were con-fronted by a large man sitting on the back of a large horse, and the man was furious. He was evidently the landowner and the one responsible for putting up the sign. There was a good deal of "What the bloody hell do you think you're doing on my land? Can't you read?" and so on. He was pompous, fleshy, tweedy. He did have a sort of authority about him, perhaps because he was on horseback, but that didn't prevent him from also appearing ridiculous.

If it had been up to me, then or now, I'd simply have lied to the man, said that I hadn't seen the sign, apologized, and retreated, but my dad didn't quite do that. He didn't deny that he'd read the sign but, he said, surely no rational person, however protec-tive he felt toward his land, could possibly object to a man such as my dad and his young son walking through their woods on a Sunday morning.

My dad was so reasonable and so utterly mistaken that the man, though still angry, was taken aback. He'd been ready for a confrontation, raised voices, an escalating argument, but my father's suggestion that he might have put up the sign without really meaning it left him flabbergasted. The best he could do was say, "How would you like it if I came and rode my horse through your garden?"

My father appeared to be giving the matter serious thought, then said, "Well, I take your point."

I didn't take any such point. Something was stirring in my bosom. Let him bring his horse to our garden, I thought. There'd just about be enough room for the horse to stand up, and his presence would surely have caused a gathering of local toughs and hooligans who, in my imagination at least, would express their class hatred, abuse the man, and probably steal his horse.

No son likes to see his father defeated, and this was certainly an argument my father couldn't have won, but I thought he'd gained a sort of victory by refusing to argue at all. We turned and walked back the way we'd come, rather slowly and overcasually. I took some comfort in thinking that even though we'd been told off, we had at least successfully trespassed on the pompous ass's land. We'd also succeeded in making him hugely angry and that had its satisfactions. My father wasn't consoled by any of this, and he continued to be genuinely amazed that anyone could be so utterly unreasonable as not to want him to walk on their land.


When I was in my early teens I was one of a small group of boys from my grammar school who met up in the center of Sheffield one evening to see our first adult film, telling our parents that we were going to one another's houses. Adult films weren't then what they are now, and the one we'd chosen to see was *The Graduate*. I'm amazed now to discover that the movie was released in 1967, and I'm sure we saw it first-run, but that would mean we were all about fourteen years old, which seems unlikely. No doubt we felt much older, and certainly tried to look it as we bought our tickets at the box office, which we did without any trouble.

*The Graduate* was far too sophisticated for our boyish tastes and we were severely disappointed. It also finished surprisingly early and we all went our separate ways, but going straight home and arriving back so soon would have made my parents suspicious. So I dawdled, eventually caught a bus back to the Longley Estate, and got off a couple of stops too early so I could walk part of the way home and kill more time. Wandering the streets at night seemed to be a safe thing for a boy to do, largely because there was nobody else on the streets.

The houses were small and tightly packed together, and there were lights on inside, and I remember I could hear televisions playing through the walls. There was a sense of quiet order. The whole area seemed to be dormant, and my presence felt sneaky and intrusive, like staring at someone while they're asleep.

I walked all around what I considered to be "my" neighborhood. I walked along all the streets that I knew, past the school, the park, and the few local shops and between the four patches of open grass in front of them known, incomprehensibly, as "the Plantation," and along one or two streets that I didn't know very well at all. I felt thoroughly detached, an unseen and unknown outsider. You might have thought there was something voyeuristic about it, although there was nothing to see.

Ultimately, however, it was all very dull. I had the sense that nothing interesting had ever happened in these streets, and that nothing much ever would. I walked for what seemed a very long time until I felt I'd exhausted all the possibilities of the neighborhood. I went home. As I walked into the house, after having had what I would later come to think of as an important moment, and having thought I'd walked for a good long time, my mother simply said, "You're back early."

Only much later did I read this passage in Jack Kerouac's *Dharma Bums:* "Walk some night on a suburban street and pass house after house on both sides of the same street each with the lamplight of the living room, shining golden, and inside the little blue square of the television, each living family riveting its attention on probably one show; nobody talking; silence in the yards; dogs barking at you because you pass on human feet instead of wheels."

I had seen no little blue television squares on my walk—this was a neighborhood where people kept their curtains tightly closed at night—but I took his point.


When, years after the event, I tried to tell my friend Steve about the way I'd felt that night, he joked that I was lucky not to have been arrested, but that was never likely to be a problem. The streets were as free of police as they were of criminals.

Steve was, and is, my oldest friend, and has been since we were both six years old. My first memories of him were as the smiling little kid who'd fallen in the schoolyard and broken his arm. Then later, the very day the cast came off, he'd fallen and broken it again. Now that both my parents were dead, Steve was my only remaining contact with Sheffield.

He was also a reminder of who and what I might have been. He'd been smart enough to go to college for four years and get a degree, but then he'd come right back, got a job in local government, married, and had two kids. He was a smart man in lots of ways, witty, thoughtful, a very talented guitar player, and yet there was something frustrated about him, and that frustration seemed to come from never having got out of the city he was born in.

Steve was also the man with whom I'd got my criminal record. We'd been hitchhiking from Sheffield to London, while at college, had made some bad decisions, and found ourselves stranded on the motorway, the English equivalent of a freeway, where walking is strictly forbidden. We walked gingerly, knowing we shouldn't be there, but were spotted by motorway police, picked up, and eventually each charged with being "a pedestrian on a motorway." As far as either of us can tell this hasn't blighted our subsequent lives.

I decided to go back to Sheffield for a long weekend of walking around the places of my youth, and it was natural that I stay with Steve and his wife, Julia. Natural, too, that I should invite Steve to come walking with me. He reckoned he could only do some of it.

These days he was suffering with his back, which sometimes

made walking too difficult and painful. He said he'd do what he could. On that basis he didn't come with me when I did my first walk around Hillsborough.

Saturday afternoons, as I was growing up, were always spent at my grandmother's house. My mother and I were deposited there while my father went off and did fatherly things. I didn't much want to be there, trapped in my grandmother's living room while she and my mother discussed the latest family scandals, and eventually a time came when I was eleven years old or so and it was reckoned that even though I was too young to be left alone in my parents' house, I was old enough to be allowed to wander the streets of Hillsborough.

My mother always told me to go to the park, but the park seemed to offer less than the scruffy but busy shops in the neighborhood. There was a single shopping street, but it changed its name halfway along, from Langsett Road to Middlewood Road, running from the park at one end to a former barracks at the other.

The shops along the street weren't really places an eleven-year-old could browse. A Woolworth's was the most kid-friendly, and I remember there being more pork butchers than any community would rightly need, one of them called Funks, a name that seems much odder to me now than it did at the time. There was also a shop that made fresh crumpets on the premises, and there was some pleasure to be had in staring in through the window watching the crumpets come to life, rise and bubble before me on a hot plate, but even with the other attractions—a place to buy comics, a newsagent that sold toys—this didn't really add up to an afternoon's entertainment.

Nevertheless, I entertained myself in a way that then seemed perfectly natural, and which now seems a bit weird. There were two automobile showrooms on the street, one at either end of the stretch of shops. The one up by the park specialized in the NSU Prinz, a small, humpy, rear-engined German car, not quite serious-looking, odd rather than exotic, but a fascinating curiosity to me. The ones I liked best were finished in a gleaming lacquered red that made them look like giant toys.

The dealership at the other end sold American cars: Nash Ramblers, mostly station wagons. At the time it did seem a little bit odd that anyone would be trying to sell Nash Ramblers in a working-class enclave of Sheffield; today it seems utterly inconceivable. Who would ever have bought one? I liked them a lot and I always looked out for them, but I don't remember ever seeing one on the road. How would you get spare parts? Which local Sheffield mechanic would be prepared to work on a car like that?

In fact, there are times when I wonder whether it was some sort of deep-cover CIA operation, that the Nash Ramblers were only there because of the NSU presence at the other end of the street. If those Germans thought they could sell weird cars in Sheffield, then they'd have to compete with American know-how.

That's a recent thought. Back then it seemed that these competing enterprises had been put there for my delight, and the two showrooms became the two poles of my Saturday afternoon walks. I would stand in front of one of them, for quite a long time, rapt, quietly excited, looking at the bright, shiny, unfamiliar cars, then I'd walk the length of the street to the other showroom, do the same thing there, then walk back to the other, then back again, and so on until the afternoon was used up.

I went back to Hillsborough on a rainy afternoon in September. In the intervening years Hillsborough had become infamous around certain parts of the world. Hillsborough is not only the name of a district, it's also the name of a soccer ground where the Sheffield Wednesday Football Club is based, and where the "Hillsborough disaster," or sometimes "Hillsborough tragedy," took place. On April 15, 1989, at a sold-out cup match between Nottingham Forest and Liverpool, thousands of fans packed into a limited standing area that was simply too small to accommodate them. As people packed in from the rear, those at the front were crushed. In all, ninety-six people were killed, and some of them died standing up, unable to fall to the ground because of the density of the crowd; hundreds more were injured.

The Liverpool fans are famous for singing "You'll Never Walk Alone," a song of Christian, or at least spiritual, consolation when sung in *Carousel* that becomes a war chant in the mouths of football supporters.

I began to walk the length of the Hillsborough shopping street. It was cold, it was raining, but my curiosity drove me on. It would have been amazing to find there were two car showrooms still in business, and I was not amazed. The building that had housed the NSU dealership was now Meade House, belonging to something called the Sheffield City Council's Children and Young Peoples' (that apostrophe is all theirs) Directorate Social Care Services. The showroom windows through which

I'd once looked at cars were gone, and blank, insubstantial, cream-colored walls had been built in their place. The effect was bleak and characterless, and I could only guess at what terrible good works were planned and executed there.

Naturally the Rambler showroom wasn't there either. Even the building that had contained it had gone and there was now a bus station in its place. And so again I walked between these two poles: between the bus station and the outpost of the Young Peoples' Directorate. There was a lot about the place and its atmosphere that had stayed the same. The pokey, failing little shops were still pokey and failing, even if they offered goods and services that hadn't been available when I'd been a boy, such as the crystal-selling shop, now closed, and the Hollywood Nail Bar, "American Style," it claimed. But the newsagents and the betting shops and the place selling gas fires didn't seem to have changed at all.

The pubs weren't much different either. When I was growing up, the name "Shakespeare" had been spoken daily by some family members since The Shakespeare was the name of one of the local pubs they drank in. It had now changed its name to The Shakey, but it looked as unwelcoming to me now as it had back then.

And there was still an excess of pork butchers, including Funks. In business since 1890, it said on the canopy outside, and clearly not about to give up now. There was a line of people queuing up to buy hot pork sandwiches with applesauce, stuffing, and crackling. I joined the line, and as I waited I checked my GPS to see how far apart the twin poles of my childhood actually were. I knew that my eleven-year-old's horizons were limited, but I now discovered that the distance between the two showrooms had been scarcely more than a quarter of a mile.

I got served, but eating a hot pork sandwich in the street in the rain, with stuffing and applesauce running down your chin and wrists, seemed just a little too difficult. I headed for the park, where I hoped to find a bit of shelter. I was prepared for Hillsborough Park to be smaller than I remembered it, but it seemed as big as ever, with an athletics track and a boating lake and a library in one corner.

But there, next to the library, was a wall and a gateway that looked completely unfamiliar yet enticing. I stepped through the gateway and found myself in another world, in a classic walled garden, something that could have been from an English country house, decked out with bowers and trellises, raised beds and benches. And I found a place with a bit of shelter overhead, sat down, and ate my pork sandwich, and I was amazed.

I don't know that my eleven-year-old self would have appreciated a classic English walled garden, but my contemporary self found it a wonder, an oasis of calm and elegance, with (let's face it) thoroughly non-working-class values. And there was nobody in there but me. Maybe that was because of the rain, but I suspected not. The people who enjoyed The Shakey and the pork butchers and the betting shops probably weren't the people who appreciated traditional English walled gardens.

I finished my sandwich, left the garden, and walked into the main area of the park through a metal arch. I looked back and saw some words, a motto shaped into wrought iron. The words said "You'll never walk alone," as sung by Liverpool fans: this gateway was in memory of the dead football fans.

I was only briefly a football supporter. I pretty much gave it up when I discovered "literature." In any case I think I would rather walk alone than walk in the company of any number of football fans. In Hillsborough, in Sheffield, in my childhood, it seemed I had never done anything else but walk alone.

Even so, the next morning my old friend Steve and I set off to explore the Longley Estate. I admit I was wary of going back. There was a theory, not mine, that people like my parents, like me, like Steve, were no longer to be found in public housing. Yes, the council estates had once been full of decent, honest, hardworking people, but they'd all moved on and moved up, the way my parents had, and those left behind were the scroungers, the criminals, the crackheads and crack whores.

Steve supported this theory. His parents, who had stayed much longer than mine in the estates, had finally tired of the crime, the graffiti, the drugs, and the rumors of drugs, and had fled to live in a trailer park twenty miles away.

On the ground there wasn't much evidence to support the "left behind" theory. Longley looked very much as I remembered it. Apart from a few style changes, some newfangled doors and double-glazed windows, and some late-model cars, a time traveler from the 1960s wouldn't have seen anything to surprise him.

We walked past my parents' old house, the center of a block of three, very traditional, red brick and slate, with a door right in the middle, windows arranged symmetrically on either side. It seemed familiar, far more than I expected it to, given that I hadn't been there for over thirty years, and yet there was no great pang of nostalgia. I well remembered what it had felt like to live here, to have walked around this area, to have been bored and restless and eager to get out. Neither I nor the place had changed very much.

And on the surface, that applied to the whole neighborhood. Steve and I walked and looked and noted what had changed but also how much had stayed the same. As in Hillsborough, the shops were a good indicator. What had been an old-fashioned grocery store was now something called Streetwise Youth Central. There was a hair salon, and although it was offering Power Tan Sunbeds, which was surely a recent development, it looked much like the hair salon my mother had gone to. And there was also a thoroughly old-fashioned shop called Sew Craft, Cross-Stitch and Wool, which seemed to be thriving.

From time to time we did see tough-looking young men with tough-looking young dogs, the international signifier of the demand for "respect." First we saw three spindly lads in baseball caps walking or being walked by some sort of customized, slavering bull terrier. Then there was a family group: young dad and mom, two small kids, and an Akita, the Japanese fighting dog, as big as a pony. Then we saw a pair of squat, pierced, tattooed heavies, their style somewhere between heavy-metal fans and apocalypse survivors, with cans of beer and a dog on a leash that if I didn't know better I would have thought was a dingo. How we respected them. Perhaps if we'd walked farther we'd have seen dog lovers with their jackals, their hyenas, their timber wolves. Our respect would have known no limits.

Steve and I reckoned these dogs were far more vicious than the ones that had menaced us when we were kids, and that their owners were no doubt much more vicious than the bullies we'd encountered. It might almost have made us nostalgic. Then we found ourselves talking about child abuse. We said, not exactly for the first time, that when we were kids, the place was quite the hotbed of grown men doing, or attempting to do, dodgy things to boys. Any lad walking on his own was fair game. Our school friend Brian had had his leg stroked by a man in the local movie theater. We all knew that was wrong, even if we didn't quite know why, but that still didn't stop us finding it hilarious.

Walking home from the library, a regular half-hour walk in each direction, I'd once met a man who claimed to be a doctor. He had a black bag and a stethoscope visible in his pocket, and he just may really have been a doctor, but he stopped me and talked to me in a way that now makes me suspicious. The man asked me what school I went to and what my favorite subjects were. He claimed to know a couple of my teachers, and possibly he did. What was so seductive was the way he talked to me, as though I were an adult, and that was incredibly flattering, so much so that I mentioned it rather proudly to my father when I got home. I could immediately see I'd told him something that would have been better left untold. He told me to be careful walking on my own, but I had no idea what there was to be careful about.

The real prize, however, went to our friend Rob, who told me about something odd that had happened to him in Longley Park. He'd met a man who invited him into the public lavatory and taught him how to masturbate. Rob hadn't been a complete novice but was glad of some extra instruction, and even passed on a few tips to me, but he still felt there was something puzzling about the episode, and I shared his puzzlement. Neither of us saw anything frightening or dangerous or morally wrong in what had happened. We did think it was a bit weird, but then so many things that adults did seemed a bit weird. I haven't seen Rob in decades, and from time to time over the years I've often wondered if he continued to shrug off the episode with such equanimity.

My walk with Steve took us into Longley Park, and we saw that the public toilet where Rob was violated and educated had been demolished and removed, and yet the footprint of the building was still absolutely clear. The grass surrounding it was green and healthy, but the flat rectangle of earth where the toilet had once stood was a damp, muddy, grassless rectangle. We were careful not to see anything too symbolic in this.

The day after Steve and I explored Longley I took a walk by myself, a necessary walk but not one that I was looking forward to. I'd decided to walk up what in my mind had become "the hill that killed my mother."

My mother had long had a heart condition, a damaged valve caused by a childhood bout of rheumatic fever. By the time I was a teenager she was suffering from shortness of breath and having trouble walking far, and by the time I was in college she could barely walk up a flight of stairs. Then she had an operation to replace the defective valve and was fine for the next decade, after which she was increasingly less fine until she had another operation to replace the replacement, and then she was fine again, as far as we knew.

She'd been out to Sunday lunch with my uncle. It was a regular thing. He was the one with the car and he picked her up and drove her to and from their favorite restaurant on the other side of the city. But this time, while they were having lunch, they and the whole of Sheffield were caught in a sudden, fierce, unexpected blizzard. The roads weren't gritted or salted and there was no way my uncle could drive her back to her house: his car simply wouldn't make it up the hills—that old problem. He took her as far as he could, which was not really very far, just to the bottom of a hill called Gleadless Road, a horribly steep road at the best of times, one that demands you drive up it in second gear, a road that buses and trucks struggle to negotiate even in good weather. It wasn't a road that anybody, least of all my mother, would ever choose to walk up, and definitely not in the middle of a blizzard, but in this situation she thought she had no option.

She made it to the top; I was never quite sure how. When she told me about it later I was horrified, and we discussed what else she might have done: knocked on doors until she found someone who'd offer her shelter, but that still wouldn't have got her home; called the police, but it didn't seem likely they'd have been willing to provide a chauffeur service for her; called an ambulance and told them about her weak heart—well, maybe they'd have helped. But she was far too proud to do any of these things. She didn't want to present herself as a cripple. There was also, surely, the option that my uncle might have driven her to his house, but this never crossed her, or my uncle's, mind. In the end we agreed that anyone would probably have done the same and walked home, but then "anyone" wasn't necessarily a sixty-nine-year-old lady with a heart condition.

"It damn near killed me," she said.

Well, it did and it didn't. It didn't destroy her but it definitely didn't make her stronger. Over the next few months it became clear, and clearer still given subsequent events, that this enforced hill climb had done some damage to my mother's heart. The valve appeared to be leaking, and there wasn't enough blood or oxygen flowing through my mother's veins. She couldn't get around as well as she once had: walking and breathing were becoming a problem again. This in itself wasn't a great surprise. It would have happened anyway, sooner or later. We knew the valves were only good for a decade or so, and although something obviously needed to be done, there didn't seem any great urgency. My mother wasn't going to insist on surgery unless and until it was strictly necessary.

My mother died a short while later, quickly it appears, and although there must have been some pain, it couldn't have been prolonged. She died trying to get up from the armchair in her living room. She never quite made it. She got halfway, struggled, and fell back awkwardly, half in the chair, half against the radiator beside her, where she was found the next morning by a neighbor.

I was a long way from England when she died, and I'm told it would have done no good even if I, or anyone, had been in the same room at the time. There was nothing anybody could have done. The doctors told me this sort of thing just happens. Damaged hearts like my mother's sometimes simply stop working. So, to be absolutely correct, the walk up Gleadless Road hadn't in itself killed my mother, but the sudden overexertion had been enough to cause undue wear on some vital part of her system, a part that would later give up the ghost.

I was wandering and walking through the deserts of Arizona at the time of her death. You might imagine you'd feel some psychic twinge, receive some supernatural message of disconnection when your mother dies, but I received nothing. I flew home a week or so later, with no reason to think that my mother wasn't alive, and found a phone message from my uncle, which was odd, and if you thought about it, only likely to mean one thing. But even so it took me some time to put two and two together.

I tried to think where I'd been at the time of my mother's death. I worked out that I was in a motel on the outskirts of Tucson, my morning, my mother's evening, and I would have been planning the details of a day's walk in the Organ Pipe Cactus National Monument in the Sonoran Desert. While her body was lying slumped in the chair I was enjoying a good though apparently unexceptional day's walking.

Now, a good decade after my mother's death, I was going to walk up Gleadless Road, the hill that killed my mother. I left Steve's house and made my way to the bottom of the hill and, frankly, from that vantage point, it didn't look so steep after all. Perhaps my mother, and my memory, had exaggerated: maybe the hill wasn't so scary, maybe it hadn't affected her so badly after all. I began my walk.

There was a sidewalk going up on either side of the hill and I tried to think which one my mother would have chosen for her ascent. To the left of the road was a wooded area and a flat, open, grassy expanse. On the other side were houses in rows that ran across the hillside at right angles from the road. This was the Gleadless Valley Estate, a public housing development that had once had a reputation for being the best in Europe, and had won all sorts of architectural awards from people who didn't live in public housing. I felt pretty sure my mother would have chosen this more built-up side. The houses provided a little protection, some shelter from the wind, and in places there were steps and a handrail. If you were making your way up here in a blizzard you'd be grateful for those things.

And as I went on, I realized the hill was every bit as steep as I'd previously thought. It was a cool day in September and I had on just a light jacket, but before I was halfway up the hill I was sweating and panting like a hog. I was impressed that my mother had made it at all. By the time I got to the top, which was still some way from where my mother actually lived—she'd have had another thirty-minute walk before she got home—I was in absolute awe of her determination and tenacity, amazed that she'd had the strength and the legs and the guts to keep going. What a strong, brave, game old lady she'd been. It even occurred to me as I gritted my way upward, feeling my temperature and heartbeat rise, the blood rushing into my face, sweat breaking out on my forehead, that the God of Ironic Deaths might find it amusing to strike me down with a heart attack right there and then as I walked. He didn't. Evidently he's biding his time.

At the top of the hill I stopped, turned around, and went down again, walking back this time through part of the Gleadless Valley Estate. It looked rougher than Longley, despite its awards. There was more graffiti, more broken and barred windows, more litter, some smashed bottles here and there. When I got back to the house Steve asked me how my walk was.

"It damn near killed me," I said, and he probably thought I was joking.

# PERFECT AND IMPERFECT WALKS, LAST WALKS, THE WALKS WE DIDN'T TAKE

In the course of my walking life I've often wondered if there's any such thing as a perfect walk, in the way that there's a perfect storm, a perfect wave, or a perfect inning; the one walk that is utterly different from all the other walks we'll ever take in our lives, a walk that is personal and universal, that makes a giant leap from the ordinary to the extraordinary, a walk that is everything you ever wanted a walk to be and yet is something more than that, too.

Being the first person ever to set foot on some piece of terra incognita would surely have a kind of perfection about it. Inevitably, it's an option that's denied to the vast majority of us—walking in fresh snow or on fresh sand is as close as most of us will ever get—and perhaps we're lucky, since perfect or not, a great deal of bitterness and conflict can come out of this kind of exploration.

Matthew A. Henson is now widely considered to be the first American ever to have set foot on the North Pole. In 1909 he was part of an expedition led by Commander Robert Peary. This was Peary's eighth such attempt, and along the way he fell ill and became unable to walk. As they neared their goal Henson was regularly sent ahead on foot as a scout while Peary continued on a dog sled, tended by four Eskimo guides.

Thus, by definition, Peary wasn't ever going to be the first man to walk on, much less walk to, the North Pole. Henson inevitably got there first. Nevertheless, Peary wanted all the credit for himself and he wanted Henson to have none. Henson writes, "From the time we knew we were at the Pole, Commander Peary scarcely spoke to me."

I have just the very slightest sympathy with Peary. Henson was a great man to have with you, no doubt, but he didn't conceive of the expedition, didn't organize it, finance it, or lead it. Whether Peary was justified in regarding Henson as at best an employee, probably more as a servant, is another matter. Completely unjustifiable was the rage Peary expressed when Henson wrote his own account of events in his book *A Negro Explorer at the North Pole*. Yes, the first American to set foot on the North Pole was black, and only long after the event did he receive his due. It wasn't until 1944 that Congress gave him a duplicate of the silver medal they'd awarded to Peary decades earlier. The four Eskimos remain undecorated.

Recently, the author Robert Bryce has claimed that nobody on the Peary expedition got within a hundred miles of the Pole. He has, unsurprisingly, been denounced in certain quarters as a racist.

Things were less racially charged at the South Pole, if only because the notion of a racially integrated expedition was unimaginable to its explorers. A Frenchman, Jules-Sébastien-César Dumont d'Urville, was the first man to set foot on Antarctica, and Roald Amundsen, a Norwegian, was the first man to walk to the South Pole, shortly followed, though not literally, by the Englishman Robert Scott.

Amundsen's description of walking across an area he named the Devil's Ballroom gives some idea of his chilly Scandinavian stoicism. "Our walk across this frozen lake was not pleasant. The ground under our feet was evidently hollow, and it sounded as if we were walking on empty barrels. First a man fell through, then a couple of dogs; but they got up again all right." Insouciance is certainly part of the perfect walk, I think.

However, when it comes to chilly reserve, along with nobility, self-sacrifice, and British understatement, none can beat Captain Lawrence "Titus" Oates, a member of Scott's expedition. Oates, suffering from frostbite, and realizing that he was a burden that threatened to destroy the mission, walked out of the tent and into the oblivion of an Antarctic blizzard on March 17, 1912, having said to Scott and the others, "I am just going outside and may be some time."

There is a kind of perfection about this walk, and of course none of the other members of the expedition said, "Hey, steady old man, don't go out for a walk, stay here with us. What does it matter if the expedition gets ruined? Your health's the most important thing." That would have ruined things in quite a different way.

There seems to have been little insouciance or selflessness when it came to the first moon walk; I mean the literal sort, not the Michael Jackson version. The original plan for the Apollo 11 mission had Buzz Aldrin slated to be the first man to walk on the moon, but Neil Armstrong, as team leader, changed that plan so that he could be first. Aldrin was understandably furious, so much so that he refused to take any pictures of Armstrong walking on the moon: a gloriously petty revenge. This moon-walking disappointment is sometimes offered as an explanation for Aldrin's descent into depression and alcoholism, from which he later recovered.

The man who emerges with the most dignity from the moon landing and walk is Michael Collins, the third member of the Apollo team, the one who remained in the orbiting craft and never got to walk on the moon at all. Collins does have the minor distinction of being the third man ever to walk in space, in 1966 on Gemini X when he left the craft to perform a couple "extra-vehicular activities," but let's face it, a gravity-free space walk really isn't any kind of a walk, it's more of a float.

In any event Collins had enough of the right stuff not to be disappointed, or at least not to let the disappointment spoil his life. No doubt it helped that he knew all along that he wouldn't be walking on the moon, and wouldn't be thwarted at the last minute the way Aldrin was. According to Collins, "I think he [Aldrin] resents not being the first man on the moon more than he appreciates being the second."

As Armstrong walked on the moon he fluffed his big line. He said, "That's one small step for man, one giant leap for mankind," when he should have said, "one small step for *a* man." Did anybody care? There is, however, footage in circulation indicating that Armstrong's initial reaction was far more colloquial and unscripted. On the sound track to a blurred bit of moon footage he's heard to say quite clearly, "Jesus H. Christ, we're on the fucking moon." And Houston, getting into the spirit of the thing, replies, "You're cleared to hook up lunar equipment conveyor to walk, fucking walk, on the moon." This has an air of believable authenticity about it, though for all we know it may have been faked. Of course there are sources, not all of them certifiably insane, claiming that man has never set foot on the moon at all. This, too, has been offered as an explanation for Buzz Aldrin's drinking. Having to *pretend* that you'd walked on the moon when you hadn't would surely create every bit as much anguish as having been the second person to walk there.

Buzz Aldrin has been known to punch out people who accuse him of being part of a hoax, and while I'm not immune to the joys of a conspiracy theory, I find it hard to understand the pleasure some people take in believing that the moon walk never happened. Nevertheless, the not-quite-real walk, the walk that doesn't quite take place, that takes place largely or solely in the imagination, that contains an element of fantasy or fraud, is a curious phenomenon and more common than you'd suppose.

In September 1954, Albert Speer, Hitler's chief architect and then his Minister for Armaments, made up his mind to walk from Berlin to Heidelberg, a distance of 620 kilometers. Since he was incarcerated in Spandau prison at the time, and was to remain there until 1966, his walk had to be an entirely theoretical and imaginary one.

He paced out a circular course of 270 meters in the prison garden, which he had designed, and began a journey that would require him to make just over 2,296 circuits of that course. He set himself the task of walking seven kilometers seven times a week. If he fell behind one day he'd try to make it up the next, and he kept detailed, some would say obsessive, records of his walking, noting the distances covered, along with daily and overall averages. Rudolf Hess, Hitler's deputy in the Nazi party, also an inmate of Spandau, helped him keep count.

Speer completed his "journey" to Heidelberg on March 19, 1955, his fiftieth birthday. He then decided he might as well continue and make another imaginary walking trip, this time to Munich and beyond. Again Hess tried to be helpful and suggested he could walk all the way to Asia, though Speer fretted that almost any route he might take would involve having to walk through some dreaded communist countries.

According to Speer's diary, he and Hess had some discussions about whether or not this sort of walking was inherently sane. Speer at first claimed it wasn't and writes, "I insisted on my claim to have a screw loose," an odd thing to insist on unless he thought that incipient insanity might speed up his release. Hess, however, was having none of it. "That just happens to be your pastime," he said, quite reasonably, and this is surely one of the very rarest moments in history when one sides with Hess rather than Speer.

By September 18, 1956, Speer had come round to Hess's point of view and was able to record, "I have walked 3326 kilometres; counting the winter that makes a daily average of 9.1 kilometres. As long as I continue my tramping, I shall remain on an even keel."

A perfect walk is certainly one that keeps you on an even keel, and Speer, for all his claims to have a screw loose, wasn't perpetrating any deception about where and when he was walking. He was telling no lies, and the fact is, a single lie may be all that's required to utterly destroy a walker's reputation and credibility.

Ffyona Campbell was a British walker (she now describes herself as a retired pedestrian) who first came to public attention in 1983, at the age of sixteen, when she walked the 875 miles from John o' Groat's in the North of Scotland to Land's End in Cornwall.

This was to become the first phase of a round-the-world walk that would take eleven years and cover 20,000 miles. She crossed America east to west. She crossed Australia, from Sydney to Perth, in ninety-five days, faster than any man had ever done it. She walked from Cape Town to Tangiers, about 10,000 miles, in a little over two years. And then she walked through Europe, from Algeciras in Spain back to London to complete the trip. If you find yourself asking how a round-the-world trip can entirely avoid Asia, I share your puzzlement.

I lived in England throughout this period and I don't remember Campbell being exactly front-page news, though those of us who took notice of these things were well aware of her two travel books, *Feet of Clay* (1991) and *On Foot Through Africa* (1994).

However, I do remember, in 1996, when she published a third book called *The Whole Story*, that all hell broke loose and she became tabloid fodder. Being a good-looking blonde was both a blessing and a curse for her; being by all accounts a thoroughly difficult and unsympathetic character made her toast.

This third book was a confession. She could no longer live a lie, she said. She revealed that early in her walking career, while she was on the American part of her journey, at age eighteen, she became pregnant by a member of her support team, a driver named Brian Noel, whom she was regularly "bonking" (her word). Being pregnant slowed her down. She could no longer complete the grueling daily requirements to keep on schedule. She had commitments to a sponsor, Campbell's soup (no relation), that was organizing events at stops along the way.

So, by her own account, Ffyona Campbell rode in the truck with Noel for about a thousand miles of the journey, appearing on foot only at the beginning and end of the day when people were looking. The fact that she was able to get away with this certainly suggests that the American media spotlight wasn't trained on her with any great brightness.

Later she terminated the pregnancy and continued walking around the world. Only after she'd walked another 16,000 miles or so did the guilt really hit her. By her own account she became a depressive and a user of heroin. Then she tried to exorcise her guilt by telling all.

The scorn and contempt poured upon her by the English press in the wake of her confession was staggering. The London *Evening Standard* called her "a self-serving ninny," which was the least of it. Campbell seems to have been surprised; I can't think why. To be conned is one thing; to have the confidence trickster then turn around and point out how gullible you are is simply unbearable. Revenge is called for. And naturally, once someone tells you they were lying about a certain part of their story, there's no reason to believe they are telling the truth about any of the rest. That record-breaking Australian walk suddenly starts to look suspect. Perhaps the confession itself is just another deception. Maybe Campbell really is a great walker, who told one lie and later suffered and made up for it. But by what means can we now tell whether or not that's the case?

The great contemporary British explorer Sir Ranulph Fiennes once called Campbell "the greatest walker of them all." I wonder what he calls her now. I also suspect that even at the time he was being uncommonly generous, since by Fiennes's standards very few people in the world are real walkers at all. Fiennes was the first man to cross the whole of Antarctica on foot, and in 2000 he attempted, and failed, to do a solo walk to the North Pole, losing his fingertips as a result. He cut them off himself because he was impatient with the doctors who were treating him.

Campbell's title *On Foot Through Africa* echoes, accidentally I think, that of a memoir written by James Augustus Grant, a Victorian explorer of equatorial Africa, and sometime companion of John Speke in his search for the source of the White Nile. Grant called his book, published in 1864, *A Walk Across Africa*, but in fact he by no means walked all the way across. For five months he had an excruciating condition in his right leg, what is now thought to have been Buruli ulcer, that caused abscesses, pain, swelling, and foul discharge. He could barely straighten his leg, much less walk.

Eventually he was carried on a stretcher from the kingdom of Karague in Abyssinia to Uganda, where he was to meet up with Speke. Grant recounts that the stretcher bearers, members of the Waganda tribe, conveyed him at shoulder height, at six miles an hour, "jostling and paining my limb unmercifully."

Speke himself was no more merciful when Grant joined him. He was about to set off into the Ugandan interior and wanted to know if Grant was capable of making a "flying march" of twenty miles a day. Grant knew he wasn't, and Speke knew it, too. Speke traveled without him and therefore didn't have to share the glory of being the first white man ever to see the source of the White Nile.

The title of Grant's book may then seem at best an exaggeration, but given that Grant himself is the one who reveals the fact of his incapacity it would be churlish to object, especially since it was inspired by Lord Palmerston, who greeted Grant on his return from Africa with the words "You have had a long walk." Call it poetic license.

It certainly seems more forgivable than the conduct of Mao Zedong during the Long March of 1934–1935. As 90,000 Red Army troops retreated north from Jiangxi to Shanxi province, dwindling by 90 percent along the way, Mao was one of only two people who did no marching, or walking, whatsoever. (The other was Otto Braun, a Prussian advisor, and an ideological opponent of Mao.) According to Dick Wilson's *The Long March*, Mao "would never march, and either rode a horse along the route or else, if it were a long stretch, would be carried on a wooden litter by four carriers."

The Long March remains one of the great national myths of China. Writing in late 1935, Mao declared, "The Long March is the first of its kind. It is a manifesto, a propaganda force, a seeding machine." Well, only up to a point.

It wasn't until 2002 that anyone tried to repeat the exercise. In that year two Englishmen, Ed Jocelyn and Andy McEwan, retraced the steps of the Long March, and although their, and apparently everyone else's, knowledge of the route depended on educated guesswork, they calculated that the march was some 4,000 kilometers shorter than had generally been claimed. The Long March is said to have been 10,000 kilometers long (a nice round figure), but Jocelyn and McEwan only clocked 6,000. They covered the route in 370 days; the Red Army took 384.

The two Englishmen were not iconoclasts, and they didn't set out to disprove or debunk the myth. Nevertheless, they've been denounced by Chinese officials. Gao Zhiyin, a spokesman for the Yan'an Foreign Affairs Department, is quoted as saying, "Can they change history? The whole world acknowledges these facts." That's all right then. Print the legend.


Which brings me to one of the world's most enigmatic (and let's face it, perfectly silly) walkers, an English playboy, womanizer, and gambler named Harry Bensley. The story, and it comes in several versions, is that on January 1, 1908, Bensley set off from Trafalgar Square in London wearing a four-and-a-half-pound iron mask in order to test whether or not a man could walk around the world without being "identified." One version has John Pierpont Morgan and Lord Lonsdale debating the matter at the London Sporting Club, which was briefly the name of a boxing venue in Manhattan, though there were surely other places with the same name. Lonsdale said it could be done; Morgan said it couldn't. Bensley overheard the debate, and being a sporting man, offered to demonstrate that it could. He stood to win £21,000 of Morgan's money if he succeeded. Another version has Bensley in enormous debt to the two men and being forced to do the walk as a forfeit.

There are problems with both these versions, and either way the whole proposition is surely an absurd one, and not much of a bet, since the matter of identification depends so largely on who the man is and precisely what parts of the world he walks around. But the real issue is the wearing of the mask, which seems to be a cheat in a couple of ways. Yes, in one way it prevents the wearer's being recognized, but in another way it doesn't. After a while people might well see him walking down the street and say, "There goes that guy in the iron mask," which is surely a sort of recognition. More crucially it means nobody could ever be certain it was actually Bensley inside the mask and doing the walking. Perhaps this was his intention.

But even assuming there was a bet to be made, would anyone, however sporting, really be inclined to give up several years of his life to travel around the world wearing a mask, even for that amount of money? If Bensley was doing it as a forfeit, that makes Morgan and Lonsdale a couple of very creepy guys indeed. Both versions do, of course, suggest that Bensley might have been thoroughly broke.

The conditions laid down for the walk were extremely strict and occasionally bizarre, and could be read in a pamphlet that Bensley sold while traveling in order to finance himself. They included details of how he was to dress, how much money he was allowed to spend (very little, although if he was broke this wouldn't have been much of an issue). He was to push a baby carriage in front of him, not a particularly onerous condition since he could carry his belongings in it, but far more problematically he had to find himself a wife en route, one who had never seen his face.

The conditions also dictated the route. It was an interesting version of "the world." Bensley was to visit over 150 towns in Britain, fifty or so in continental Europe, three in Canada, eight in the United States, four in the whole of South America, eight in South Africa, six in Egypt (though none in the rest of Africa), and a handful each in India, China, Australia, and New Zealand. It was precisely the sort of route a son of the British Empire might take. Whether Bensley actually took it is anybody's guess.

He surely did go to some of the places dictated. A number of postcards were made depicting the iron-masked walker, and messages on the backs of the surviving ones indicate that Bensley covered at least some parts of England. Legend has it that he was arrested in Bexleyheath, in Kent, for selling his postcards without a license, and that he once sold one to King Edward VII for the staggering sum of five pounds. I find it hard to believe any king of England would pay one of his subjects so much for so little, but it's a story that does him credit.

Whether Bensley went abroad is more doubtful. The final part of the legend has him in Genoa at the outbreak of the First World War, at which point he abandons the frivolous business of walking and enlists in the British army, to be invalided out a year later. In another version the start of hostilities moves Morgan to call off the bet, although since Morgan had died in 1913 this is a variant we can reasonably discount.

I suspect that Bensley wasn't much of a walker, and certainly didn't walk around very much of the world. Rather, he was a sort of showman and self-made fairground attraction, who had probably never set eyes on Morgan or Lonsdale. He'd turn up at gatherings around England on high days and holidays and make a spectacle of himself, be the center of attention, sell some postcards and pamphlets, then go on his way. The walking, or the claim to be a great walker, was a way of drawing a crowd, part of the shtick, like the baby carriage and the mask. He made a weird and wonderful sight, and sometimes I wonder if the whole exercise wasn't just a photo opportunity, an excuse to make a zany postcard.

Bensley's round-the-world walk was, I think, imaginary, and it existed not so much in Bensley's imagination as in the minds of his public. Yes, Bensley was a sort of fake, a sort of con man, not a true walker, but he could see the appeal of being a great pedestrian, and although money was part of the equation, the invention of the walker in the iron mask must surely have appealed to some private need and fantasy of his. He is surely not a great walker, but he is one of the very greatest nonwalkers. His imaginary walking had a perfection about it that remained unassailed by reality.

I realize that much of the above makes walkers appear to be a vain, duplicitous, lying bunch. Wasn't walking, especially walking straight and tall, supposed to be synonymous with honesty and plain dealing? Well, only up to a point. Perhaps all great walks involve the imagination to some extent and contain a nagging element of self-dramatization and self-aggrandizement that may not have much to do with the facts. Perhaps if we're in search of perfection we need to look for something more local and less ambitious.

I have found one walk that strikes me as perfect and perfectly honest, the more so because it is essentially modest and small scale, and doesn't make any unnecessarily large claims for itself.

One Sunday afternoon in the summer of 1948, George de Mestral took a life-changing walk in the mountains of his native Switzerland. De Mestral was an inventor by trade and an enthusiastic weekend hiker. He and his dog walked all the time, and as they set off that day he had no reason to believe that this walk would be different from any of the others, and in truth the walk itself was unexceptional enough.

The walk took him through brush and undergrowth, and when he got home he began the tedious process of removing the cockleburs that had attached themselves to his clothes and his dog's coat. Again, this was a common experience; it happened every time he walked. This time, however, as he picked off the burs he found himself wondering, as he'd never wondered before, just why they stuck so firmly.

He took one of the cockleburs to his study, put it under a microscope, and made the discovery that changed his and, to a strictly limited extent, all our lives. He saw that the burs had hooks on them, and these hooks attached themselves to the fibers of his clothes and to the coat of his dog. He thought there must be some practical application for such a hook-and-loop system. There was. George de Mestral had made the discovery that enabled him to invent Velcro. The rest is social history.

De Mestral's walk has a modest perfection about it. Something local and quotidian becomes the source for something ubiquitous, if not, in the more grandiose sense, universal. It's the simple domesticity that's so appealing. Almost none of us will ever know what it's like to walk on the moon or the North Pole. We won't walk around the world or across continents, we won't complete a 10,000- or even a 6,000-kilometer march. But most of us can imagine, and aspire to, a short walk in familiar territory that might provide us with our great idea, our great moment of inspiration.

And for a writer that's especially alluring. We know that when William Wordsworth was in the throes of composition he would stride up and down the garden path outside his home in Grasmere; walking and writing had for him become synonymous. And I do believe that there's some fundamental connection between walking and writing. In the broadest sense I've always found walking to be inspiring. When I need to solve a problem that's arisen in something I'm writing, to work out a plot point, to decide what character A might say or do if she found herself in a room with character Z, then going for a walk will usually clarify matters. The pace of words is the pace of walking, and the pace of walking is also the pace of thought.

Both walking and writing are simple, common activities. You put one foot in front of the other; you put one word in front of another. What could be more basic than a single step, more basic than a single word? Yet if you connect enough of these basic building blocks, enough steps, enough words, you may find that you've done something special. The thousand-mile journey starts with the single step; the million-word manuscript starts with a single syllable.

With writing as with walking you often find that you're not heading exactly where you thought you wanted to go. There'll be missteps and stumbles, journeys into dead ends, the reluctant retracing of your steps. And you have to tell yourself that's just fine, that it's a necessary, and not wholly unenjoyable, part of the process. It's an exploration.

Even the most determined and committed walker finds that there are certain walks he always intends to take yet never quite does. For instance, I have always meant to walk the length of the River Thames in London, crossing from one side to the other each time I encounter a bridge. In New York, I fully intend to walk the entire length of Broadway, but have never quite got around to it. A walk along the Great Wall of China remains an ambition, and not an unrealizable one. None of these is a particularly original or unusual walk; they have all been done many times by others. But that shouldn't be a reason for me not to do them. And I tell myself there's plenty of time. I have plenty of years ahead of me; perhaps I will do these walks after all. Still, it is one of the intimations of mortality to realize that we only have a certain number of walking miles in us. There are walks we simply won't make. We're guaranteed to end our walking days with certain routes and paths still untrodden.

For now I continue to walk constantly, mostly in Los Angeles because that's where I live most of the time, but I also walk wherever else I am. Walking continues to be a great pleasure. It also continues to be a form of self-medication. It stops me from getting depressed. It keeps me more or less healthy, more or less sane. It helps me to write.

And so far I've managed to remain upright as I walk. Like anyone else I've occasionally tripped or slipped, lost my footing for a moment here and there, but so far I haven't fallen down again, not since that day when I was walking in the Hollywood Hills and broke my arm in three places. This is a small achievement but a real and welcome one.

Walking is not a risk-free activity, and we probably don't want it to be. We may fall down along the way. Something may get broken. People get lost, people walk into oblivion, some willingly, some not. Some return to tell lies about where they've been and what they've done; they create myths for themselves and others. This may not be strictly a good thing, but it's hard to see how it can be prevented. For many of us the perfect walk may simply be the one that we come back from in one piece. For a writer the perfect walk may simply be one he can write about.

Perhaps also, in both writing and walking, each word, each step takes you a little nearer to the end of things, to the last sentence, the last walk. Sooner or later everybody takes their last step. However, because walking is able to make us healthier, happier, slightly fitter, certain steps in fact take us just a little further away from the end, at least for a while.

# A Walking Bibliography

Abibliography of a thousand volumes begins with a single citation. But who would want a bibliography of a thousand volumes? I've therefore limited this list to items that are actually discussed in the text, or that I've genuinely used in writing the book. Literary works mentioned in passing, *Ulysses*, *Swann's Way*, or *Lessness*, for example, are omitted, and their bibliographical details are surely easy enough to find elsewhere.

I'd been planning to write something on the subject of walking for a very long time. And then, in 2000, Rebecca Solnit published the book *Wanderlust*, subtitled "A History of Walking," which got attention and good reviews, and which I approached reluctantly, afraid that the author might have said everything I wanted to say. Fortunately, and not so surprisingly, she didn't. The book contains, for instance, a chapter called "Aerobic Sisyphus and the Suburbanized Psyche," which made me tend to believe we weren't on precisely the same walking path.

Then, in 2004, Joseph Amato published a book called *On*

*Foot*, also, incredibly, subtitled "A History of Walking," which again didn't feel like direct competition. It has a chapter called "Choose Your Steps—Reflections on the Transformation of Walking from Necessity to Choice."

Neither the Solnit book nor the Amato book contains a bibliography as such, but each has an extensive notes section: twenty-five pages in the case of Solnit, forty pages in the case of Amato. Amato says in his notes that Solnit's book "proved useful" to him. There's obviously a serious temptation to strew footnotes all over a text about walking, but as you can see, I resisted.

I'm aware of two texts called "The Art of Walking." One is a short piece by Christopher Morley in the 1918 collection *Shandygaff*, subtitled "A number of most agreeable Inquirendoes upon Life & Letters, interspersed with Short Stories & Skits, the whole most Diverting to the Reader." Morley writes, "Now your true walker is mightily 'curious in the world,' and he goes upon his way zealous to sate himself with a thousand quaintnesses. When he writes a book he fills it full of food, drink, tobacco, the scent of sawmills on sunny afternoons, and arrivals at inns late at night."

The other is an anthology titled *The Art of Walking*, actually rather slender, edited by Edwin Valentine Mitchell, and published in 1934. It contains works by many of the usual suspects— Dickens, Leslie Stephen's "In Praise of Walking," Max Beerbohm's "Going Out for a Walk," as well as a piece by Christopher Morley called "Sauntering." Thus: "It is entrancing to walk...and catalogue all that may be seen. I jot down on scraps of paper a list of all the shops on a side street; the names of tradesmen that amuse me; the absurd repartee of gutter children. Why? Because it amuses me and that is sufficient excuse."

It's interesting to compare the contents of that anthology with those of a more recent one, *The Vintage Book of Walking*, edited by Duncan Minshull, published in 2004. Dickens, Stephen, Beerbohm all hold their places, though there's no room for poor old Morley. It seems that even in the world of walking, of walking anthologies and walking bibliographies, there are no such things as eternal vérités.

Abbey, Edward. *Desert Solitaire: A Season in the Wilderness*. New York: McGraw-Hill, 1968.

———. *The Journey Home: Some Words in Defense of the American West*. New York: Dutton, 1977.

Ainslie, Scott, and Dave Whitehill. *Robert Johnson: At the Crossroads—the Authoritative Guitar Transcriptions*. Milwaukee: Hal Leonard Publishing, 1992.

Alstruther, Stephen. *The Mindful Hiker: On the Trail to Find the Path*. Camarillo, Calif.: DeVorss Publications, 2004.

Amato, Joseph A. *On Foot: A History of Walking*. New York: New York University Press, 2004.

Arturian, Judy, and Mike Oldham. *Movie Star Homes: The Famous to the Forgotten*. Santa Monica, Calif.: Santa Monica Press, 2004.

Aslan, Reza. *No God But God*. New York: Random House, 2005.

Atget, Eugene. *Atget Paris.* Carte Madera, Calif.: Gingko Press, 1992.

Auster, Paul. *The New York Trilogy.* New York: Penguin, 1987.

Banham, Peter Reyner. *Scenes in America Deserta.* Salt Lake City: Gibbs Smith, 1982.

————. *Los Angeles: The Architecture of Four Ecologies.* Harmondsworth, England: Allen Lane, Penguin Press, 1971.

Baudrillard, Jean. *America.* Translated by Chris Turner. London: Verso, 1988.

Bean, J. P. *The Sheffield Gang Wars.* Sheffield, England: D and D, 1981.

Bein, Alex. *The Jewish Question: Biography of a World Problem.* Translated by Harry Zohn. Rutherford, N.J.: Fairleigh Dickinson University Press, 1990.

Bellos, David. *Georges Perec: A Life in Words.* London: Harvill Press, 1993.

Benjamin, Walter. "The Flâneur" (1938). In *Charles Baudelaire: A Lyric Poet in the Era of High Capitalism.* Translated by Harry Zohn and Quintin Hoare. London: NLB, 1973.

————. *The Arcades Project.* Translated by Howard Eiland and Kevin McLaughlin. Cambridge, Mass.: Belknap Press, Harvard University Press, 1999.

Bradbury, Ray. "The Pedestrian" (1951). In *S Is for Space.* London: Hart-Davis, 1968.

Brinnin, John Malcolm. *Dylan Thomas in America: An Intimate Journal.* London: Dent, 1956.

Brook, Stephen. *L.A. Lore.* London: Sinclair-Stevenson, 1992.

Brownlow, Kevin. "Brownlow on Beckett (on Keaton)." In *Film West* 22, Autumn 1995.

Burton, Richard. *Personal Narrative of a Pilgrimage to El-Medinah and Meccah*, 3 vols. London: Longman, Brown, Green and Longmans, 1855–57.

Burton, Robert. *The Anatomy of Melancholy* (1621). New York: New York Review of Books, 2001.

Campbell, Ffyona. *Feet of Clay: Her Epic Walk Across Australia*. London: Heinemann, 1991.

———. *On Foot Through Africa*. London: Orion, 1994.

———. *The Whole Story: A Walk Around the World*. London: Orion, 1996.

Chandler, Raymond. *The Big Sleep*. New York: Alfred A. Knopf, 1939.

———. *Farewell, My Lovely*. New York: Alfred A. Knopf, 1940.

———. *The High Window*. New York: Alfred A. Knopf, 1942.

———. *The Lady in the Lake*. New York: Alfred A. Knopf, 1943.

———. *The Little Sister*. London: Hamish Hamilton, 1949.

———. *The Long Goodbye*. London: Hamish Hamilton, 1953.

———. *Playback*. London: Hamish Hamilton, 1958.

———. *Selected Letters*. Edited by Frank MacShane. London: Jonathan Cape, 1981.

Chatwin, Bruce. *The Songlines*. London: Jonathan Cape, 1987.

———. *What Am I Doing Here*. London: Jonathan Cape, 1989.

Clark, David. *L.A. On Foot, a Free Afternoon*. Los Angeles: Camaro Publishing, 1972.

Coverley, Merlin. *Psychogeography*. London: Pocket Essentials, 2006.

Davis, Mike. *City of Quartz: Excavating the Future in Los Angeles*. New York: Vintage, 1992.

————. *Ecology of Fear: Los Angeles and the Imagination of Disaster*. New York: Vintage, 1999.

Debord, Guy Ernest. *Panegyric: Volumes 1 and 2* (1989 and 1997). Translated by James Brook and John McHale. London: Verso, 2004.

————. *Society of the Spectacle*. Translated by Donald Nicholson-Smith. New York: Zone Books, 1995.

————. "Theory of the Dérive." *In Guy Debord and the Situationist International: Texts and Documents*. Edited by Tom McDonough. Cambridge, Mass.: MIT Press, 2004.

————. "Introduction to a Critique of Urban Geography" (1955). In *The Situationist International Anthology*. Translated by Ken Knabb. Berkeley, Calif.: Bureau of Public Secrets, 2006.

De Quincey, Thomas. *Confessions of an English Opium Eater* (1862). Harmondsworth, England: Penguin, 2003.

Dickens, Charles. "Night Walks" (1860). Chapter XIII in *The Uncommercial Traveller*. London: Chapman and Hall, 1901.

Drummond, Bill. *45*. London: Little, Brown, 2000.

Dunaway, David King. *Huxley in Hollywood*. New York: Harper and Row, 1989.

Duncan, Andrew. *Secret London*. London: New Holland Publishers, 1995.

Edmunds, Lowell. *Martini Straight Up.* Baltimore: Johns Hopkins University Press, 1998.

Fletcher, Colin. *The Complete Walker.* New York: Knopf, various editions from 1968 to 1984.

Foster, Lynn. *Adventuring in the California Desert.* San Francisco: Sierra Club Books, 1987.

Francis, John. *Planetwalker: How to Change Your World One Step at a Time.* Point Reyes Station, Calif.: Elephant Mountain Press, 2005.

Freeman, Judith. *The Long Embrace: Raymond Chandler and the Woman He Loved.* New York: Pantheon Books, 2007.

Fuchs, R. H. *Richard Long.* London: Thames and Hudson, 1986.

Gebhard, David, and Robert Winter. *Los Angeles: An Architectural Guide.* Salt Lake City: Gibbs-Smith, 1994.

Gilden, Bruce. *Facing New York: Photographs by Bruce Gilden.* New York: power-House, 1992.

———. *Coney Island.* New York: Trebruk, 2002.

———. *A Beautiful Catastrophe.* New York: powerHouse, 2005.

Grant, James Augustus. *A Walk Across Africa; or Domestic Scenes from My Nile Journal.* London: Blackwood, 1864.

Gray, Christopher. *Streetscapes: Tales of Manhattan's Significant Buildings and Landmarks.* New York: Abrams, 2003.

Gross, Miriam, ed. *The World of Raymond Chandler.* London: Weidenfeld and Nicholson, 1977.

Harmon, Ruth, and Minnis, John. *Sheffield*. New Haven and London: Pevsner City Guides, Yale University Press, 2004.

Harrison, Jim. "Westward Ho." In *The Beast God Forgot to Invent*. New York: Grove, 2000.

Henson, Matthew. *A Negro Explorer at the North Pole* (1912). New York: Invisible Cities, 2001.

Herzog, Werner. *Of Walking in Ice: Munich–Paris 23 November–14 December 1974*. Translated by Marje Herzog and Alan Greenberg. New York: Tanam Press: 1980.

———. *Herzog on Herzog*. Edited by Paul Cronin. London: Faber, 2002.

Hiney, Tom. *Raymond Chandler: A Biography*. London: Chatto and Windus, 1997.

Jakle, John A., and Keith A. Sculle. *Lots of Parking: Land Use in a Car Culture*. Charlottesville and London: University of Virginia Press, 2004.

Jarvis, Robin. *Romantic Writing and Pedestrian Travel*. London: Macmillan, 1997.

Jay, Ricky. *Jay's Journal of Anomalies*. New York: Quantuck Lane Press, 2003.

Jencks, Charles. *Post-Modern Triumphs in London*. London: Academy Editions, 1991.

Joyce, Julie, and Sandra Q. Firmin. *Mudman: The Odyssey of Kim Jones*. Cambridge, Mass.: MIT Press, 2007.

Kayton, Bruce. *Radical Walking Tours of New York City*. New York: Seven Stories Press, 2003.

Kazin, Alfred. *A Walker in the City*. New York: Harcourt, Brace, 1951.

Keaton, Buster, with Charles Samuels. *My Wonderful World of Slapstick*. Garden City, N.Y.: Doubleday, 1960.

Kerouac, Jack. *On the Road*. New York: Viking Press, 1957.

———. *Dharma Bums*. New York: Viking Press, 1958.

Klein, Jim. *The Complete Films of Buster Keaton*. New York: Citadel Press, 1993.

Lawson, Kristan, and Anneli Rufus. *California Babylon: A Guide to Sites of Scandal, Mayhem, and Celluloid in the Golden State*. New York: St. Martin's Griffin, 2000.

Lelyveld, Nita. "He Has His Walking Points: Neil Hopper Navigates the L.A. Area with His Feet." *Los Angeles Times*, September 16, 2004.

Lewis, Percy Wyndham. *The Childermass* (1928). New York: Riverrun Press, 2000.

Long, Richard. *Walking the Line*. London and New York: Thames and Hudson, 2002.

———. *Richard Long: Selected Statements and Interviews*. Edited by Ben Tufnell. London: Haunch of Venison, 2007.

———. *Walking and Marking*. Edinburgh: Scottish National Gallery of Modern Art, 2007.

Machen, Arthur. *The London Adventure or the Art of Wandering*. London: Secker, 1924.

MacShane, Frank. *The Life of Raymond Chandler*. New York: Dutton, 1976.

Mahoney, Erin. *Walking In L.A.* Berkeley, Calif.: Wilderness Press, 2005.

Manley, William Lewis. *Death Valley in '49*. San Jose, Calif.: Pacific Tree and Vine Co., 1894.

Minshull, Duncan. *The Vintage Book of Walking*. London: Vintage, 2000.

Mitchell, Edwin Valentine, ed. *The Art of Walking* (1934). Great Neck, N.Y.: Core Collection Books, Inc., 1978.

Morgan, Bill. *The Beat Generation in New York: A Walking Tour of Jack Kerouac's City*. San Francisco: City Lights, 1997.

Muybridge, Eadweard. *The Human Figure in Motion* (1901). New York: Dover, 1955.

Neil, Charles Lang. *Walking: A Practical Guide to Pedestrianism for Athletes and Others*. London: C. Arthur Pearson, 1903.

O'Hara, Frank. *Standing Still and Walking in New York*. Bonias, Calif.: Grey Fox Press, 1975.

———. "Let's Take a Walk." In *Selected Poems*. Edited by Donald Allen. New York: Knopf/Vintage, 1974.

Olson, Brian, and Bonnie Olson. *Tailing Philip Marlowe*. St. Paul, Minn.: Burl-write, 2003.

Parr, Martin. *Martin Parr*. London and New York: Phaidon, 2002.

———. *The Phone Book*. London: Rocket, 2002.

Peiper, Albrecht. *Cerebral Function in Infancy and Childhood*. London: Pitman Medical Publishers, 1963.

Poetzsch, Markus. "Walks Alone and 'I Know Not Where': Dorothy Wordsworth's Deviant Pedestrianism." Presented at the 13th Annual Conference of the North American Society for the Study of Romanticism: Deviance and Defiance, August 13–17, 2005.

Porter, Roy. *London: A Social History*. London: Hamish Hamilton, 1994.

Radford, Peter. *The Celebrated Captain Barclay: Sport, Gambling and Adventure in Regency Times*. London: Headline, 2001.

Rice, Edward. *Captain Sir Richard Francis Burton*. New York: Scribner, 1990.

Rousseau, Jean-Jacques. *The Reveries of the Solitary Walker* (1782). Translated by Charles E. Butterworth. Indianapolis and Cambridge: Hackett Publishing Company, 1992.

Rubenstein, Raphael. "Snap Judgments: Exploring the Winogrand Archive." *Art in America*, February 2002.

Sacks, Oliver. *A Leg to Stand On*. New York: Harper and Row, 1984.

Sardar, Ziauddin. "How Mecca Became a Death Trap." *New Statesman*, March 26, 1999.

Saward, Jeff. *Labyrinths and Mazes: A Complete Guide to Magical Paths of the World*. New York: Lark Books, 2003.

Sebald, W. G. *The Rings of Saturn*. Translated by Michael Hulse. London: Harvill, 1998.

Sinclair, Iain. *Lights Out for the Territory: 9 Excursions in the Secret History of London*. London: Granta Books, 1997.

———. *London Orbital: A Walk Around the M25*. London: Granta Books, 2002.

———. *Lud Heat*. London: Albion Village Press, 1975.

Snow, Sebastian. *The Rucksack Man*. London: Hodder and Stoughton, 1976.

Solnit, Rebecca. *Wanderlust: A History of Walking*. New York: Penguin Books, 2000.

————. *Motion Studies: Eadweard Muybridge and the Technological Wild West*. London: Bloomsbury, 2003.

Speer, Albert. *The Spandau Secret Diaries*. Translated by Richard and Clara Winston. New York: Macmillan, 1976.

Sutherland, John. "Clarissa's Invisible Taxi," in *Can Jane Eyre Be Happy? More Puzzles in Classic Fiction*. London: Oxford University Press, 1997.

Tatley, Roger. "In the Studio: Richard Long." *Art + Auction*, February 2006.

Thom, Walter. *Pedestrianism; or, an Account of the Performances of Celebrated Pedestrians During the Last and Present Century; with a Full Narrative of Captain Barclay's Public and Private Matches; and an Essay on Training*. Aberdeen: NP, 1808.

Thomson, David. *The Big Sleep* (BFI Film Classics). London: British Film Institute, 1997.

Thoreau, Henry David. "Walking." *Atlantic Monthly*, June 1862.

Tomkins, Calvin. *Duchamp: A Biography*. New York: Henry Holt, 1996.

Underhill, Paco. *Call of the Mall*. New York: Simon and Schuster, 2004.

Van Dyke, John C. *The Desert* (1901). New York: Gibbs Smith, Scribners, 1980.

Waldie, D. J. *Holy Land: A Suburban Memoir*. New York: W. W. Norton, 1996.

Ward, Elizabeth, and Alain Silver. *Raymond Chandler's Hollywood*. Woodstock, N.Y.: Overlook Press, 1987.

Westbury, Virginia. *Labyrinths: Ancient Paths of Wisdom and Peace*. Cambridge, Mass.: Da Capo Press, 2001.

Westerbeck, Colin, and Joel Meyerowitz. "Afterword: The Sidewalk Never Ends." In *Bystander: A History of Street Photography*. London: Thames and Hudson, 1994.

White, Edmund. *The Flâneur: A Stroll Through the Paradoxes of Paris*. London: Bloomsbury, 2001.

Williams, George. *Guide to Literary London*. London: Batsford, 1973.

Wilson, Dick. *The Long March: The Epic of Chinese Communism's Survival*. New York: Viking Press, 1972.

Winogrand, Garry. *Figments from the Real World*. Edited by John Szarkowski. New York: Museum of Modern Art, 1988.

———. *1964*. Edited by Trudy Wilner Stack. Santa Fe, N.M.: Arena Editions, 2002.

Wood, Dennis. *The Power of Maps*. New York: Guilford Press, 1992.

Woolf, Virginia. *Mrs. Dalloway*. London: Hogarth Press, 1925.

———. "Oxford Street Tide" (1931). In *The London Scene: Six Essays on London Life*. New York: Ecco, HarperCollins, 2006.

Wordsworth, Dorothy. *Journals of Dorothy Wordsworth*. London: Oxford University Press, 1971.

Wrigley, J. R. *A Hillsborough Camera*. Sheffield, England: Pickard Publishing, 2003.

Ziegler, Philip. *London at War 1939–1945*. London: Sinclair-Stevenson, 1995.

Zochert, Donald, ed. *Walking in America*. New York: Knopf, 1974.

## SOME ONLINE SOURCES

A serious academic bibliography on walking, though with some unexpected and very welcome quirks, by Andie Miller of the University of Witwatersrand, Johannesburg.
http://web.wits.ac.za/Academic/Humanities/SLLS/Holistic/
BibliographyWalking/

Neil Hopper's website recording his walks around Los Angeles.
http://www.walkinginla.com

A short bibliography of sources relating to psychogeography, from the sociology department of Manchester Metropolitan University.
http://www.sociology.mmu.ac.uk/driftnet_bibliography.php

A bibliography and a collection of links and quotations compiled by Michael Garofalo.
http://www.egreenway.com/wellbeing/walk.htm

A weblog about the uses of walking in art, including a bibliography, initiated by the Tate Modern, run by Ana Laura.
http://walkart.wordpress.com/bibliography/

The people behind the walking tours of the parking lots of America. I'm still uncertain whether this is art pretending to be urban studies or vice versa, but the uncertainty is all part of the fun.
http://temporarytraveloffice.net/main.html

This website, which I made, includes a small percentage of the visual materials I assembled while writing this book.

http://www.flickr.com/photos/32373413@N00/

## Acknowledgments

The following people have all helped with the making of this book, sometimes by giving help and information, sometimes by acting as much-needed walking companions. A big thank-you to them all.

Yvonne Antrobus
Thomas Berger
Stephen Chambers
Neil Coulbeck
Sue Coulbeck
Johanne Fronth-Nygren
Bruce Gilden
Leila Hamidi
Dian Hanson
Laura Howard
Kim Jones
Steve Kenny

Keith Kinsella

Robert Klenner

Michael Kupperman

Richard Lapper

Matthew Licht

Nina Lubbren

Joanna Moriarty

Mark Newgarden

Martin Parr

Scott Peake

Sally Kurosawa Russell

Ethel Sena

David Stromberg

Marianne Thompson

Mel Thompson

St. John Walker

# About the Author

**Geoff Nicholson** is the author of twenty books, including *Sex Collectors, Hunters & Gatherers, The Food Chain,* and *Bleeding London,* which was shortlisted for the Whitbread Prize. He divides his time between Los Angeles and London.